Make Mine a Mystery II

Recent Titles in Genreflecting Advisory Series

Diana Tixier Herald, Series Editor

Hooked on Horror III
Anthony J. Fonseca and June Michele Pulliam

Caught Up in Crime: A Reader's Guide to Crime Fiction and Nonfiction
Gary Warren Niebuhr

Latino Literature: A Guide to Reading Interests
Edited by Sara E. Martínez

Teen Chick Lit: A Guide to Reading Interests
Christine Meloni

Now Read This III: A Guide to Mainstream Fiction
Nancy Pearl and Sarah Statz Cords

Gay, Lesbian, Bisexual, Transgender and Questioning Teen Literature: A Guide to Reading Interests
Carlisle K. Webber

This Is My Life: A Guide to Realistic Fiction for Teens
Rachel L. Wadham

Primary Genreflecting: A Guide to Picture Books and Easy Readers
Susan Fichtelberg and Bridget Dealy Volz

Teen Genreflecting 3: A Guide to Reading Interests
Diana Tixier Herald

Urban Grit: A Guide to Street Lit
Megan Honig

Historical Fiction for Teens: A Genre Guide
Melissa Rabey

Graphic Novels for Young Readers: A Genre Guide for Ages 4–14
Nathan Herald

Make Mine a Mystery II

A Reader's Guide to Mystery and Detective Fiction

Gary Warren Niebuhr

Genreflecting Advisory Series

Diana Tixier Herald, Series Editor

 LIBRARIES UNLIMITED

AN IMPRINT OF ABC-CLIO, LLC
Santa Barbara, California • Denver, Colorado • Oxford, England

Library of Congress Cataloging-in-Publication Data

Niebuhr, Gary Warren.
    Make mine a mystery II : a reader's guide to mystery and detective fiction /
  Gary Warren Niebuhr.
       p. cm. -- (Genreflecting advisory series)
    Includes bibliographical references and indexes.
    ISBN 978-1-59884-589-1 (acid-free paper)
    1. Detective and mystery stories--Bibliography. 2. Detective and mystery stories--Stories,
  plots, etc. I. Title. II. Title: Make mine a mystery 2. III. Title: Make mine a mystery two.
  Z5917.D5N54 2011
  [PN3448.D4]
  016.8093'872--dc23   2011017226

ISBN: 978-1-59884-589-1

15 14 13 12 11   1 2 3 4 5

Visit www.abc-clio.com for details.

Libraries Unlimited
An Imprint of ABC-CLIO, LLC

ABC-CLIO, LLC
130 Cremona Drive, P.O. Box 1911
Santa Barbara, California 93116-1911

This book is printed on acid-free paper ∞
Manufactured in the United States of America

Dedicated with all my love to Barbara Jo and Robert Crocker: two people, two hearts, one courageous spirit.

Contents

Acknowledgments

This book would not exist except for the pioneering work *Genreflecting* and the work done by Betty Rosenberg and Diana Tixier Herald. This is a debt that can never be paid. I would like to thank Barbara Ittner for the opportunity to produce this work, and thank all the hard-working folks at Libraries Unlimited. A big thank you to Sharon DeJohn, who edited this book with precision, and to Emma Bailey for her steady hand on the tiller.

Some of these annotations may have previously appeared in print in one or more of the following sources: *A Reader's Guide to the Private Eye Novel* (G. K. Hall, 1993), *Booklist, Dapa-Em, Deadly Pleasures, Mystery News,* or *The Poisoned Pen.*

Any errors or omissions in this work are unintentional, and in the spirit of maintaining the level of research intended to do a revision, I would appreciate receiving any comments readers may have to improve a later edition. My e-mail address is gniebuhr@wi.rr.com.

I would like to thank my wife, Denice, who provides for me in ways that no one else can understand.

Introduction

An Overview of This Book

This book is the second volume of this title intended to help readers' advisors, librarians, and others develop a greater understanding of the mystery genre. By referring to both volumes, they can make reading recommendations and successfully answer questions raised by readers who enjoy mysteries. The book covers mystery detective novels in which a fictional character tries to solve a puzzle concerning a crime to the administration of justice. It does not cover crime, intrigue, thrillers, suspense, adventure novels, or true crime stories.

In the original work I was attempting to represent the entire mystery detective genre, and I included titles from its entire history. This book covers, in the main, publications from the twenty-first century. Because the authors' works represented here are in series, under each series I have listed those titles that were annotated in the previous volume. Titles in the series that were not annotated in the previous volume are annotated here. For each author, all books in a series are included, listed in publication order. Books written by the author in other areas of the mystery field (such as suspense or crime) and those written outside the mystery genre are not included. (Sources listed in the appendix can help you find additional titles by these authors).

Many of the titles listed in this book are in print. However, some will only be found by searching a quality collection in a large public library or by haunting specialty mystery or used bookstores. Because of their loyalty to series characters, mystery readers are quite willing to track down older and out-of-print titles featuring those characters. Readers who are intrigued should not hesitate to use interlibrary loan at their local library or use the World Wide Web to search for out-of-print book dealers that carry mystery fiction.

Each entry provides publisher, publication date, and ISBN for the American edition. In the rare instances where there is no American edition, the bibliographic information is for the edition from the country of origin. Alternate bibliographic information is given after the American edition for the original edition published in a non-American country or if the work was published with an alternative title. Additional bibliographic information is contained in parentheses. An asterisk (*) at the beginning of the entry indicates that the title was not located for review in time for this publication.

Although this book is intended for professionals who advise readers, it will also be useful to fans of the genre, mystery bookstore owners, educators who teach literature courses in mystery, mystery publishers, and writers who want to publish in the genre.

The Appeal of a Series Character

After years of participating in the mystery genre, as a readers' advisor in my library, a fan of the mystery genre, and an educator in the field, I believe that this genre's greatest appeal is the attraction to the detective character featured in a mystery series. The majority of the entries in this book exhibit this appeal. There are a few exceptions, but not many. The organization of this book reflects this premise, classifying approximately 700 titles by lead character type: amateur detective, public detective, and private detective. Series detectives make up the majority of titles in the genre, and readers' advisors will be able to suggest a series to a reader using the appeal of a series character. Character introductions and annotations throughout the book give brief background sketches of the detectives and offer further glimpses into the content and appeal of the series. If readers' advisors can understand the appeal of the character to the reader, they can find other series characters with similar jobs, attitudes, styles, or mannerisms. The readers' advisors can then connect readers to a book that will give them a similar and enjoyable reading experience.

In discussing why readers like mysteries, the appeal of the main character cannot be overemphasized. Readers form an emotional attachment to their favorite characters and enjoy reading books in series about the same character. Point of view becomes an important consideration. First-person narration certainly provides a greater opportunity to bond the character to the reader, as the discussion is a direct one. Third-person narration allows authors to further exploit their characters' psyche and offer readers increased objectivity and a broader understanding of the story.

Throughout the history of the mystery, many character types have been allowed into the detective club. Today's mysteries have the freedom to use any type of individual to combat crime. This book is based on the premise that character is mystery's primary appeal, and it is organized around this love of character. This book's bibliography is organized according to the type of mystery characters featured in series. These are the basic character types:

Amateur Detectives

    Traditional amateur detectives

    Eccentric amateur detectives

Public Detectives

    Police detectives

    Lone wolf police

    Detectives who support the police

    Lawyer detectives

Private Detectives

    Private investigators

    Crime specialist detectives

Ex-cop detectives

Rogue detectives

Mystery fans will have a predilection for specific types within these broad ranges—for example, academic amateur detectives, detectives who work in teams, or even detectives who are aided by cats. To find characters with more specific features, users are encouraged to consult the subject index. All users of this book, no matter what their level of expertise, will question the inclusion of certain authors and the exclusion of others. The authors covered in this book represent some aspect of the development and maintenance of the genre. They may be included because they are benchmark authors whose works define a style within the genre. They may be included because of their popularity, even if that popularity was only in their own time period. Authors of single titles may be included because that single title is important in the history of the genre. Likewise, some contemporary authors may not be listed because time has not defined their role in the genre. (The sources listed in the appendix will help you discover the potential significance of contemporary authors and their work.)

Additional Appeals of the Mystery Series

Character is not the only appeal of mystery fiction. Additional appeals include plot, setting, location, theme, and subjects. Access to titles through these features is provided through the annotations, the subjects listed at the end of the annotations, specific icons or symbols that appear in the annotations, and the indexes. Some of these appeals are discussed in chapter 1 of the first *Make Mine a Mystery* volume, "Advising the Mystery Reader."

Hopefully the annotations for each title, and the indexes in this book, will provide additional clues to readers' advisors about what the appeals of a particular series or an individual title are. Each series entry begins with an explanation of how some of these appeals extend over the entire series. Also, the detectives are divided into the type of action that is typical in the series or whether a series can be considered soft-boiled, traditional, or hard-boiled, indicated by the following acronyms at the end of the annotation:

SB soft-boiled mysteries

TM traditional mysteries

HB hard-boiled mysteries

Entries for books that have won awards are identified with an award symbol 🎗 preceding the title, and the specific awards are listed following the annotation, using these symbols:

AG The Agatha Awards winners

AN The Anthony Awards winners

BA The Barry Award winners

DA The Dagger Award winners

DI The Dilys Award winners

ED The Edgar Award winners

MA The Macavity Award winners

SH The Shamus Award winners

Chapter 1

Amateur Detectives

Traditional Amateur Detectives

With one short story, "Murders in the Rue Morgue," Edgar Allan Poe established many of the parameters that still determine the well-written detective story. Poe created his eccentric detective with superior abilities and placed him in opposition to an ineffectual police force. He also created a faithful partner and chronicler for the great detective, so that he would not have to record his own exploits, but ensured that a respectful individual would. Poe fashioned a murder with confusing details, included a list of wrongly suspected suspects, and manipulated the story so that the great detective was left alone to deliver the verdict at the end of the story. Poe did one other courageous thing: he brought his detective back for a second adventure and established series fiction as the norm for the detective hero.

The development of the detective as a fictional hero continued from these beginnings in three directions: amateur, public, and private. The extensions into the area of detectives who do investigations as a part of their job or those who do investigations for a profit are logical.

If fictional detectives bear any relationship to reality, those furthest from the realities of criminal investigations are the amateurs. Yet in the history of mystery fiction, amateur detective characters developed more rapidly than police or private detective characters. This may be partially explained by the rather slow evolution of legitimate police forces and the time it took to develop scientific methods for investigations. Although private investigations were an option for some people in need of a detective, private investigations of murder have always been a fantasy reserved for fiction.

The amateur has a few advantages over public and private detectives. First, amateurs are independent operators who answer only to themselves. Second, the amateur operates outside any restrictions, including the law or the cost of an investigation. Third, amateurs have all the time in the world to investigate a case and can focus all of their attention on the case while ignoring the rest of the world.

But the disadvantages are numerous. An amateur would normally never be allowed anywhere near a murder scene, nor would an amateur have access to any of the evidence. Amateurs do not have the resources available to a public or private detective, including all the scientific methodologies used in modern investigations. They lack the resources to conduct an investigation, including the finances to carry it out.

Yet amateurs continue to play a major role in the world of the fictional detective. Their appeal lies strictly in their personalities, which outweigh any doubts the reader might have about their ability or duty to investigate crimes. They can create the most reader identification among all the types of detectives. By being the least equipped to investigate the crime, they are probably most like the average reader. If reading mystery fiction is an escape, perhaps the ability to suspend disbelief is easiest for readers when the detective is an average individual with amateur status who also has uncommon abilities, a pleasing persona, and continuous access to crime.

Why would reasonable people who are not professional detectives investigate a crime? Perhaps it is because there is no better person for a reader to identify with than another member of society with the courage to act when others are standing by. Maybe it is the need to believe that individuals can still matter, and that society is not completely dependent on organizations, but rather on the courage and tenacity of its individual members. Perhaps it is because reading about the amateur is more fun.

Churchill, Jill (pseud. of Janice Young Brooks) ✍

Jane Jeffry

Jane Jeffry is a single mother with three kids, living in the Chicago area. The amazing thing about her life is that despite all her domestic and social entanglements, she still has time to investigate an occasional crime. Eventually she develops a relationship with Mel VanDyne, a detective on the local police force, which will keep her close to crime. Churchill's fans may also enjoy Katharine Hall Page and Valerie Wolzien. See the author's Web site at http://www.jillchurchill.com. **SB** Series subjects: **Illinois, Chicago**

Grime and Punishment. Avon, 1989.

A Farewell to Yarns. Avon, 1991.

A Quiche Before Dying. Avon, 1993.

The Class Menagerie. Avon, 1994.

Knife to Remember. Avon, 1994.

From Here to Paternity. Avon, 1995.

Silence of the Hams. Avon, 1996.

War and Peas. Avon, 1996.

Fear of Frying. Avon, 1997.

The Merchant of Menace. Avon, 1998.

A Groom with a View. Avon, 1999.

Mulch Ado About Nothing. Morrow, 2000.

The House of Seven Mabels. Morrow, 2002. 0380977362.

Bitsy Burnside has talked Jane Jeffry into remodeling her mansion, insisting that the work crew be all women. Drafting her best friend Shelley Nowack, Jeffry takes on the task with gusto, only to find her project sabotaged. When one of the pranks leaves the contractor dead, Jane and Shelley are eager to play detective to capture a murderer.

Remodeling

Bell, Book, and Scandal. Morrow, 2003. 0060097973.

Jane Jeffry and her friend Shelley Nowack are attending a mystery writers' conference when death strikes an editor named Sophie Smith. As Jane and her pal investigate the poisoning, more incidents happen to other attendees while Jane is trying to shop her manuscript to some agents.

Authors • Publishing

A Midsummer Night's Scream. Morrow, 2004. 0060097981.

Jeffry's best friend Shelley Nowack and her husband have purchased a theater for a local community college and are mounting a production. With Jane roped in to do the catering, she is on the spot when one of the young actors is killed, and her boyfriend Mel VanDyne begins an investigation. The violence should be no surprise considering that the mix of amateur and professional actors includes an egomaniacal writer/director named Steven Imry and the stage stars John and Gloria Bunting. This case must decide whether the show will survive as well as the cast.

Catering • Theater

The Accidental Florist. Morrow, 2007. 9780060528454.

Jane Jeffry has decided to marry Detective Mel VanDyne, and all should be bliss, until her mother decides to take control of every aspect of the wedding. Even Mel's mom wants to chip in. While the preparations move forward, Mel convinces Jane and her pal Shelley to take a self-defense course, which leads to a corpse. Now Jane has to balance a murder investigation against her wedding while keeping the two mothers from killing each other.

Mothers and daughters • Weddings

Coben, Harlan ✍

Myron Bolitar

A combination of detective work, sports, and humor is featured in the early paperback originals about the sports agent Bolitar. These books were well received, but as the series migrated to hardcover, the themes became darker and dealt less with sports. The character Win Horne, the psychotic sidekick, may be one of the more disturbing allies a detective has ever had, but his choice of morality lends depth to Coben's themes. Bolitar's office team includes Esperanza and Big Cindy, two wonderful female characters, each with her own definite sense of self. Readers who enjoy Coben's work may also enjoy Simon Brett (Charlie Paris), Robert Crais, or Laura Lippman. See the official Harlan Coben Web site at http://www.harlancoben.com. **TR** **HB**

> *Deal Breaker.* Dell, 1995.
>
> *Dropshot.* Dell, 1996.
>
> *Fade Away.* Dell, 1996.
>
> *Backspin.* Dell, 1997.
>
> *False Move.* Delacorte, 1998.
>
> *The Final Detail.* Delacorte, 1999.
>
> *Darkest Fear.* Delacorte, 2000.

Promise Me. Dutton, 2006. 9780525949497.

> For six years, Bolitar has been out of the life: no adventures. When he offers aid to two teenage girls, he does not expect to be the last person seen with one of them when she goes missing. To save himself he resurrects himself and once again finds himself on dark paths to try to save the innocent.
>
> *Children in jeopardy • Missing persons • New Jersey*

Long Lost. Dutton, 2009. 9780525951056.

> When Bolitar's former girlfriend Terese Collins calls from Paris, where she is under suspicion of having murdered her ex-husband, he flies to her rescue. Terese's husband Rick was a journalist on the trail of a hot story, and his death is complicated when clues include the DNA of Terese and Rick's dead daughter. Bolitar must chase the leads across the face of Europe to reveal the story behind the headlines.
>
> *DNA • France, Paris • Journalists • Terrorism*

Cross, Amanda (pseud. of Carolyn Heilbrun) ✍

Kate Fansler

English professor Kate Fansler solves mysteries with a literary style. It is often noted that Cross's books may be the modern equivalent of Dorothy L. Sayers's, in that they are witty and crisp in their social commentary. Her thoroughly modern feminist heroine is not shy about expressing opinions or solving crimes. Readers may also enjoy Colin Dexter, Terence Faherty, Antonia Fraser, Reginald Hill, Nancy Pickard, or Dorothy L. Sayers. **TR**

> *In the Last Analysis.* Macmillan, 1964.
>
> *The James Joyce Murder.* Macmillan, 1967.
>
> *Poetic Justice.* Knopf, 1970.
>
> *The Theban Mysteries.* Knopf, 1971.
>
> *The Question of Max.* Knopf, 1976.
>
> *Death in a Tenured Position.* Dutton, 1981 (UK title: *A Death in the Faculty*).
>
> *Sweet Death, Kind Death.* Dutton, 1984.
>
> *No Word from Winnifred.* Dutton, 1986.
>
> *A Trap for Fools.* Dutton, 1989.
>
> *The Players Come Again.* Random House, 1990.
>
> *An Imperfect Spy.* Ballantine, 1995.
>
> *The Collected Stories.* Ballantine, 1997.
>
> *The Puzzled Heart.* Ballantine, 1998.
>
> *Honest Doubt.* Ballantine, 2000.

The Edge of Doom. Ballantine, 2002. 0345452364.

> From her eldest brother Laurence, Fansler learns that a man named Jason "Jay" Ebenezer Smith is claiming to be Fansler's biological father. DNA evidence proves him right, but evidence mounts that the man may not really be Smith. Then Smith disappears.
>
> *DNA • New York, New York • Parents*

Davidson, Diane Mott ✍

Goldy Bear Schulz

Cooking was the hook that brought Davidson's heroine to the attention of readers, and her books contain recipes for those readers who want to challenge themselves in the kitchen. The books do a good job of blending humor with suspense. Based in the fictional Colorado' town Aspen Meadow, this caterer never finds herself far from a mysterious death. It also helps that Goldy's husband, Tom Schulz, is a police detective. Readers may also enjoy Katherine Hall Page or Valerie Wolzien. **SB TR** Series subjects: **Catering • Colorado, Aspen Meadow • Food • Humor**

> *Catering to Nobody.* St. Martin's, 1990.
>
> *Dying for Chocolate.* Bantam, 1992.

The Cereal Murders. Bantam, 1993.

The Last Suppers. Bantam, 1994.

Killer Pancake. Bantam, 1995.

The Main Corpse. Bantam, 1996.

The Grilling Season. Bantam, 1997.

Prime Cut. Bantam, 1998.

Tough Cookie. Bantam, 2000.

Sticks & Scones. Bantam, 2001.

Chopping Spree. Bantam, 2002. 0553107305.

Goldy is preparing a catering job for the Princess Without a Pricetag party at the local mall. When a runaway truck nearly kills her and her staff, she valiantly proceeds to cater the event anyway. Then a fight breaks out. However, finding the dead body of the organizer Barry Dean, killed with one of her own knives, puts a further damper on the day.

Malls

Double Shot. Morrow, 2004. 0060527293.

Schulz has battled her ex-husband Dr. John Richard Korman throughout the series, but never with such consequences as in this entry, when he ends up dead after a disastrous luncheon at which she and he were seen fighting. Neither her son Arch's grief nor an approaching wildfire can keep her from trying to defend herself against a murder charge.

Spousal abuse

Dark Tort. Morrow, 2006. 9780060527310.

Schulz finds the dead body of paralegal Dusty Routt at the law firm where she caters breakfast. Routt's brother has just died in police custody, so the family asks Schulz to investigate Dusty's death. The clues lead Schulz to the paintings of food artist Charlie Baker, which provide the lead to a murderer.

Art

Sweet Revenge. Morrow, 2007. 9780060527334.

Catering a Christmas event at the Aspen Meadow Public Library should be worry free, but not when the caterer is Schulz, and not when a dead body is found in the stacks. The man, disgraced D.A. Drew Wellington, was trying to sell a rare map, and the sale may involve an old nemesis of Schulz. With her husband leading the police investigation, it seems likely that Schulz will stay involved to the end.

Christmas • Libraries • Maps

Fatally Flaky. Morrow, 2009. 9780061348136.

Schulz has many weddings to cater, so her hands are full when Harold "Doc" Finn dies en route to the first one. As she tries to balance all that she does, she also needs to be a detective, especially when her godfather Jack is also attacked. What does all this have to do with a malpractice suit, and how does it all tie into the Golden Gulch spa, run by the less than forthright Victor Lane? With the help of her police officer husband Tom and her assistant Julian Teller, she intends to find out.

Weddings

Dunning, John ✍

Cliff Janeway

Book lovers and book collectors have fallen in love with the insider information gained by reading the adventures of Cliff Janeway, a Denver homicide detective, who quits his job to open the rare book shop Twice Told Tales. Janeway's passion for first editions comes from the fact that the author operated the Old Algonquin Bookstore in Denver for a decade. Readers who enjoy Dunning may also enjoy Lawrence Block's Bernie Rhodenbarr, Jonathan Gash's Lovejoy, or Denver area cop novels like those of Rex Burns. **TR** Series subjects: **Book collecting** • **Bookstores** • **Colorado, Denver** • **Rare books**

Booked to Die. Scribner, 1992. 0684193833.

Denver homicide detective Cliff Janeway has been on the trail of a sociopath named Jackie Newton, whom he believes murders the homeless on Denver's streets. When his overzealousness with Newton gets him suspended from the force, Janeway quits and opens Twice Told Tales, a rare book shop. Determined to create a link between the death of a book scout named Bobby Westfall, who has been beaten to death, and the aforementioned Newton, Janeway begins to follow a trail of first editions that could lead to the clues he needs while also placing his new business in danger.

Homeless

The Bookman's Wake. Scribner, 1995. 0684800039.

When Eleanor Rigby jumps bail and runs to Seattle, ex-cop Clydell Slater hires Janeway to go to Seattle and bring her back. Her crime is that she stole a rare edition of Edgar Allan Poe's *The Raven*, but when Janeway meets the suspect, he begins to believe he has been sent on a wild goose chase. Then Eleanor disappears again, and Janeway finds himself on the hot seat and partnered with Trish Aandahl, a biographer who may have the secret to the whole mystery.

Poe, Edgar Allan • *Washington, Seattle*

The Bookman's Promise. Scribner, 2004. 0743249925.

Janeway's excitement about buying a signed first edition by Sir Richard Francis Burton turns into despair when Josephine Gallant claims it is the long-missing copy owned by her grandfather. She believes her grandfather, a traveling companion of Burton's, had a large collection of memorabilia that is now missing, and she wants Janeway to locate the items and return them to her. When Gallant dies, Janeway continues the search and discovers that there may be others on the same path he is.

Burton, Richard Francis, Sir

The Sign of the Book. Scribner, 2005. 0743255054.

When his lawyer girlfriend Erin D'Angelo asks Janeway to look into the murder charges pending against her old friend Laura Marshall, it is because they have not spoken since Laura broke up the relationship between Erin and the newly deceased, Bobby Marshall. Although Janeway may love Erin, he loves the fact that Bobby Marshall was a book collector more. Does Erin want to forgive and forget and become Laura's defense attorney? Can Janeway free her from the charges, when the police have her confession?

Affairs • Colorado, Paradise • Husbands and wives

The Bookwoman's Last Fling. Scribner, 2006. 9780743289450.

In Idaho to appraise the famed children's book collection of the H. R. and Candice Geiger estate, Janeway discovers that something is amiss in the quality and quantity of the collection. What he discovers is that the life story of Candice, who died twenty years before her husband, may provide clues to who has the collection today and why it was moved.

California, Arcadia • California, San Francisco • Golden Gate Race Track • Horses • Idaho • Santa Anita Race Track

Fluke, Joanne ✍

Hannah Swensen

Hannah Swensen returns to her hometown of Lake Eden in Minnesota after her father's death. She and partner Lisa Herman open The Cookie Jar, a bakery and coffee shop, and it becomes a popular establishment and her office for amateur detective investigations. Through her sister Andrea's husband, Deputy Sheriff Bill Todd, Swensen always has an opening into the small town's criminal scene, to the horror of her mother, Delores. Mother also worries because Swensen cannot decide between Detective Mike Kingston and the local dentist, Norman Rhoades. Swensen's best efforts come when she can move about the community, learning the secrets she will need to solve the crimes. These books include great cookie recipes. Readers may also enjoy Dianne Mott Davidson. **SB** Series subjects: **Baking • Minnesota, Lake Eden • Recipes**

The Chocolate Chip Cookie Murder. Kensington, 2000. 1575665247.

When the milkman, Ron LaSalle, is murdered in the alley behind The Cookie Jar, Swensen joins forces with her brother-in-law, Deputy Sheriff Bill Todd, to investigate. When the owner of the Cozy Cow Diary, Nat Turner, disappears, it seems that the town may be dealing with a crime wave.

Loan sharks • Milkmen

The Strawberry Shortcake Murder. Kensington, 2001. 1575666448.

Swensen is eager to serve as the judge in the Hartland Flour's Dessert bake-off in Lake Eden. When last-minute substitute judge and high school basketball coach Boyd Watson is murdered, Swensen and her sister Andrea begin to dig into the reasons, to keep her friend Danielle, the coach's wife, out of jail. At the same time, a case of blackmail keeps Swensen running after clues.

Blackmail • Coaches • Cooking contests • Husbands and wives • Romance

Blueberry Muffin Murder. Kensington, 2002. 157566707X.

During Lake Eden's annual winter carnival, best-selling cookbook author Connie MacIntyre is found dead inside The Cookie Jar, and Detective Mike Kingston shuts the place down. Hannah and Andrea feel it is up to them to save the reputation of the bakery and launch an investigation. How will the romance between Mike and Hannah work out when he specifically tells her not to investigate?

Authors • Carnivals • Winter

Lemon Meringue Pie Murder. Kensington, 2003. 0758201508.

When the body of beautiful Rhonda Scharf is found in the basement of a recently inherited home, it peaks Swensen's interest, and she is off on another investigation. Did her lemon meringue pie, shared at a meal on the night of Scharf's murder, have anything to do with the crime? Could her sometime boyfriend, dentist Norman Rhodes, be a suspect because he just bought the home from Scharf?

Real estate

Fudge Cupcake Murder. Kensington, 2004. 0758201524.

When Sheriff Grant ends up dead in a dumpster, the number one suspect is the man who announced he would be running against him for election, Bill Todd. Now it is up to Swensen and the pregnant Andrea to defend one of their own against a charge of murder, when Mike Kingston suspends Todd from the force.

Elections • False accusation • Sheriffs

Sugar Cookie Murder. Kensington, 2004. 075820681X.

Everyone is on hand for the special Christmas recipe book release party thrown by Swensen, when Martin Dubinski's new trophy wife, Brandi, is murdered with a cake knife. With Andrea about to have her baby, Hannah is on her own to solve this snowbound mystery.

Christmas • Holidays • Winter

Peach Cobbler Murder. Kensington, 2005. 9780758201546.

> When the Magnolia Blossom bakery opens across the street from her place, Swensen is in a black mood, because Mike is smitten with Shawna Lee Quinn, one of the new owners. Then someone shoots Vanessa Quinn, and Swensen becomes suspect number one.
>
> *False accusation • Love triangles*

Cherry Cheesecake Murder. Kensington, 2006. 9780758202949.

> When Ross Barton, Swensen's' old flame, turns up in Lake Eden to film *Crisis in Cherrywood*, he does not expect murder. When Dean Lawrence shoots himself to death with a prop pistol intended to be used by actor Anson Burke, it is up to Swensen to save the reputation of her old boyfriend and the production company, in order to save the show.
>
> *Actors • Motion pictures*

Key Lime Pie Murder. Kensington, 2007. 9780758210180.

> While judging the baking contest at the Tri-County Fair, Swensen is present when fellow judge Willa Sunquist is murdered. Now it is up to her to find the suspects from the economics teacher's world to determine who was mad at this gentle woman.
>
> *Contests • Fairs • Teachers*

Carrot Cake Murder. Kensington, 2008. 9780758210203.

> When friend Marge Beeseman's Uncle Gus dies at their family reunion, it inspires Swensen to launch a thorough investigation to find out who murdered her friend's relative. Since he left Lake Eden thirty years ago, it seems unlikely that anyone would want Gus dead now. As Swensen investigates, she discovers that Gus is now wealthy, a fortune he built up from leaving with the family's small fortune and borrowing money from relatives he never repaid.
>
> *Family reunions*

Apple Turnover Murder. Kensington Books, 2010. 9780758234896.

> With college professor Bradford Ramsey in town, Swensen now has to juggle the attentions of three men. When she agrees to be a magician's assistant for a charity event, she finds Ramsey dead backstage. Does this have anything to do with the fact that her youngest sister Michelle was also once involved with him?
>
> *Charity events • Love triangles*

Hambly, Barbara ✍

Benjamin January

Benjamin January is a free man of color who has lived in Paris for many years. Both a doctor and a musician, he has lived a good life. Then his wife dies, and he decides to return to New Orleans. Once he is back in America of the 1830s, he is beset

with all the problems of a man who will be judged not by his contributions and talents but by the color of his skin. He finds that he is often asked to aid his friend, Abishag Shaw of the New Orleans City Guards, and work with his white musician friend, Hannibal Sefton. Readers may also enjoy C. S. Harris, Anne Perry, Robert E. Skinner, David Fulmer, Walter Mosley, or Kris Nelscott. **TR**
Series subjects: **African American • Historical (1800–1899) • Louisiana, New Orleans • Physicians • Race relations • Slavery**

A Free Man of Color. Bantam, 1997. 0553102583.

> While working as a piano player at a Carnival revelry, Benjamin becomes involved in the search for Madeleine Trepagier's family jewels when the white woman attends the octoroon, or the ball for people of color. The jewels are in the possession of Angelique Crozat, mistress to Madeleine's dead husband. When Angelique is murdered, January takes up the cause of finding the murderer. Allying himself with a sympathetic policeman named Abishag Shaw, January tries to retain his dignity and solve the crime.
>
> *Mardi Gras*

Fever Season. Bantam, 1998. 0553102540.

> Benjamin January is applying his medical skills at the Charity Hospital in a vain attempt to stem the tide of the cholera epidemic of 1833, while still giving music lessons for money. When the lover of a servant in the home of one of his pupils asks him for help, January begins to ask the wrong questions. Cora Chouteau may be a runaway herself, and she is now accused of murdering her master, Otis Redfern, and nearly killing his wife Emily with poison. When Cora disappears, January discovers that he must look at both Cora and Emily as potential murderers.
>
> *Cholera*

Graveyard Dust. Bantam, 1999. 0553102591.

> When Benjamin's sister Olympe has been arrested for murder, accused of providing the poison that killed Isaak Jumon, he attempts to clear her. Also on trial is Isaak's wife Célie, who stands accused by Isaak's brother Antione. Mixed into the stew of this case is the fact that Olympe practices the dark arts of voodoo, which may get her hanged when Célie admits to ordering a curse. Meanwhile, a killer named Killdevil is trying to make sure that Benjamin helps no one, while the city suffers a cholera epidemic.
>
> *Cholera • Husbands and wives • Voodoo*

Sold Down the River. Bantam, 2000. 0553102575.

> Benjamin has decided to investigate the strange happenings on the Simon Fourchet sugar plantation by going undercover as a field hand. This is especially scary for Benjamin because he was sold from this plantation when he was a seven-year-old boy and now is returning to work for his former master, who is convinced he has a slave revolt on his hands. Arson

and murder are rampant on the plantation, and voodoo is in the air. Benjamin must try to watch both the overlords and the slaves for potential sources of all the happenings that are haunting this homestead.

Plantations • Voodoo

Die Upon a Kiss. Bantam, 2001. 0553109243.

Lorenzo Belaggio has opened the American Theater to present opera to the society of New Orleans, and Benjamin finds himself hired to play in the orchestra. During an attack on the new concert master, Benjamin is injured as well, and eventually a sponsor is murdered. Belaggio believes the rival owner of another opera company tried to murder him, but January thinks perhaps the real clues lie in the basic plot of the first opera that Belaggio is to present, *Othello*.

Opera • Othello • Shakespeare, William

Wet Grave. Bantam, 2002. 0553109359.

It appears that Benjamin is the only one who cares when an old hag named Hesione LeGros is found murdered in the depths of despair that is the worst of New Orleans. He remembers the days when she moved in the best of society as a white man's mistress and is troubled enough by her death as a penniless whore to seek a reason. While he also spends time chasing the fair Rose Vitrac, a second murder leads him down a dark path that questions the roots of some of New Orleans's finest families.

Mistresses • Prostitutes

Days of the Dead. Bantam, 2003.

Now married to the fair Rose, Benjamin takes her on a mission in Mexico City to help their musician friend, Hannibal Sefton. Sefton is charged with the murder of Fernando, the son of Don Prospero de Castellon, a prosperous landowner. What the couple finds is that this culture is not easy to sift through when seeking a murderer among the convoluted family relationships at the Hacienda Mictlán, especially when the Don expects all to be revealed when his son returns on the Day of the Dead.

Day of the Dead • Mexico, Mexico City

Dead Water. Bantam, 2004. 0553109545.

The Januarys are now operating a school for girls of color. They are approached by their banker with the distressing news that $100, 000 is missing, including all of their savings. By tracing the suspected employee, the detectives end up on the steamboat *Silver Moon*, on a short cruise to adventure, when the ship docks in Natchez-Under-the Hill with the Januarys working undercover as Hannibal Sefton's slaves.

Embezzlement • Mississippi, Natchez-under-the-Hill • Shipboard • Steamboats

Dead and Buried. Severn, 2010. 9780727868671.

When January attends a friend's funeral, he and the guests are stunned when the coffin is tipped and out rolls the body of a white man. When his friend Hannibal Sefton recognizes the corpse but appears afraid to tell the man's story, January knows he has another mystery to solve. What he does not know is that a connection to nobility will reveal the secrets of his beloved New Orleans.

Funerals • Nobility

Harris, C. S. ✍

Sebastian St. Cyr

During the Regency period in England, Sebastian St. Cyr, Viscount Devlin, is a former army officer in the Napoleonic Wars and heir to an earldom. At odds with the society that he thrives in, he takes on the role of detective to solve crimes, utilizing his skill at disguises and his willingness to defend the innocent. His most reliable ally is his lover, Kat Boleyn, while his most challenging enemy is Lord Jarvis. Readers may also enjoy Sir Arthur Conan Doyle, Bruce Alexander, Anne Perry, Charles Todd, and Rhys Bowen. See the author's Web site at http://www.csharris.net/sebastian.php. **TR** Series subjects: **England, London • Historical (1800–1899) • Nobility • Regency England**

What Angels Fear. New American Library, 2005. 9780451216694.

It is 1811 in England, and the country lives in fear of the madness of its own King George III. When Rebecca York is found murdered on the steps of a parish church not far from Westminster Abbey, a dueling pistol is found among her clothing. It belongs to Sebastian St. Cyr, Viscount Devlin, who must take up detecting in order to clear himself of the accusation of murder.

False accusation

When Gods Die. New American Library, 2006. 9780451222558.

When the Prince Regent is found with the corpse of a beautiful woman, the powers that be assign St. Cyr the task of discovering who is guilty of what. Draped around the victim's neck is an ancient necklace that once belonged to his own mother, and now the royal detective needs to probe not only the suspect's alibis but his own past to discover the clues to a killer.

England, East Sussex, Brighton • Jewels

Why Mermaids Sing. Obsidian, 2007. 9780451222268.

There is a serial killer loose in 1811, and his target is the sons of the wealthiest members of society. When the magistrate asks St. Cyr for help, he finds the clues may lie in a poem by John Donne that reveals a dark secret among the elite of Regency society. Will the sons be sacrificed for the sins of the fathers?

Fathers and sons • Serial killer

Where Serpents Sleep. Obsidian, 2008. 9780451225122.

When a Quaker safe house for prostitutes becomes a death house for eight of them, the only survivor is the daughter of the Prince Regent's cousin, Lord Jarvis. When the young woman, Hero Jarvis, turns to St. Cyr for help in investigating the crimes, the two discover that a series of murders in the darkest parts of London may lead them to a murderer in the highest strata of society.

Prostitutes

What Remains of Heaven. Obsidian, 2009. 9780451228024.

When the Bishop of London is murdered, the task of finding his killer falls to St. Cyr. It will come as no surprise that this powerful man also had some powerful enemies, and though they may be suspects for St. Cyr, they also could be the forces behind the selection of the next Archbishop of Canterbury. A confusing element in the case is the other victim: a mummified body found in the same crypt as the bishop. To make it worse, St. Cyr finds his tangled relationship with Miss Hero Jarvis will be strained because she was the last person to see the bishop alive.

Archbishop of Canterbury • Religion

Hart, Carolyn G. ✍

Annie Laurance/Max Darling

Death on Demand is a mystery bookstore owned by Laurance, located on the island of Broward's Rock off the coast of South Carolina. Part of the fun of reading Hart's books is that readers can follow clues about other great mystery novels while reading these cases. As Hart makes reference to the greats who preceded her in the field, she also creates two separate levels of enjoyment in her books. This series includes a plucky couple relationship, with Annie's eventual husband, Max Darling, the dilettante private eye, playing an equal role as detective. Readers may also enjoy Anne George, Frances Lockridge and Richard Lockridge, Joan Hess, or Katherine Hall Page. See the author's Web site at http://www.carolynhart.com. **SB** Series subjects: **Islands • South Carolina, Broward's Rock • Teams**

Death on Demand. Bantam, 1987.

Design for Murder. Bantam, 1988.

Something Wicked. Bantam, 1988.

Honeymoon with Murder. Bantam, 1989.

A Little Class on Murder. Doubleday, 1989.

Deadly Valentine. Doubleday, 1990.

The Christie Caper. Bantam. 1991.

Southern Ghost. Bantam, 1992.

Mint Julep Murder. Bantam, 1995.

Yankee Doodle Dead. Avon, 1998.

White Elephant Dead. Avon, 1999.

Sugar Plum Death. Morrow, 2000.

April Fool Dead. Morrow, 2002. 0380977745.

When Annie's plans to host mystery writer Emma Clyde go awry because someone wants her events to fail, it sets off a chain reaction that leads to murder. When two people die, Annie finds herself a suspect. As Max and Annie try to find out who is trying to sabotage them, they discover secrets on the island that will lead them to the murderer.

Authors

Engaged to Die. Morrow, 2003. 006000469X.

Jake O'Neill is murdered on the very night when his engagement to heiress Virginia Neville was to be announced at the opening of a new collection at the Neville Art Gallery. The accused is Laurance's assistant Chloe, and Darling is deputized to help solve the murder. With their loyalties split, Laurance and Darling take their separate investigations in different directions.

Art

Murder Walks the Plank. Morrow, 2004. 0060004746.

Annie has planned a fund-raising cruise off the island, with attendees costumed as their favorite characters. When one of the revealers, Pamela Potts, falls overboard and drowns, it appears to be a tragic accident. The next day, when another victim is found dead in their home, Max and Annie know they must try to discover who is killing their neighbors.

Shipboard

Death of the Party. Morrow, 2005. 0060004762.

Media mogul Jeremiah Addison has fallen down a flight of stairs inside his mansion on his private island, Golden Silk. Knowing that she has removed the trap that tripped her brother-in-law, Britt Barlow decides not to tell the police. Instead, she has a gathering of the suspects and puts Max's Confidential Commissions in charge of finding a killer. Isolated on the private island, the suspects and the detectives all fall victim to the schemes of the murderer.

South Carolina, Golden Silk

Dead Days of Summer. Morrow, 2006. 9780060724047.

When Max fails to arrive home in a timely fashion one night, a search for him turns up his car, a murder weapon, and a dead woman. When Max is arrested and the police chief is removed from the case, Annie goes undercover to clear her husband's name.

False accusation • Missing persons

Death Walked In. Morrow, 2008. 9780060724146.

Max is too busy renovating the old Franklin House to take a call, and it is left to Annie to find Gwen Jamison near death from a gunshot wound. Missing are $2 million worth of gold coins called Double Eagles that belonged to Geoffrey Grant, and the blame falls on Gwen's son Robert. But the real trouble comes when everyone assumes the coins are hidden in Franklin House.

Coins

Dare to Die. Morrow, 2009. 9780061453038.

Annie is helping her friends by managing their motel. When former resident Iris Tilford returns to the island and attends a party thrown by the Darlings, she ends up strangled in a nearby wood. Could it have something to do with a ten-year-old mystery and the disappearance of two of Iris's high school friends? Annie tries to stay clear, but when danger strikes near home, it is time for her to join her PI husband Max in the investigation.

Hotels and motels

Laughed 'Til He Died. Morrow, 2010. 9780061453090.

Broward's Rock Island has a youth recreation center that is the focus of the crime when Annie and Max take on another local mystery. First a local youth supposedly falls from a viewing platform, and then one of the center's board members is murdered. When the investigation reveals that his mistress is in charge of Haven and his wife does not care that he is dead, Annie and Max begin to assemble a cast of suspects for the murders.

Youth recreation centers

Henrie O.

Henrietta O'Dwyer Collins is a retired newspaper reporter whose cases take her all over the American landscape. This series is darker than the series featuring Laurance and Darling, listed above. Readers may also enjoy Sujata Massey or Nancy Pickard. See the author's Web site at http://www.carolynhart.com. **TR**

Dead Man's Island. Bantam, 1993.

Scandal in Fair Haven. Bantam, 1994.

Death in Lover's Lane. Avon, 1997.

Death in Paradise. Avon, 1998.

Death on the River Walk. Avon, 1999.

Resort to Murder. Morrow, 2001.

Set Sail for Murder. Morrow, 2007. 9780060724030.

Jimmy Lennox, Henrie O's former boyfriend, wants her to investigate a threat against his current wife, Sophia Montgomery. Sophia has decided to settle the issue by gathering her extended family and making a decision about their inheritances. So Henrie O finds herself on a two-week cruise in the Baltic with a ship full of Sophia's stepchildren, all of whom have reason to kill their stepmother.

Baltic • Cruises • Stepchildren • Wills

Hart, Erin ✍

Nora Gavin

American pathologist Dr. Nora Gavin has fled her Minnesota homeland to hide in Ireland after her sister Triona's unsolved murder. While she is supposed to be working in Dublin, she finds herself called away to wild lands of the bogs, where her forensic skills are put to the test by the ancient copses that surface occasionally from the peat. Finding herself attracted to the handsome archaeologist Corman Maguire, she resists settling down until she can put her ghosts to rest. Readers of this series may also like the Appalachian stories of Sharyn McCrumb. See the author's Web site at http://www.erinhart.com. **TR** Series subjects: **Pathologists**

Haunted Ground. Scribner, 2003. 0743235053.

When a bog person's head is discovered in Lough Derg, the call goes out to archaeologist Cormac Maguire and a visiting American pathologist named Nora Gavin. One of the first charges to the investigator is to try and identify in what age the red-harried woman lived and what the cause of her death was. Meanwhile, the investigators hear of the tragedy at Bracklyn House, where Hugh Osborne's Indian-born wife Mina and child have disappeared while walking in the bog. With local detective Garret Devaney on the case, there is hope the modern mystery will be solved along with the ancient puzzle.

Ireland, County Galway, Lough Derg • Peat bogs

Lake of Sorrows. Scribner, 2004. 0743247965.

Dr. Gavin is called to another bog when a long dead body is discovered and finds herself investigating alongside her lover, archaeologist Corman Maguire. The old victim appears to be a "triple death" pagan sacrifice, but everyone is shocked when a fresher corpse is found with the same ritualistic markings. As the two reluctant partners battle their own demons, they must take on the controversies of the people who work and live around the peat bogs of Loughnabrone.

Ireland, County Offaly, Loughnabrone Bog • *Peat bogs*

False Mermaid. Scribner, 2010. 9781416563761.

After her three years in Ireland, Dr. Gavin returns to St. Paul, intent on proving that her brother-in-law Peter Hallett murdered her sister Triona. With Peter about to remarry, Gavin also would like to protect her eleven-year-old niece Elizabeth. When a crucial piece of evidence indicates that Triona's murder might not have been the only one committed five years ago, it opens the door to new clues that lead to a solution for the haunted Dr. Gavin, but not before she must return to Ireland to follow the story of another haunting.

Folklore • *Ireland, Donegal* • *Minnesota, St. Paul* • *Sisters*

Littlefield, Sophie

Stella Hardesty

Stella Hardesty is a businesswoman who owns the Hardesty Sewing Machine Sales & Repair shop in Prosper, Missouri. Because she herself is a victim of domestic violence and now a widow in her fifties, her real passion is to help battered women and to make sure that their abusive partners cannot harm them again. Her method is to act as both judge and jury, often with the help of local sheriff Goat Jones and a former client, Chrissy Shaw. Readers may also enjoy Joan Hess. See the author's Web site at http://www.sophielittlefield.com. **TR** **HB** Series subjects: **Domestic abuse** • **Missouri, Prosper** • **Vigilantism**

A Bad Day for Sorry. Minotaur, 2009.

Chrissy Shaw comes to Hardesty for help because she has an abusive husband, Roy Dean Shaw. When the husband snatches their two-year-old son and disappears, Hardesty goes into action. She finds herself up against an organized crime ring specializing in auto parts, but allied with the local sheriff and a more than willing client.

Organized crime

A Bad Day for Pretty. Minotaur, 2010.

A local tornado unearths the mummified body of an abused woman from under the demolition derby track at the fairgrounds. When her friend Donna Donovan's husband Neb is accused of the crime, Hardesty jumps to his defense. Meanwhile, her relationship with Sheriff Goat Jones becomes complicated when his' ex-wife arrives in town gunning for him. Still recovering from being shot on her last case, Hardesty is happy to have Chrissy as her assistant, because the sheriff is not in the mood to cooperate.

False accusation

Massey, Sujata ✎

Rei Shimura

Rei Shimura, an English teacher living in Tokyo, is trying to understand the conflicts between her American and Japanese backgrounds. Rei's other skills lie in the area of antiques, and her cases often involve the complex relationships of a piece of antiquity to a modern drama. To her surprise, she finds herself constantly challenged by death, as well as the culture she lives in. Readers may also enjoy Carolyn G. Hart (Henrie O.), Nancy Pickard, and S. J. Rozan. See the author's Web site at http://interbridge.com/sujata. **TR**

> *The Salaryman's Wife*. HarperPaperbacks, 1997.
>
> *Zen Attitude*. HarperPaperbacks, 1998.
>
> *The Flower Master*. HarperCollins, 1999.
>
> *The Floating Game*. HarperCollins, 2000.
>
> *The Bride's Kimono*. HarperCollins, 2001.

The Samurai's Daughter. HarperCollins, 2003. 0066212901.
    Hugh Glendinning, Shimura's boyfriend, is working on a reparation case for sex slave victims of World War II. When his San Francisco investigation leads to murder, it is fortunate that Shimura is in town visiting her relatives. When a medical student named Manami Okada, who lives with her family, disappears, Shimura finds herself probing the history of her own family, some of whom may carry guilt for their own actions during World War II.
    California, San Francisco • Japan, Tokyo • World War II

The Pearl Diver. HarperCollins, 2004. 0066212960.
    Shimura has finally decided to live with her boyfriend, lawyer Hugh Glendinning, while also accepting an assignment to decorate a new Asian restaurant. When Shimura's cousin Kendall Johnson disappears from the restaurant's grand opening, the detective finds herself a temporary mother to Kendall's two children. A second case opens up when the restaurant's hostess Andrea wants her war-bride mother located more than thirty years after she disappeared.
    Washington, D.C. • Weddings • World War II

The Typhoon Lover. HarperCollins, 2005. 9780060765125.
    Takeo Kayama, Rei Shimura's former lover, is believed to be in possession of an artifact liberated from a Baghdad museum. Asked by the U.S. government to retrieve the ancient pitcher, an ibex ewer, from Takeo's collection in Japan, Shimura, who is mystified by her assignment, must leave her current lover Hugh behind. When Shimura arrives on the island,

she finds a country devastated by a typhoon and uses that as cover to infiltrate the home and heart of Takeo.

> *Artifacts • Japan, Kamakura • Japan, Tokyo • Weddings*

Girl in a Box. HarperCollins, 2006. 9780060765149.

Shimura has gone to work for the Organization for Cultural Intelligence. Her first assignment is to go undercover in a Tokyo department store, Mitsutan, where suspicions exist about the money flowing through the business. She finds it difficult to immerse herself in the life of a Japanese woman and struggles with the cultural differences. When events begin to spin out of control, Michael Hendricks arrives to rescue Shimura, which heightens the romance between the two spies.

> *Business corruption • Department stores • Japan, Tokyo • Spies*

Shimura Trouble. Severn House, 2008. 9780727866011.

Shimura's father, Toshiro, is recovering from a stroke, but that does not keep her from taking him to Hawai'i for a strange family reunion with some previously unknown relatives. Part of her family is attempting to recover land they believe was taken illegally from them during World War II. When the arrest of a nephew on a false charge of arson leads her to believe the persecution of her family may be continuing into the present, she decides to use her skills to help her newfound relatives.

> *Family reunions • Hawai'i, Oahu • World War II*

Mosley, Walter ✍

Easy Rawlins

Revealing the African American experience in America through a set of historical novels, Mosley displays the travails of Easy Rawlins as he tries to make a place for himself in America. Mosley takes cases to make money or as favors to friends, and occasionally for justice, out of a sense of outrage. His friend Mouse is one of the most interesting and dangerous sidekicks ever created for a detective. These novels should be recommended to hard-boiled mystery readers. Readers may also enjoy Terence Faherty and Don Winslow. **HB** **Historical.** Series subjects: **African American • California, Los Angeles • Historical (1900–1999)**

> *Devil in a Blue Dress*. Norton, 1990.
>
> *A Red Death*. Norton, 1991.
>
> *White Butterfly*. Norton, 1992.
>
> *Black Betty*. Norton, 1994.

A Little Yellow Dog. Norton, 1996. 0393039242.

Now the head custodian at the Sojourner Truth Junior High School in Watts, Easy is usually first in the school each day. One day he is joined by Idabell Turner, who weaves a tale of her mad husband, gives Easy a tumble, and then disappears, leaving Easy holding her dog. When a well-dressed male corpse ends up on school grounds and then another body is found, the clues lead back to Easy, who finds the good life just got hard again.

Dogs • Schools

Gone Fishin'. Black Classic Press, 1997. 1574780255.

This is a flashback story set in 1939 that will establish the early relationship between Easy Rawlins and Raymond Alexander, otherwise known as Mouse. When the two young men decide to take a road trip to Pariah, where Mouse's stepfather Reese Corn lives, it sets up a scenario that will establish their kinship for the rest of their lives. Ostensibly going to ask for money, the choices that each man makes force them to deal with issues revolving around their fathers.

Fathers and sons • Texas, Houston • Texas, Pariah

Bad Boy Brawly Brown. Little, Brown, 2002. 0316073016.

The Urban Revolutionary Party is a group of African Americans who have rejected the white man, and one of its members is an old friend of Easy's, Brawly Brown. Asked to find her son by Brawly's mom, Easy finds himself accused of murder when he finds a dead body. With the revolution in chaos and an old friendship on the line, Easy must decide how to confront a cause that may ask him to make a sacrifice he is not willing to make.

Racism

Six Easy Pieces. Atria, 2003. 0743442520.

A collection of the following stories: "Amber Gate," "Crimson Stain," "Gator Green," "Gray-Eyed Death," "Lavender," "Silver Lining," and "Smoke."

Short stories

Little Scarlet. Little, Brown, 2004. 0316073032.

After the Watts Riots of 1965, Rawlins is hired unofficially by the police when a black woman named Nola Payne, known as Little Scarlet, is murdered. It is a well-known fact in the black community that Nola had been sheltering a white man in her apartment during the riots, but could he have committed the murder? Never sure if Mouse's help is really necessary, Rawlins sets out on a quest to undercover the truth without setting the city on fire again.

Watts Riots

Cinnamon Kiss. Little, Brown, 2005. 9780316073028.

When Rawlins's daughter Feather's illness can only be cured by a trip to a Swiss clinic, he finds himself needing $35,000. He takes a job from P.I. Saul

Lynx and finds himself in San Francisco looking for a missing lawyer and his lover, Cinnamon. He is forced to hunt for the truth during the "Summer of Love."

Blonde Faith. Little, Brown, 2007. 9780316734592.

Bonnie Shay has decided to leave her lover, Rawlins, and Rawlins's friend Mouse is once again wanted for murder. Rawlins's other friend Christmas Black, a Green Beret in Vietnam, has also disappeared, leaving his adopted eight-year-old Vietnamese child with Rawlins. All of this emotional turmoil makes it hard for Easy to choose which path to follow, until he finds Faith.

Vietnamese War, 1961–1975

Newman, Sharan ✍

Catherine LeVendeur

The Middle Ages provides a rich tapestry for Newman, as her historically accurate mysteries try to dispel some of the myths about the role of women in that period. Set in twelfth-century France, this series follows LeVendeur from her days as a young novice in a convent into womanhood. They can be recommended to traditional mystery readers. Readers may also enjoy Laurie King (Mary Russell/Sherlock Holmes), Ellis Peters, and Steven Saylor. See the author's Web site at http://www.hevanet.com/sharan/ Levendeur.html. **TR** **Historical.** Series subjects: **Historical (1100–1199)** • **Religion**

Death Comes as Epiphany. Tor, 1993.

The Devil's Door. Forge, 1994.

The Wandering Arm. Forge, 1995.

Strong as Death. Forge, 1996.

Cursed in the Blood. Forge, 1998.

The Difficult Saint. Forge, 1999.

To Wear the White Cloak. Forge, 2000.

Heresy. Forge, 2002. 0765302462.

LeVendeur, pregnant and missing her husband, who has gone to Spain, decides to visit the convent run by her friend, the abbess Heloise. When Heloise's son Astrolabe is accused of the murder of a heretic named Cecile, LeVendeur decides to take action by harboring the fugitive from justice and seeking the real killer.

France, Reims

The Witch in the Well. Forge, 2004. 0765308819.

The family legend clearly states that if the well runs dry in the castle, the family will be cursed. As death begins to surround them and an evil lord seeks to take over the family homestead, Catherine seeks out the pagan ways to prevent the ultimate tragedy from coming true.

Curses • France, Boisvert • Witches

Page, Katherine Hall ✍

Faith Sibley Fairchild

Having given up a career as a caterer and moved to a small Massachusetts town to marry a clergyman, Fairchild finds that murder occurs even in a small town setting. This series manages to combine an interest in food with an interest in crime, and each book comes with recipes. It can be recommended to soft-boiled or traditional mystery readers. Readers may also enjoy Jill Churchill, Diane Mott Davidson, and Valerie Wolzien. **TR**

The Body in the Belfry. St. Martin's, 1990.

The Body in the Kelp. St. Martin's, 1991.

The Body in the Bouillon. St. Martin's, 1991.

The Body in the Vestibule. St. Martin's, 1992.

The Body in the Cast. St. Martin's, 1993.

The Body in the Basement. St. Martin's, 1994.

The Body in the Bog. Morrow, 1996.

The Body in the Fjord. Morrow, 1997.

The Body in the Bookcase. Morrow, 1998.

The Body in the Big Apple. Morrow, 1999.

The Body in the Moonlight. Morrow, 2001.

The Body in the Bonfire. Morrow, 2002.

The Body in the Lighthouse. Morrow, 2003. 038097844X.

Their cottage on Sanpere Island brings the Fairchilds into a battle over a historic lighthouse that is being threatened by developers. When a real estate agent is poisoned and the body of developer Harold Hapswell washes up at the base of the lighthouse, Fairchild finds herself driven to investigate who on the island took this vicious step to try to save the lighthouse. Her investigation brings her into personal danger, and despite the highs of the summer festival season, the island residents suffer the lows of arson and murder.

Lighthouses • Maine, Penobscot Bay, Sanpere Island

The Body in the Attic. Morrow, 2004. 9780060525316.

When her husband Tom accepts a one-year position at the Harvard Divinity School, Fairchild finds herself relocated to Cambridge. When she discovers a diary in the attic of her creepy temporary home, it leads to an investigation into the past that includes uniting with her long-lost boyfriend, Richard Morgan.

Academia • Harvard University • Massachusetts, Boston • Massachusetts, Cambridge

The Body in the Snowdrift. Morrow, 2005. 9780060525309.

The entire family is gathering for grandfather's seventieth birthday on the slopes of a Vermont ski resort called Pine Slopes. When Fairchild finds the dead body of Boyd Harrisson on the cross-country trail, it is just the beginning of a series of misadventures that try the patience of her extended family. Being friends with the Staffords, who own the resort, Fairchild is driven to determine who is committing this havoc in the vacation wonderland.

Catering • Skiing • Vacations • Vermont

The Body in the Ivy. Morrow, 2006. 9780060763657.

Barbara Bailey Bishop, best-selling author, has invited a select group of nine alumni of Pelham College to a remote island in New England. Fairchild is there to cater when a storm hits, cutting off the guests from the mainland. Then a murder occurs, and Fairchild learns it is linked to the death of Bishop's twin sister on the campus thirty years before.

Catering • Islands • New England

The Body in the Gallery. Morrow, 2008. 9780060763671.

The suggestion that she open a café in the Ganley Art Museum appeals to Fairchild, until she finds that her detective skills are needed as much as her culinary ones. Forgeries have been slipped into the museum, and Patsy Avery, the president of the museum board, would like to know how and why. So would the police, when an unidentified body ends up as a part of a new installation at the museum.

Art museums • Catering • Massachusetts, Aleford

The Body in the Sleigh. Morrow, 2009. 9780061474255.

Fairchild and her family are holidaying on Sanpere Island for Christmas. But then the dead body of Norah Taft, a local girl who changed from the apple of her grandparent's eye to a runaway with a drug problem and the new name of Zara, turns up in the Christmas display in front of the Sanpere Historical Society. Already busy because she discovered the body, Fairchild is contacted by a reclusive spinster named Mary Bethany, who has just found a babe in the manger on her goat farm.

Christmas • Maine, Penobscot Bay, Sanpere Island

Peters, Elizabeth ✍

Vicky Bliss

Art history is Bliss's specialty, and also her entrée into the world of murder. Her PhD in medieval European history also helps add some interesting aspects to her career in crime, as does the author's use of humor. Mostly it is the plucky spirit of the detective that appeals to the reader. Readers may also enjoy Aaron Elkins or Nancy Pickard. See the author's Web site at http://www.mpmbooks.com. **SB** **TR** Series subjects: **Antiquities**

> *Borrower of the Night.* Dodd, Mead, 1973.
>
> *Street of the Five Moons.* Dodd, Mead, 1978.
>
> *Silhouette in Scarlet.* Congdon, 1983.
>
> *Trojan Gold.* Atheneum, 1987.
>
> *Night Train to Memphis.* Warner, 1994.

Laughter of Dead Kings. Morrow, 2008. 9780061246241.

> Bliss is an assistant curator at the National Museum in Munich. Her lover, John Tregarth, is accused of stealing King Tut's mummy from the Valley of the Kings, which comes as a great surprise to the retired art thief. Bliss, her boss at the museum, and John all take off on a whirlwind adventure in an attempt to clear John's name of this new crime.
>
> *Egypt, Valley of the Kings • King Tut*

Rees, Matt Beynon ✍

Omar Yussef

Omar Yussef is a Palestinian who journeys from a life in politics, to teaching history, to being a detective. His daily life is affected by who he is and where he lives. The cases that he gets embroiled in serve as a background for a man with limited national identity. The series should appeal to those who like the international politically oriented stories told in other novels from Soho Press, such as those by Cara Black, Colin Cotterill, or Rebecca Pawel. The author's Web site can be found at http://www.mattbeynonrees.com. **TR**

The Collaborator of Bethlehem. Soho Press, 2007. 9781569474426.

> Omar Yussef is a schoolteacher in the Dehaisha Palestinian refugee camp in the West Bank. When one of his former students, George Saba, is taken by the ak-Aqsa Martyrs Brigade for collaborating with the Israelis, only Omar has the courage to stand up against the injustice. What he finds is that the powers that be in this city may have no power at all.
>
> *Israel, Bethlehem • Muslims • Palestinian–Israeli relations • Refugees • Teachers*

A Grave in Gaza. Soho, 2008. 9781569474723.

Omar Yussef is on a school inspection tour in the Gaza Strip when he is embroiled in the arrest of a schoolteacher on spying charges, probably brought about by his accusation of governmental corruption. When Yussef's Swedish boss Magnus Wallender is kidnapped and another UN official is murdered, Yussef's support is withdrawn. Yussef stays anyway and finds himself drawn into the governmental chaos of the region, having to deal with an ineffective leadership and the militants who oppose it.

Israel, Gaza Strip • Kidnapping

The Samaritan's Secret. Soho, 2009. 9781569475454.

When Ishaq, a Palestinian Authority official, is murdered, the Samaritan community where he lived discovers that millions in government money is missing. Yussef undertakes the investigation in the hopes of solving Ishaq's murder so the money can be recovered before the World Bank stops all aid to the Palestinian people.

Israel, Nablus • Samaritans

The Fourth Assassin. Soho, 2010. 9781569476192.

In New York City to deliver an address to the United Nations on the refugee situation in Palestine, Yussef must rise to the defense of his son Ala when he finds the decapitated body of his son's roommate in their Brooklyn apartment. While his son languishes in jail, Yussef discovers that the land of opportunity is challenging to a man like him, and the neighborhood of Bay Ridge is not a peaceful Palestinian enclave.

Fathers and sons • New York, New York • Palestinian Americans

Robotham, Michael ✍

Joe O'Loughlin

Joe O'Loughlin can help others as a psychologist, but who helps him? He suffers from Parkinson's disease. His disease surfaces just about the same time that murder does. Readers may also enjoy Ian Rankin, T. Jefferson Parker, or Minette Walters. The author's Web site can be found at http://www.michaelrobotham.com/usa/index. htm. **HB**

Suspect. Doubleday, 2005. 0385508611. (UK: Little, Brown, 2004).

Joe O'Loughlin' is dragged into a murder investigation when the victim is a former client who once charged him with sexual assault. Once Joe exhibits an interest in the case, he begins to discover that he is the most likely suspect in the girl's murder. As his personal life spins out of control and he becomes the target of the police, he is the only one who believes in his innocence.

England, London • England, Merseyside, Liverpool • Parkinson's disease • Psychologists

Lost. Doubleday, 2006. 9780385508667. (UK: Little Brown, 2005).

> When Detective Inspector Vincent Ruiz is pulled from the Thames with a bullet in his leg and no memory of how he got there, he is turned over to psychologist Joe O'Loughlin. With a boat full of blood nearby and a photograph of a long-missing seven-year-old in his pocket, the cop has some explaining to do. Facing suspicion and accusations of faking his illness, Ruiz is going to be dependent on the doctor for help in explaining why he was investigating a case in which the accused is safely convicted and in prison.
>
> *Children in jeopardy • England, London • Missing persons • Recovered memories*

Shatter. Doubleday, 2008. 9780385517911. (UK: Sphere, 2008).

> Now teaching part time at university, Joe fails to stop a suicide attempt; the woman leaps to her death from a bridge. Disturbed by his failure, he tries to play detective. When the woman's daughter contacts him with crucial information, he turns to his friend Vincent Ruiz, a retired detective, for help. Then another death occurs, and Joe begins to think this all may be tied to his practice.
>
> *England, Somerset, Bath • Suicide*

Spencer-Fleming, Julia ✍

Reverend Clare Fergusson

As the first female priest of the St. Alban's Episcopal Church in Millers Kill, New York, Reverend Clare Fergusson faces all the daily challenges of a representative in her calling. Add to that her second calling, detective. Her toughness comes from her training in the U.S. Army as a helicopter pilot during Desert Storm. Working in and around her rural home in the Adirondacks, she finds herself in an association with Chief of Police Russ Van Alystyne. Eventually this series becomes about these two individuals and their unique relationship. Readers may also enjoy Kate Charles's Callie Anson, Diane Mott Davidson's Goldy Bear, and Janet Evanovich's Stephanie Plum. See the author's Web site at http://www.juliaspencerfleming.com/index.html. **TR** Series subjects: **Adirondack Mountains • Affairs • Churches • Clergy • Episcopal Church • New York, Millers Kill • Religion**

In the Bleak Midwinter. St. Martin's Minotaur, 2002. 0312288476.

> When the new priest at St. Alban's finds an abandoned baby on her doorstep, she gets in contact with Millers Kill Chief of Police Russ Van Alstyne. A few days later, when the mother is found murdered, a murder investigation is opened that will involve Clare Ferguson in her first round of detective work.
>
> **AG** **DI**
>
> *Children in jeopardy*

A Fountain Filled with Blood. St. Martin's Minotaur, 2003. 0312304102.

When gay bashing rears its ugly head in Millers Kill, Reverend Clare is pitted against Van Alstyne, the chief of police. She wants action, but he wants it all to go away. When murder occurs too often, Clare takes things into her own hands and finds that the investigation will place her in danger as she seeks the truth.

Homosexuality

Out of the Deep I Cry. St. Martin's Minotaur, 2004. 0312312628.

When a local philanthropists tries to shifts funds to Clare's church from a project at the local free clinic, it leads to the disappearance of Dr. Rouse, the director. This leads Clare to launch another investigation that will bring to light her relationship with the town's chief of police, Russ Van Alstyne. Also brought to light is the dark past of the Ketchum family, whose secrets are linked to the clinic and may explain why the doctor is missing.

Clinics • Philanthropy • Physicians

To Darkness and to Death. St. Martin's Minotaur, 2005. 9780312334857.

November 14 is Chief of Police Russ Van Alstyne's fiftieth birthday, but his relaxing day is spoiled when he gets a report of a woman who has gone missing. Rev. Clare is asked to join a search party for Millicent, the sister of Eugene van der Hoeven, a recluse who owns a massive amount of land and timber in the area of Millers Kill. Told over the period of one day, this crime tale reveals how greed and blackmail can lead to attempted murder.

Lumber • Missing persons

All Mortal Flesh. St. Martin's Minotaur, 2006. 9780312312640.

Clare, under direction from her superiors, has decided to abandon her interest in Chief Russ Van Alstyne. Russ is separated from his wife Linda when he is summoned to the scene of her murder. With the New York State Police homicide unit focusing on the chief as the main suspect, it is up to Clare to launch a private investigation to clear his name. With their relationship now out in the open in this small town, Clare's happiness is threatened.

False accusation

I Shall Not Want. St. Martin's Minotaur, 2008. 9780312334871.

When it appears that someone is murdering migrant works around Millers Kill, Chief Russ Van Alstyne is drawn out of his funk. Besides dealing with his own personal problems, he has personnel problems in his department. Meanwhile, across town Reverend Clare is also dealing with her personal feelings as she finds herself drawn into the mystery behind the murders.

Immigration • Migrant workers • Serial killer

White, Stephen ✍

Alan Gregory

As a clinical psychologist in Boulder, Dr. Alan Gregory uses his professional talents to profile the murderers who cross his path. Paired with his girlfriend, Lauren Crowder, a deputy D.A., he explores the reasons behind the crimes that occur within his purview. His cases can be recommended to traditional and hard-boiled mystery readers. Readers may also enjoy Jonathan Kellerman. See the author's Web site at http://www.authorstephenwhite.com. **HB** **TR** Series subjects: **Colorado, Boulder • Psychologists**

> *Privileged Information.* Viking, 1991.
>
> *Private Practices.* Viking, 1993.
>
> *Higher Authority.* Viking, 1994.
>
> *Harm's Way.* Signet, 1996.
>
> *Remote Control.* Dutton, 1997.
>
> *Critical Conditions.* Dutton, 1998.
>
> *Manner of Death.* Dutton, 1999.
>
> *Cold Case.* Dutton, 2000.
>
> *The Program.* Doubleday, 2001.
>
> *Warning Signs.* Delacorte, 2002.
>
> *The Best Revenge.* Delacorte, 2003.
>
> *Blinded.* Delacorte, 2004.

Missing Persons. Dutton, 2005. 0525948597.

> Alan Gregory has shared office space with Hannah Grant and considers her a friend, so he is shocked when she is apparently murdered at work. Does this have anything to do with the disappearance of their mutual friend Diane? As he probes into the reasons for Hannah's death, he discovers that the clues lead to a missing teenager named Mallory Miller and her schizophrenic mother, who is obsessively attending weddings in Las Vegas. Or could it all be explained by the schizophrenic whom he is treating?
>
> *Missing persons • Nevada, Las Vegas*

Kill Me. Dutton, 2006. 9780525949305.

> Alan Gregory has a patient who has signed a pact with the Death Angels to terminate his life should he ever reach a point where that is needed because of a reduction in the quality of his life. The problem is, the patient does not agree with the timetable of the people he has hired. This book is narrated by the anonymous patient, and Gregory has only a minor role.
>
> *Euthanasia • Terminally ill*

Dry Ice. Dutton, 2007. 9780525949978.

In *Privileged Information*, the very first time we met Alan Gregory, he helped put away a deadly killer named Michael McClelland. Now McClelland has broken out of the mental hospital that has been his jail for all these years. His target may be Gregory and his family, and that puts a terrible strain on the good psychologist and his prosecutor wife Lauren, who already has to deal with her multiple sclerosis. When it appears that Gregory may be guilty of a series of crimes, he realizes the clever killer is setting him up.

Escaped prisoners • False accusation • Serial killer

Dead Time. Dutton, 2008. 9780525950066.

When Alan's ex-wife Meredith seeks his help, he is conflicted. She needs to find her missing surrogate mother, whom she shares with her fiancé, Eric Leffler. The issue is that years ago, in the Grand Canyon, another young woman went missing. With the help of his cop friend Sam Purdy, Alan launches an investigation.

Arizona, Grand Canyon • Husbands and wives • Surrogate mothers

Wolzien, Valerie ✍

Susan Henshaw

An upscale member of Hancock, Connecticut, Henshaw is in a position to help out when murder affects her community. With the same precision as any Golden Age traditional, each player in these books assumes a position in the community that is being disturbed, and the fun is in knocking down each suspect to get to the criminal. Readers may also enjoy Jill Churchill, Diane Mott Davidson, Joan Hess, and Katherine Hall Page. See the author's Web site at http://www.nmomysteries.com. **SB** **TR** Series subjects: **Connecticut, Hancock**

Murder at the PTA Luncheon. St. Martin's, 1988.

The Fortieth Birthday Party. St. Martin's, 1989.

We Wish You a Merry Murder. Gold Medal, 1991.

All Hallow's Evil. Gold Medal, 1992.

An Old Faithful Murder. Gold Medal, 1992.

A Star-Spangled Murder. Gold Medal, 1993.

A Good Year for a Corpse. Gold Medal, 1994.

'Tis the Season to Be Murdered. Gold Medal, 1994.

Remodeled to Death. Gold Medal, 1995.

Elected for Death. Gold Medal, 1996.

Weddings Are Murder. Fawcett, 1998.

The Student Body. Fawcett, 1999.

Death at a Discount. Fawcett, 2000.

An Anniversary to Die For. Fawcett, 2002. 0449007170.

When Susan Henshaw and her husband Jed decided to spend their thirtieth anniversary at the Landing Inn where they honeymooned, little did they know that a body would be found under the gifts on their bed. Ashley Marks was not the most popular of people, but who from her past would use this occasion to poison her?

Anniversaries • Connecticut, Oxford Landing • Poisons

Death in a Beach Chair. Fawcett, 2004. 0449007197.

Susan Henshaw and Jed are staying at the Compass Bay resort in the Caribbean with their friends Kathleen and Jerry. When a beautiful blonde is found murdered and she turns out to be Jerry's first wife's sister, the police believe it could hardly be a coincidence. Now it is up to the Henshaws to find the evidence needed to clear their best friend's reputation and solve a murder.

Caribbean • Vacations

Death in Duplicate. Fawcett, 2005. 0345468082.

The Henshaws discover their children can go home again when their daughter Chrissy, her husband Stephen, and the twins all move into their home accompanied by a nanny. When their neighbor, Nadine Baines, identifies the nanny as a suspect in some nursing home deaths, she is quickly dispatched. While trying to solve the deaths at the Perry Island nursing home, Henshaw discovers a mysterious connection to the land the old folks' home rests on.

Nannies • Neighbors

Eccentric Amateur Detectives

The most notable attributes of these detectives may be their personal eccentricities, rather than their detective skills. All the great thinking detectives had the skill necessary to solve the crime, but that ability seemed to handicap them in normal society. Perhaps this can be dismissed as a literary necessity to set one great thinker apart from another, but the model of the detective as an unusual character was established early. During the golden age of mystery writing, some authors continued the tradition of giving their characters odd and unusual behaviors. The good news for readers is that as time progressed, odd detectives became more human (during the golden age), and that made their stories more readable. Today, authors may still add quirky attributes to their characters, but the better authors handle it in a natural way, adding depth and dimensions to the characters.

Andrews, Donna ✍

Meg Langslow

Amateur investigator Meg Langslow cannot seem to distance herself from her extended family, and they cannot seem to distance themselves from murder. A sculptor/blacksmith by trade, Meg spends little time working her craft and most of her time investigating crimes. The series blends romance and crime and should appeal to readers of M. C. Beaton and Carolyn G. Hart. The author's Web site can be found at http://www.donnaandrews.com. **SB** Series subjects: **Humor • Virginia, Caerphilly**

> *Murder with Peacocks.* St. Martin's, 1999.
>
> *Murder with Puffins.* St. Martin's, 2000.
>
> *Revenge of the Wrought-Iron Flamingos.* St. Martin's Minotaur, 2001.

Crouching Buzzard, Leaping Loon. St. Martin's Minotaur, 2003. 0312277318.

Langslow's brother Rob turned his Lawyers from Hell computer game into a multimillion-dollar game company called Mutant Wizards, but when things get weird, he needs his sister to staff the switchboard at the front desk. The switchboard is shared with a company called Eat Your Way Skinny, and the space is shared with a number of animals, including a one-winged buzzard named George. When Ted, the office mail boy and practical joker, is found dead while playing one of his jokes, Langslow finds herself being a detective to free her brother from the accusation of murder.

Animals • Computer games

We'll Always Have Parrots. St. Martin's Minotaur, 2004. 0312277326.

When Langslow's boyfriend Michael has to attend a fan convention for his television program, *Porfiria, Queen of the Jungle*, the two find themselves in Northern Virginia locked into a hotel with rabid fans and a gaggle of parrots. Michael's goal for the weekend is to get out of his contract, to which he is being held by the show's prima donna, Tamerlaine Wynncliffe-Jones. However, when she is murdered, he finds himself trying to avoid being suspect number one.

Actors • Television • Virginia, Loudoun County

Owls Well That Ends Well. St. Martin's Minotaur, 2005. 9780312329389.

Langslow and her boyfriend Michael have just invested in a three-story Victorian painted lady they call The House. The former owner, Edwina Sprocket, was a collector, and the plucky couple's first task is to clean out all of Emma's junk from their new house and barn. Although it sounds simple to have a yard sale, things get so complicated that an antiques dealer named Gordon McCoy ends up dead—not to mention concern about the endangered owls in the barn!

Antiques • Endangered animals • Home ownership • Owls • Victorian houses

No Nest for the Wicket. St. Martin's Minotaur, 2006. 9780312329402.

While playing extreme croquet, Meg's errant shot lands in a briar patch near the dead body of Lindsay Tyler, a former history professor who had a romantic interlude with Meg's fiancé, Michael. Does the death tie into plans to develop the pasture land into an outlet mall?

Croquet • Extreme sports • Land development

The Penguin Who Knew Too Much. St. Martin's Minotaur, 2007. 9780312329426.

When Meg's Dad agrees to give temporary shelter to the bankrupt zoo's penguins in her new house's basement, no one expects that to lead to a dead body. While Michael and Meg contemplate an elopement, they find that the animals have a different plan. Forced to save the critters and their new home, they launch an investigation that will both save the zoo and determine who murdered the zoo owner.

Penguins • Zoos

Cockatiels at Seven. St. Martin's Minotaur, 2008. 9780312377151.

While trying to get ready for a big show, Langslow reluctantly agrees to watch her friend Karen's two-year-old son Timmy. When Mommy fails to return to claim her son, Langslow sets out on a search for the missing mother. The central question becomes whether Karen is deeply involved in a crime or a victim on the run from a crime committed at the campus where Langslow's new husband Michael works. Meanwhile, Langslow's family continues to be challenging, and Michael discovers what parenthood may hold for this plucky couple.

Babysitting

Six Geese A-Slaying. St. Martin's Minotaur, 2008. 9780312536107.

Langslow and her husband Michael are the marshals for the annual Caerphilly Christmas parade. Organizing things is already hard enough; then Santa Claus, local curmudgeon Ralph Doleson, ends up dead. Now it is not just a matter of solving a murder but of saving the Christmas spirit of this small town.

Christmas • Holidays

Swan for the Money. Minotaur, 2009. 9780312377175.

The Caerphilly Garden Club is sponsoring its first rose show on Raven Hill Estate, and Meg's parents have asked her to help with the festivities. When it becomes evident that someone has murder in mind, and the victim is none other than the host of the show, Philomena Winkleson, Meg decides she needs to plow the ground for clues. Issues about the treatment of animals and sabotage of roses make everyone irritated, and the tension culminates in Meg discovering a dead corpse who is not who she thought it would be.

Animal rights • Flower shows • Roses

Stork Raving Mad. Minotaur, 2010. 9780312621193.

> As if being eight months pregnant with twins was not enough of a challenge, Meg's husband Michael has announced that he has invited a Spanish playwright to stay at their house while one of his plays is being produced at Caerphilly College. Wild nights ensue, leading to an announcement of the play's eminent cancellation and the murder of the dean. Now Meg has to race against her biological clock to solve the murder before the arrival of the twins.
>
> *Academia • Plays • Pregnancy*

Bradley, Alan

Flavia de Luce

The year is 1950, and Flavia de Luce is an overly curious eleven-year-old girl who likes to play detective. She lives in an old Victorian mansion in England, which comes equipped with its own chemistry lab, a convenience for someone who will run across challenging mysteries as she grows up. Raised by her widowed father, Flavia must deal with her older sister's relentless sibling rivalry and her own obsession with death. Fans of this series may enjoy other works with young protagonists, such as *The Shadow of the Wind* by Carlos Ruiz Zafón, *The Final Solution: A Story of Detection* by Michael Chabon, or *The Curious Incident of the Dog in the Night-Time* by Mark Haddon. See the character's Web site at http://www.flaviadeluce.com. **SB Historical.** Series subjects: **Chemistry • Children as detectives • England, Bishop's Lacey • Fathers and daughters • Historical (1900–1999) • Humor**

🏵 *The Sweetness at the Bottom of the Pie*. Delacorte, 2009. 9780385342308.

> It is 1950, and eleven-year-old amateur chemist Flavia de Luce experiences death for the first time when a man dies in the cucumber patch of Buckshaw mansion. When her single parent father, the Colonel, is accused of the murder, she goes into action, using her scientific interests to begin to accumulate clues. When her father confesses to a secret from his past, the case begins to solidify.
>
>
>
> *Children in jeopardy*

The Weed That Strings the Hangman's Bag. Delacorte, 2010. 9780385342315.

> When his van breaks down near Bishop's Lacey, the famous television puppeteer Rupert Porson is talked into giving a performance in the village by de Luce. When Rupert is electrocuted, de Luce takes an interest in solving his murder. Her knowledge of chemistry comes in handy as she follows clues that lead her to Rupert's current traveling companions and to a death in the past that may be the key.
>
> *Puppets*

Braun, Lilian Jackson ✍

Jim Qwilleran/Koko/Yum Yum

No one can question the power of cats and crime in the 1990s, and the leader in this field was Braun. Her human detective, Qwilleran, may not be as popular as his two Siamese cats, Koko and Yum Yum. Qwilleran's skills as a detective are developed when he is a crime reporter, a job he eventually is forced by his life circumstances to give up. When he recovers from these traumas, and as the series begins, he is able to land a job as a reporter with the *Daily Fluxton* in a city vaguely defined as "down there." Qwilleran is a throwback to the dilettante detectives; after he inherits a large sum of money, he eventually leaves the rat race of the big city and moves somewhere north to Pickax, in Moose County. Readers may also enjoy Carole Nelson Douglas. See a fan site for this author at http://home.att.net/~RACapowski. **SB** Series subjects: **Cats • State Unknown, Pickax (Moose County) • Teams**

> *The Cat Who Could Read Backwards.* Dutton, 1966.
>
> *The Cat Who Ate Danish Modern.* Dutton, 1967.
>
> *The Cat Who Turned On and Off.* Dutton, 1968.
>
> *The Cat Who Saw Red.* Jove, 1986.
>
> *The Cat Who Played Brahms.* Jove, 1987.
>
> *The Cat Who Played Post Office.* Jove, 1987.
>
> *The Cat Who Knew Shakespeare.* Jove, 1988.
>
> *The Cat Who Had 14 Tales.* Jove, 1988.
>
> *The Cat Who Sniffed Glue.* Putnam, 1988.
>
> *The Cat Who Went Underground.* Putnam, 1989.
>
> *The Cat Who Lived High.* Putnam, 1990.
>
> *The Cat Who Talked to Ghosts.* Putnam, 1990.
>
> *The Cat Who Knew a Cardinal.* Putnam, 1991.
>
> *The Cat Who Moved a Mountain.* Putnam, 1992.
>
> *The Cat Who Wasn't There.* Putnam, 1992.
>
> *The Cat Who Went into the Closet.* Putnam, 1993.
>
> *The Cat Who Blew the Whistle.* Putnam, 1994.
>
> *The Cat Who Came to Breakfast.* Putnam, 1994.
>
> *The Cat Who Said Cheese.* Putnam, 1996.
>
> *The Cat Who Tailed a Thief.* Putnam, 1997.
>
> *The Cat Who Sang for the Birds.* Putnam, 1998.

The Cat Who Saw Stars. Putnam, 1998.

The Cat Who Robbed a Bank. Putnam, 1999.

The Cat Who Smelled a Rat. G. P. Putnam's, 2001.

The Cat Who Went up the Creek. Putnam, 2002.

The Private Life of the Cat Who: Tales of Koko and Yum Yum (from the Journal of James Mackintosh Qwilleran). Putnam, 2003. 039915132X.

A collection of the following stories: "Enter: Kao K'o Kung, Howling," "Enter: Yum Yum, Shrieking," "Confessions of a Cat-Illiterate," "The Cat Who Had 60 Whiskers," "Yum Yum the Paw," "Koko and the Siamese Rope Trick," "Yum Yum and the Interior Designer," "Koko and the Rum Tum Tugger Syndrome," "Cats! Who Can Understand Them!" "The Matter of the Silver Thimble," "Cool Koko's Almanac," "Why Can Cats Do What They Do?" "Do Cats Have a Sense of Humor?" "The Day Yum Yum Got Out," "Limericks: Fun in the Boondocks," "Cool Koko Also Says," "The Fine Art of Naming Cats," "Yum Yum and the Queen-size Bed," "Koko's Unique Social Graces," "Kidnapped!" "More Cool Kokoisms," and "Yum Yum Discovers Her Wings."

Short stories

The Cat Who Brought Down the House. Putnam, 2003. 0399149422.

The abandoned opera house in downtown Pickax has been purchased by native daughter Thelma Thackeray, returning to Moose County from Hollywood for her retirement. When she decides to remodel the building into a film club, a number of suspicious activities occur. Does all of this tie into the death a year before of Thelma's twin brother, Thurston?

The Cat Who Went Bananas. Putnam, 2004. 0399152245.

The Pirate's Chest is a new bookstore in Pickax City, to be run by former librarian Polly Duncan, thanks to the Klingenschoen Fund, Qwilleran's philanthropic efforts. But the grand plans for this new business and his relationship with Polly are strained when a local Theater Club production of *The Importance of Being Earnest* brings actor Alden Wade to town. When Alden marries a local heiress who is part of the Hibbard House history being written by Qwilleran and death occurs, Koko and Yum Yum's crime-solving abilities are going to be needed once again.

Actors • Theater

The Cat Who Talked Turkey. Putnam, 2004. 0399151079.

While the festive bicentennial is going on in the town of Brrr, a body is discovered on the Qwilleran property. Hopefully that will not distract from the celebration, or from the hunt for some wild turkeys, the opening of a new bookstore, and a radio play about the big storm of 1913. All of these things distract Qwill from the crimes and keep his focus on local activities, while Yum Yum and Koko continue to detect.

Bicentennial celebrations

The Cat Who Dropped a Bombshell. Putnam, 2006. 9780399153075.

Pickax Now is the sesquicentenary celebration of Qwill's home town, and it is in full swing when the bodies of Nathan and Doris Ledfield are discovered.

Sesquicentenary celebrations

The Cat Who Had 60 Whiskers. Putnam, 2007. 9780399153907.

When the late Nathan Ledfield's mansion is about to be remodeled into a senior center, all of his belongings are sold for the benefit of the needy children in Moose County. But then "The Old Hulk" is burnt to the ground, a young woman dies from a bee sting, and Quill and the cats find themselves writing a play called *The Cat Who Was Elected Dogcatcher* while leading an investigation.

Arson • Theater

Douglas, Carole Nelson ✍

Temple Barr/Midnight Louie

Along with Lilian Jackson Braun, Douglas uses the popularity of cats and mysteries for the sleuthing feline Midnight Louie, a nineteen-pound black cat capable of telling his own side of the story. Teamed with Temple Barr, a Las Vegas freelance publicist, the two follow the clues to the solution. These cases can be recommended to soft-boiled mystery readers. Douglas's fans may also enjoy Lilian Jackson Braun. See the author's Web site at http://www.fastlane.net/cdouglas. **SB** Series subjects: **Cats • Nevada, Las Vegas • Teams**

Crystal Days. Bantam, 1990 (also published as *The Cat and the King of Clubs*. Five Star, 1999; *The Cat and the Queen of Hearts*. Five Star, 1999).

Crystal Nights. Bantam, 1990 (also published as *Jill of Diamonds*. Five Star, 2000; *The Cat and the Jack of Spades*).

Catnap. Tor, 1992.

Pussyfoot. Tor, 1993.

Cat on a Blue Monday. Forge, 1994.

Cat in a Crimson Haze. Forge, 1995.

Cat in a Diamond Dazzle. Forge, 1996.

Cat with an Emerald Eye. Forge, 1996.

Cat in a Flamingo Fedora. Forge, 1997.

Cat in a Golden Garland. Forge, 1997.

Cat on a Hyacinth Hunt. Forge, 1998.

Cat in an Indigo Mood. Forge, 1999.

Cat in a Jeweled Jumpsuit. Forge, 1999.

Cat in a Kiwi Con. Forge, 2000.

Cat in a Leopard Spot. Forge, 2001.

Cat in a Midnight Choir. Forge, 2002. 0312857977.

A renegade band of magicians called The Synth is raising havoc for both the human detective Temple and the feline Louie. Meanwhile, homicide lieutenant C. R. Molina is hunting the Stripper Killer, with the two chief suspects being either her own ex-husband, Rafi Nadir, or Temple's current boyfriend, Max.

Magicians

Cat in a Neon Nightmare. Forge, 2003. 0765306808.

A hooker named Vassar is found dead on the ceiling of a Las Vegas casino, and her last client was the famous radio psychiatrist, Matt Devine. Midnight Louie and his "possible" daughter, Midnight Louise, are on the case, knowing that the Stripper Killer (from the previous book) still stalks. While Lt. Molina watches for the magician Synth, who may be behind some of this, he also has his eye on Max Kinsella, which stirs the interest of Barr.

Magicians

Cat in an Orange Twist. Forge, 2004. 0765306816.

Maylords, a new furniture store, is opening in Las Vegas, and Barr is in charge of its public relations when a shooter kills Simon Foster. This is a surprise, because it was Amelia Wong, media maven, whose life had been threatened. Foster was the life partner of Barr's friend Danny Dove, so the investigation is personal, and it moves forward with the help of Louie, the feline P.I.

Furniture • Retail

Cat in a Hot Pink Pursuit. Forge, 2005. 9780765313997.

Teen Idol is a TV reality show, and C. R. Molina's thirteen-year-old daughter wants to compete for the crown. In order to provide her protection from a stalker who has been leaving mutilated Barbie dolls as a warning, Barr goes undercover on the show as a teenage contestant named Xoe Chole Ozone. Midnight Louie lends a paw as well when a number of deaths occur in the haunted mansion where the competition is held.

Reality television • Television

Cat in a Quicksilver Caper. Forge, 2006. 9780765314000.

Public relations expert Temple Barr is responsible for the opening of the Russian Czars exhibit at the New Millennium Hotel. An aerial magic act, scheduled for the same space, leads to a death that threatens the exhibit. A second death and the disappearance of a priceless object lead the two detectives toward a complicated international solution or the realization that local talent may have pulled off the perfect caper.

Art • Public relations

Cat in a Red Hot Rage. Forge, 2007. 9780765314017.

During the Red Hat Sisterhood's national convention in Las Vegas, Temple's landlady Electra Lark is accused of murder when a conventioneer is strangled. While Temple agrees to investigate, it is Louie who finds an ex-lover on the spot and needs to scramble to clear the innocent and nail a killer.

Conventions • Red Hatters

Cat in a Sapphire Slipper. Forge, 2008. 9780765318619.

Temple's romance-writing aunt Kit Carlson has found a man of her own: an ex-mobster with a heart of gold named Aldo Fontana. When the bachelor party takes place out at Sapphire Slipper, a cathouse in the desert, it is no surprise that one of the prostitutes ends up dead. This is an uncomfortable situation for two of the attendees: ex-priest and Temple's fiancé, Matt Devine, and the cat detective Midnight Louie.

Bachelor parties • Prostitutes • Weddings

Cat in a Topaz Tango. Forge, 2009. 9780765318626.

Las Vegas is being stalked by The Barbie Doll, who is attacking teens who show some talent. When Barr's fiancé Matt Devine decides to be a part of the charity dance contest called "Dancing with the Celebs," Barr goes behind the scenes to try to prevent any mayhem. When Lt. Molina's daughter Mariah becomes involved, all the characters need to step up their game to protect one of their own, including Midnight Louie.

Charity events • Dance • Teenagers at risk

Cat in an Ultramarine Scheme. Forge, 2010. 9780765318633.

Barr, in her real-life job as a publicist, is involved in the opening of a mob-controlled museum and casino. But when the fun and games of designing an underground tour of the underworld uncover a body in a safe, Barr must switch into detective mode. With neither Matt nor Max around, Barr is only supported by the Vegas Strip Irregulars, her network of cats.

Casinos • Museums • Organized crime

Hess, Joan ✍

Claire Malloy

One of two Arkansas series that Hess writes (see also the Police Chief Arly Hanks series), this one features a bookstore owner named Claire Malloy. One of the appeals of the series is Malloy's troubled relationship with her teenage daughter Caron. Light but not entirely cozy, the stories take advantage of the unique landscape and the secondary characters to create the proper atmosphere in The Book Depot. The use of humor and humorous situations is a strength of this series. The cases can be recommended to soft-boiled and traditional mystery readers. Readers may also enjoy M. C. Beaton (Agatha Raisin), Anne George, or Carolyn G. Hart (Annie Laurance/Max Darling). See the author's Web site at http://www.joanhess.com. **SB** **TR** Series subjects: **Arkansas, Farberville • Humor**

> *Strangled Prose.* St. Martin's, 1986.
>
> *The Murder at the Murder at the Mimosa Inn.* St. Martin's, 1986.
>
> *Dear Miss Demeanor.* St. Martin's, 1987.
>
> *A Really Cute Corpse.* St. Martin's, 1988.
>
> *A Diet to Die For.* St. Martin's, 1989.
>
> *Roll Over and Play Dead.* St. Martin's, 1991.
>
> *Death by the Light of the Moon.* St. Martin's, 1992.
>
> *Poisoned Pins.* Dutton, 1993.
>
> *Tickled to Death.* Dutton, 1994.
>
> *Busy Bodies.* Dutton, 1995.
>
> *Closely Akin to Murder.* Dutton, 1996.
>
> *A Holly, Jolly Murder.* Dutton, 1997.
>
> *A Conventional Corpse.* St. Martin's Minotaur, 1999.

Out on a Limb. St. Martin's Minotaur, 2002. 0312266804.

Emily Parchester has chained herself to a platform in a tree to protest the developments sponsored by Anthony Armstrong. When Armstrong is killed, Malloy is left with a baby to care for and the child's teenage mom as the number one suspect.

Environment

The Goodbye Body. St. Martin's Minotaur, 2005. 9780312313043.

When rodent removal forces Malloy to temporarily abandon her apartment, she and her daughter Caron move into the home of Dolly Goforth. Dolly is gone on a cruise with her husband, but subsequent events make Malloy think that Dolly may actually be on the run. When a corpse keeps showing up at inconvenient times and then disappearing, the intrepid amateur sleuth must set aside her bookselling ways and seek the truth.

Damsels in Distress. St. Martin's Minotaur, 2007. 9780312315016.

Claire is getting married to Detective Peter Rosen. Wedding plans are hard to make when a Renaissance fair arrives in town and one of the members, Edward Cobbinwood, may be the son of Claire's ex, Carlton. When an arson leaves a woman dead, Claire realizes there is more to this case than just heredity.

Arson • Biological parents • Reenactments • Renaissance fairs

Mummy Dearest. St. Martin's Minotaur, 2008. 9780312363604.

Finally married to cop Peter Rosen, Malloy finds herself on her honeymoon in Luxor, Egypt. Along for the ride are the teenagers Caron and Inez. Odd things begin to happen to the group, who feel like they are being followed, while Peter begins communication with the Egyptian government. Then the group meets Lady Amelia Peabody Emerson, an archaeologist who knows something about detecting.

Egypt, Luxor • Honeymoons

Peters, Elizabeth ✍

Amelia Peabody

Dilettante spinster Peabody is free to roam the late Victorian world as an explorer of Egyptology, and her match with archaeologist Radcliffe Emerson makes for an interesting mystery duo. Eventually Amelia and Radcliffe have a son named Ramses, and as more time goes by, the minor characters begin to take major places on the mystery stage in this series. As historicals, these cases also provide a canvas for the changing picture as the world prepares for war. Readers may also enjoy Aaron Elkins, Sharyn McCrumb (Elizabeth MacPherson). and Anne Perry. See the author's Web site at http://www.mpmbooks.com. **SB TR Historical.** Series subjects: **Archaeology • Egypt (Ancient) • Historical (1900–1999)**

Crocodile on the Sandbank. Dodd, Mead, 1975.

The Curse of the Pharaohs. Dodd, Mead, 1981.

The Mummy Case. Congdon, 1985.

Lion in the Valley. Atheneum, 1986.

The Deeds of the Disturber. Atheneum, 1988.

The Last Camel Died at Noon. Warner, 1991.

The Snake, the Crocodile and the Dog. Warner, 1992.

The Hippopotamus Pool. 1996.

Seeing a Large Cat. Warner, 1997.

The Ape Who Guards the Balance. Avon, 1998.

The Falcon at the Portal. Avon, 1999.

He Shall Thunder in the Sky. Morrow, 2000.

Lord of the Silent. Morrow, 2001.

The Golden One. Morrow, 2002. 0380978857.

On another visit to the tombs of Egypt, Peabody's party is angered by another tomb desecration. But when the body of a tomb robber is discovered at the site, Peabody must go to work as a detective. Meanwhile her son Ramses is spying in Gaza, and while he is on his mission, his life is in danger every moment. When his mission to find Sethos falters, his family rides to his rescue.

Egypt, Luxor • Gaza • Spies • World War I

Children of the Storm. Morrow, 2003. 0066214769.

The end of the First World War finds the Emerson family in the Valley of the Kings hoping for a peaceful time on a new dig. But the end of the war has not ended unrest in Egypt, and some artifacts are stolen from the site, sabotage occurs, and someone is murdered. When Peabody's son Ramses is kidnapped, she must investigate to save her family.

Egypt, Luxor

Guardian of the Horizon. Morrow, 2004. 0066214718.

The family returns to the mountainous site of the Lost Oasis, which they have kept secret since it was discovered in *The Last Camel Died at Noon*. Prince Tarek, who is the ruler of this significant religious and historical area, is in need of their help again, but the journey from England is fraught with danger. The mission is to save the prince from being overthrown, and more adventures await Peabody, Emerson, Ramses, and Nefret when they arrive at the secret site. This novel is a recounting of an adventure of our heroes that took place during 1907–1908, a period heretofor not recounted in this series.

Shipboard

The Serpent on the Crown. Morrow, 2005. 0060591781.

It is now 1922, and the Emerson family is approached by novelist Magda Petherick, widow of antiquity collector Pringle Petherick, who wants to get rid of a cursed piece of work her husband had in his collection. When Sethos, Emerson's illegitimate half-brother, arrives on the scene, it appears that those who want to deal in artifacts are not afraid of the curse. Maybe they should be, because something has killed Magda, and now the family must investigate the artifact and a crime.

Tomb of the Golden Bird. Morrow, 2006. 9780060591809.

> This series has reached the point when Tutankhamen's tomb is to be opened. As Emerson negotiates for the rights that would lead him to this treasure, others descend on the Valley of the Kings ahead of him and bar him from the site. Emerson's half-brother Sethos is also on the scene, this time carrying a secret that will threaten Emerson and Peabody's family.
>
> *Tutankhamen*

A River in the Sky. Morrow, 2010. 9780061246265.

> Jumping back in time to 1910, this novel tells the tale of the time when Amelia and Emerson set out to Palestine to uncover the Temple of Jerusalem and find the Ark of the Covenant. Teamed with the English discoverer George Morley, our heroes nevertheless know that he may be a spy for the German government. But their hearts are really focused on discovering the fate of their son Ramses, kidnapped by evil forces and out of touch with his parents.
>
> *Ark of the Covenant* • *Jerusalem* • *Palestine* • *Temple of Jerusalem*

Chapter 2

Public Detectives

The concept of a publicly supported police force is only about 200 years old. The French must receive some credit for beginning a police force with the work of François Eugene Vidocq. Figuring it was best to send a thief to catch a thief, Napoleon hired the former criminal as his first chief of police. Vidocq was eventually forced from office and opened one of the first private detective businesses. His adventures and reputation proved so great that several Honoré de Balzac novels featured a character named Vautrin, based on Vidocq, and Vidocq himself authored several reminiscences that were sensationalized accounts of his own career.

In most of the early great thinking detective series, in which the hero stood outside the formal police departments, the policeperson was a figure of ridicule. The policeperson as hero was slow to develop. Following the success of the eccentric private detective or amateur detective, the first police series found their heroes functioning within the system for their access to the cases, but often outside the system in the methods they used to solve them.

Ed McBain is credited with having created the contemporary police procedural with his <u>87th Precinct</u> novels in the 1950s. Besides basing their case work on police procedure, his books feature more than one case that more accurately reflects the actual workload of a police department. Avoiding the lone wolf concept, McBain established a vigorous and vibrant crew of cops working out of the same department.

Since McBain's work, the police detective has evolved into a full-fledged hero, including all types of police officers in all types of police forces. Stories are now be set in cities as widespread as Hong Kong and Maggody, Arkansas. The inclusion of women and minority characters throughout the 1960s and 1970s has broadened the palette with which these cases can be drawn.

Of the three main directions that mystery fiction took in the development of its detectives, this category is the closest it gets to reality. This may be one of its strongest appeals. Unlike the amateur and private detectives, who are cut off from all the legitimate resources for an investigation, the public detectives are fully vested in institutions that can provide the necessary resources to conduct an investigation. All the functionaries whose jobs are created to support them as they investigate also aid these detectives. This subgenre also has the appeal of watching a team work together to solve a crime, with plenty of social interaction, sometimes supportive and sometimes challenging, to go with it. All this effort lends an air of legitimacy to the process that validates these fictional characters as capable and believable detectives.

Police Detectives

Police often functioned as buffoons in the great detective's cases. The use of police procedure parallels the establishment of the policeman as the hero. Using scientific methods, once the sole purview of the great thinking detective, moves to the police force as the procedures become more complex and the methodologies become too difficult to be replicated by a detective outside the police department.

The characters listed in this section basically follow standard procedures within a fairly well-functioning institution. They may, on occasion, act independently of their departments, but usually they are dependent on the department and their fellow officers to help them solve the crimes. These officers stand in contrast to the lone wolf police, who function more independently than a standard police officer.

The Modern Practitioners

Aird, Catherine (pseud. of Kinn Hamilton McIntosh) ✍

Christopher Sloan

Aird's works features CID Inspector Sloan, sardonic and brash, who works his cases in the fictional town of Berebury in the county of Calleshire, England. His world includes his wife Margaret; his companion on his cases, Constable William Crosby; and his boss, Superintendent Leeyes. Rehashing the typical British whodunit format, these novels can be recommended to readers looking for that type of mystery. **SB TR** Series subjects: **England, Calleshire, Berebury**

> *The Religious Body.* UK: Macdonald, 1966 (US: Doubleday, 1966).
>
> *Henrietta Who?* UK: Macdonald, 1968 (US: Doubleday, 1968).
>
> *The Complete Steel.* UK: Macdonald, 1969 (US title: *The Stately Home Murder.* Doubleday, 1970).
>
> *A Late Phoenix.* UK: Collins, 1970 (US: Doubleday, 1971).
>
> *His Burial Too.* UK: Collins, 1973 (US: Doubleday, 1973).

Slight Mourning. UK: Collins, 1975 (US: Doubleday, 1976).

Parting Breath. UK: Collins, 1977 (US: Doubleday, 1978).

Some Die Eloquent. UK: Collins, 1979 (US: Doubleday, 1980).

Passing Strange. UK: Collins, 1980 (US: Doubleday, 1981).

Last Respects. UK: Collins, 1982 (US: Doubleday, 1982).

Harm's Way. UK: Collins, 1984 (US: Doubleday, 1984).

A Dead Liberty. UK: Collins, 1986 (US: Doubleday, 1987).

The Body Politic. UK: Macmillan, 1990 (US: Doubleday, 1991).

A Going Concern. UK: Macmillan, 1993.

Injury Time. UK: Macmillan,1994 (US: St. Martin's Press, 1995).

After Effects. UK: Macmillan, 1996 (US: St. Martin's Press, 1996).

Stiff News. UK: Macmillan, 1998 (US: St. Martin's Press, 1999).

Little Knell. UK: Macmillan, 2000 (US: St. Martin's Minotaur, 2001).

Amendment of Life. St. Martin's Minotaur, 2003. 0312290802. (UK: Macmillan, 2002).

At Aumerle Court, people pay for the privilege of walking in the Tudor-era maze of yew that decorates the grounds. When Daphne Pedlinge views a body in the maze from her wheelchair in the manor, Sloan is called in to investigate. The body is Margaret Collins, wife of the owner of Double Felix, the sound and light company that manages the maze.

Mazes

Chapter and Hearse. St. Martin's, 2004. 0312290845. (UK: Macmillan, 2003).

A collection of the following stories: "A Change of Heart," "Chapter and Hearse," "Dummy Run," "Examination Results," "Like to Die," "Preyed in Aid," "Time, Gentlemen, Please," "Touch Not the Cat," "The Trouble and Strife," and "The Wild Card." This edition also includes twelve non-Sloan stories.

Hole in One. St. Martin's Minotaur, 2005. 9780312342296. (UK: Allison & Busby, 2005).

Sloan and Crosby are handed a case involving a corpse found buried in a golf course bunker known as "Hell's Bells." When it is discovered that the club's members are in competition not only on the links but also for some prime real estate that needs development, Sloan and Crosby begin to see the motive for the murder.

Golf

Losing Ground. St. Martin's Minotaur, 2008. 9780312368890. (UK: Allison & Busby, 2007).

Tolmie Park is desired by developers, but the locals are reluctant to see their past given up. When an eighteenth-century painting is taken from the house minutes before it goes up in flames, Detective Inspector Sloan and Detective Constable Crosby are called in. When bones are found in the ruins, the case becomes one of murder.

Beaton, M. C. (pseud. of Marion Chesney) ✍

Hamish Macbeth

Scotland provides the backdrop for Hamish Macbeth, a village constable in the Scottish Highlands. Charmer that he may be, Macbeth seems to have a dark cloud following him around, now matter how hard he tries. An eligible bachelor, he eventually is promoted to sergeant. These police novels are written with a decidedly light feel. Readers may also enjoy Joan Hess (Arly Hanks) and H. R. F. Keating. See a Web site about this author at http://www.booksnbytes.com/authors/beaton_mc.html. **SB** Series subjects: **Humor • Scotland, Lochdubh**

Death of a Gossip. St. Martin's Press, 1985.

Death of a Cad. St. Martin's Press, 1987.

Death of an Outsider. St. Martin's Press, 1988.

Death of a Perfect Wife. St. Martin's Press, 1988.

Death of a Hussy. St. Martin's Press, 1990.

Death of a Snob. St. Martin's Press, 1991.

Death of a Prankster. St. Martin's Press, 1992.

Death of a Glutton. St. Martin's Press, 1993.

Death of a Travelling Man. St. Martin's 1993.

Death of a Charming Man. Mysterious Press, 1994.

Death of a Nag. Mysterious Press, 1995.

Death of a Macho Man. Mysterious, 1996.

Death of a Dentist. Mysterious, 1997.

Death of a Scriptwriter. Mysterious Press, 1998.

Death of an Addict. Mysterious Press, 1999.

Death of a Dustman. Mysterious, 2001.

Death of a Celebrity. Mysterious Press, 2002.

Death of a Village. Mysterious Press, 2003. 0446613711.

When the residents of the village of Stoyre begin to act odd, Constable Macbeth decides to vacation among the villagers to find out why. Reporter Elspeth Grant's theory is that people are being frightened out of their homes. When Macbeth almost becomes a victim during his investigation, and after an elderly woman is frightened to death, he finds his investigative skills are needed to root out the cause.

Scotland, Stoyre • Submarines

Death of a Poison Pen. Mysterious, 2004. 0892967889.

The small town of Braikie is disturbed by a series of poison pen letters that are circulating among the population. The letters attack everyone, revealing old secrets and the possibility of two homicides, while leading to the suicide of one of the letter's victims. Meanwhile, Macbeth faces a fierce battle on the romantic front when confronted by a woman who has designs on him.

Blackmail • Scotland, Braikie

Death of a Bore. Mysterious, 2005. 0892967951.

Author John Heppel has arrived in Scotland to give a writing course, promising that it will bring attendees riches. But his harsh critical style proves unpopular, and when he is murdered, the most likely suspects are the students in his class. Macbeth looks to a manuscript written by the dead man for the clues he needs to solve this murder.

Authors

Death of a Dreamer. Mysterious Press, 2006. 9780892967896.

A new arrival to Lochdubh, artist Effie Garrard, has apparently committed suicide, but Macbeth does not believe that is true. Able to survive the harsh winter, Effie may not have been able to survive her tempestuous relationship with local artist Jock Fleming. When another death occurs, this time of an American tourist, it leads to the revelation that Effie may not have been everything she claimed to be.

Artists

Death of a Maid. Mysterious Press, 2007. 9780892960101.

Mavis Gillespie is the Jane Marple of Lochdubh in her ability to pick up all the town gossip while working as a housecleaner. But when she is bludgeoned to death with her own cleaning pail, Macbeth finds she was more inclined to walk on the dark side than the light, and there is no end to the list of clients who are now suspects in her death.

Blackmail • Maids

Death of a Gentle Lady. Grand Central, 2008. 9780446582605.

Is it love or duty that makes Macbeth offer to marry the lovely Turkish maid Avesha to prevent her being deported? It does not matter, because her employer, Margaret Gentle, may be trying to get Macbeth's station closed. Then this woman, whom the community sees as kind and gentle, is first blackmailed and then murdered. While Macbeth tries to balance love and death, he finds himself under the scrutiny of his boss, Detective Chief Inspector Blair.

Blackmail • Deportation

Death of a Witch. Grand Central, 2009. 9780446196130.

Back home from a vacation, Macbeth finds his local town disturbed by a witch named by Catriona Beldame, who has cast a sexual spell over the village's men. Her recipe for sexual potency only makes the men sick and angry. When she dies in a house fire, suspicion falls on Macbeth. But when more women begin to die, it appears a serial killer is loose in the Highlands.

Herbalists • Serial killer • Witches

Death of a Valentine. Grand Central, 2010. 9780446547383.

Annie Fleming, the Highlands' Lammas Festival queen, is killed when she receives a bomb in a package on Valentine's Day. As Sergeant Macbeth begins his investigation, he finds that the queen may not have been what most people assumed. His partner in the investigation is the attractive Constable Josie McSween, a woman who soon could be Lady Macbeth.

Holidays • Romance • Valentine's Day

Bland, Eleanor Taylor ✍

Marti MacAlister

Lincoln Prairie, Illinois, is the home of African American female cop Marti MacAlister, who is often partnered with Vik Jessenovik. As a single mother of two children, she struggles to maintain a home life and a professional career. The crimes in Lincoln Prairie are as serious as in the neighboring city of Chicago, and MacAlister needs to call on all her skills, and the skills of her support organization, to solve the cases. Eleanor Taylor Bland passed away in June 2010. Readers may also enjoy J. A. Jance (Joanna Brady), Laurie King (Kate Martinelli), and Margaret Maron (Sigrid Harald). See the author's Web site at http://home.earthlink.net/~etbland. **TR** Series subjects: **African American • Illinois, Lincoln Prairie**

Dead Time. St. Martin's Press, 1992.

Slow Burn. St. Martin's, 1993.

Gone Quiet. St. Martin's, 1994.

Done Wrong. St. Martin's, 1995.

Keep Still. St. Martin's Press, 1996.

See No Evil. St. Martin's Press, 1998.

Tell No Tales. St. Martin's Press, 1999.

Scream in Silence. St. Martin's Minotaur, 2000.

Whispers in the Dark. St. Martin's Minotaur, 2001.

Windy City Dying. St. Martin's Minotaur, 2002. 0312300980.

> MacAlister and her new husband Ben have moved to Lincoln Prairie, where she hopes to lead a more peaceful life, but her job threatens her family when the murder of a sixteen-year-old intrudes. The death of Graciela Lara may mean someone MacAlister's first husband had put away is back on the streets and seeking vengeance. Despite that threat, MacAlister finds time to counsel some of Chicago's troubled children.
>
> *Children in jeopardy*

Fatal Remains. St. Martin's, 2003. 0312300972.

> Idbash Smith was a conductor on the Underground Railroad and an early white founder of Lincoln Prairie, which already was home to the Potawatomi Indians. MacAlister and partner Matthew "Vik" Jessenovik are handed a case involving the death of a young archaeology student murdered on the estate of Smith heir Josiah. The clues lead the cops to some Native Americans and a black man who has converted to Judaism, and they find themselves haunted by the past.
>
> *Native Americans • Potawatomi Indian Tribe • Underground Railroad*

A Cold and Silent Dying. St. Martin's Minotaur, 2004. 9780312326654.

> MacAlister must deal with her jealous new boss, Lieutenant Gail Nicholson, while trying to put together her investigation of the death of a homeless woman and an assault on a city alderman. With echoes from *Whispers in the Dark*, her days turn even darker when MacAlister's girlfriend Sharon's ex-husband DeVonte Lutrell comes back, seeking revenge on MacAlister and Sharon.
>
> *Revenge • Serial killer*

A Dark and Deadly Deception. St. Martin's Minotaur, 2005. 9780312326678.

> MacAlister and her partner, Vik Jessenovik, are assigned the task of determining who killed African American actress Savannah Payne-Jones and dumped her body in the Des Plaines River during a film shoot in Lincoln Prairie. Another case has them trying to determine why someone killed a man and walled his body up in a building fifty years ago. While the detectives both try to reconcile with personal illness in their families, the two cases surprisingly begin to merge.

Blunt, Giles ✍

John Cardinal

John Cardinal never has an easy day. He tries to do his job despite a wife suffering from depression and connections to a local drug dealer, which have the police believing he may be on the take. When the series begins, his own belief in a case has resulted in his being demoted, and he is depressed. Saddled with an officer who may be doing an internal investigation, he finds his new partner Lise Delorme is more than she initially seems. Setting his stories in a region of Canada that is remote and challenging, Blunt uses the landscape and the people to create the themes and tones of his books. Readers of this series might enjoy Stephen Booth, James Lee Burke, and Peter Robinson. See the author's Web site at http://www.gilesblunt.com. **TR** Series subjects: **Canada, Ontario, Algonquin Bay**

Forty Words for Sorrow. Putnam, 2001. 0399147527.

> Demoted because of his obsession with a missing persons case, homicide detective John Cardinal is so down he believes his new partner, Lise Delorme from the Office of Special Investigations, has been sent to spy on him. Cardinal is redeemed when the body of Katie Pine is discovered in an old mine shaft. This reopens interest in the cases of other teens who have gone missing and sets the two reluctant partners on the trail of a serial killer.
>
> *Children in jeopardy • Serial killer*

The Delicate Storm. Putnam, 2003. 0399148655.

> With the spring thaw comes the discovery of a man's arm; he was an American. Then the body of woman who was raped is found; she was the town doctor. While Cardinal and his partner Delorme are trying to figure out the reason for these two murders, they discover a clue that leads them back to a similar murder in the past. When it may lead to unsettling times in Quebec history, the two find themselves trying to sort out the present from the past.
>
> *Rape • Terrorism*

Black Fly Season. Putnam, 2005. 9780399152559.

> A woman with no memory walks into Algonquin Bay, covered in black fly bites and suffering from exposure. Nicknamed "Red," she lands in the lap of the police when it is discovered that she is carrying a bullet in her brain. Now Cardinal and Delorme must determine who wanted Red dead, and who may want to finish the job.
>
> *Brain injuries • Memory loss*

By the Time You Read This. Henry Holt, 2006. 9780805080612. (UK: The Fields of Grief. HarperCollins, 2006).

> Setting aside his personal grief, Cardinal plunges into the investigation of his wife's death when he receives messages that hint that her death might have

been a homicide. Meanwhile, Delorme is investigating a case of child pornography whose victim appears to live in Algonquin Bay. Then there is another suicide, and it seems that Cardinal's sense of danger was correct.

Grief • Pedophilia • Pornography • Suicide

Booth, Stephen ✍

Ben Cooper and Diane Fry

When DC Ben Cooper and DC Dian Fry first meet, they both have baggage in their personal lives and are both interested in the same promotion. As the tension builds between them while they work cases together, the pair must deal with their mutual distrust and mounting personal issues. Readers of this series may also enjoy Giles Blunt, Ian Rankin, Peter Robinson, and Minette Walters. See the author's Web site at http://www.stephen-booth.com. **TR** Series subjects: **England, Derbyshire, Edendale • England, Derbyshire, Peak District**

Black Dog. Scribner, 2000. 068487301X. (UK: Collins, 2000).

Teenager Laura Vernon has gone missing, and the search is on for her in the Peak District. When DC Ben Cooper and his reluctant partner Diane Fry are assigned to the case, they must decide whether she is a runaway or they are searching for her body. When an uncooperative man named Harry Dickinson finds the body, his actions make him suspect number one. But Cooper and Fry are not satisfied that the case ends with Harry. Instead, it may only begin with him. As each cop faces a personal challenge, they must try to keep their own weaknesses from wrecking the investigation.

Teenagers at risk

Dancing with the Virgins. Scribner, 2001. 0743216903. (UK: Collins, 2001).

The body of cyclist Jenny Weston is found in the ancient ruins of The Nine Virgins. Is she a victim of the same person who attacked Maggie Crew a few weeks earlier, leaving her scarred and with no memory of the attack? While Booth investigates this complex case, he still resents newly promoted Detective Sergeant Diane Fry.

Moors

Blood on the Tongue. Scribner, 2002. 0743236181. (UK: Collins, 2002).

The Edendale police do not lack for bodies. Marie Tennent has frozen to death on Irontongue Hill, the same spot where a plane crashed during World War II. Only the pilot, Danny McTeague, survived, and he supposedly absconded with a large amount of money. His granddaughter, Alison Morrissey, has arrived in Derbyshire to clear her grandfather's name. But what is to be made of the unidentified body dug up by a snowplow and the missing baby?

Grandparents • Suicide • World War II

Blind to the Bones. Scribner, 2003. 074323796X. (UK: HarperCollins, 2003).

Cooper is in the village of Withens investigating house break-ins, while the rest of the force and Fry are working on the case of Emma Renshaw. Her blood-covered cell phonehas been found, the first clue to her disappearance. When Cooper is on the spot at the discovery of a death connected to Emma, he begins to delve into the clues to find the reason for her being missing.

England, Derbyshire, Withens • Missing persons

One Last Breath. Bantam, 2006. 9780385339056. (UK: HarperCollins, 2004).

When ex-con Mansell Quinn returns to the Castleton area, he may be seeking revenge for his long stay in prison for the murder of his lover, a crime of which he still claims he is innocent. Cooper and Fry are on the hunt for him after a new murder occurs, and the caves under the town may provide a perfect hiding spot for a killer. Is Quinn intent on seeking revenge, and will one of the victims be Cooper, the son of the cop who arrested Quinn all those years ago?

Caves • England, Derbyshire, Castleton • Revenge

The Dead Place. Bantam, 2007. 9780385339063. (UK: HarperCollins, 2005).

An anonymous phone call warns the force of an imminent death. Then a local woman goes missing. A corpse is found, but it is a year old, and Cooper and Fry must reconcile why the description from the tip matches the older death, after an autopsy proves she was not murdered. As more bodies are found, the case becomes a public nightmare for the force.

Serial killer

Scared to Live. Bantam, 2006. 9780385339070. (UK: HarperCollins, 2006).

Why would someone want to murder an agoraphobic? This is the question that confounds Cooper and Fry as they try to determine whether the death was a random accident of bad karma or there is something in the life of the dead woman to explain her murder. At the same time, a house fire kills a mother named Lindsay Mullen and her children, and the force has to determine if her missing husband Brian is to blame.

Agoraphobia • Arson

*Dying to Sin. UK: HarperCollins, 2007. 9780007243426.

The Kill Call. UK: HarperCollins, 2009. 9780007243457.

When an Eden Valley fox hunt turns up the body of a man who has been killed, it reveals one thing about Fry and Cooper: they know nothing about horses and hunts. But they will have to learn fast, because the tips they are receiving are deceiving, and the local hunters are not cooperative. Although the victim may have not been a model citizen, the question arises about the involvement of those who wanted to stop a fox hunt at all costs. But perhaps a more disturbing revelation is the way meat is being delivered to the market and how a horse dealer may be involved.

Fox hunts • Horses • Hunts • Meat

Cleeves, Ann ✍

Jimmy Perez

The remote island of Shetland proves to be tough ground for Detective Jimmy Perez to tred. As an outsider, he finds breaking down years of tradition daunting. His discovery of love with girlfriend Fran Hunter can prove to be either a help or a distraction in carrying out his duties. See the author's Web site at http://www.anncleeves.com. Readers may also enjoy Carolyn Hart's Annie and Max, Margaret Maron, or Nancy Pickard. **TR** Series subjects: **Islands • Scotland, Shetland Island**

🏵 *Raven Black*. St. Martin's Minotaur, 2006. 9780312359669. (UK: Macmillan, 2006).

Teenager Catherine Ross has been found murdered on the island of Shetland on a snowy winter day. From the mainland arrives Detective Jimmy Perez, ready to investigate the crime. What Perez is not ready for is the close-knit community, which tries to lock him out of the process while they try to blame the killing on the slightly odd Magnus Tait, who might also be a suspect in an eight-year-old murder. **DA**

Teenagers at risk

White Nights. St. Martin's Minotaur, 2008. 9780312384333. (UK: Macmillan, 2008).

The Herring House gallery is having a midsummer opening for artist Bella Sinclair and Perez's girlfriend Fran Hunter. The party is disrupted when a man breaks down in front of one of the paintings and confesses he has amnesia. The next morning the man is found hanged to death in a fishing shed. Perez believes it is murder rather than suicide, and while he investigates, a second murder tied to the art community occurs. Now if he could only explain the clown masks.

Amnesia • Art • Suicide

Red Bones. Minotaur, 2009. 9780312384340. (UK: Macmillan, 2009).

When an archaeologist named Val Turner's dig uncovers human remains, the island of Whalsay is curious about the find. When Sandy Turner's grandmother Mima is murdered a few weeks after the discovery, Detective Inspector Jimmy Perez comes back to the island to investigate. What he finds is a closed and guarded community, so small that everyone knows everyone else's business, except who shot Mima.

Archaeology

Blue Lightning. Minotaur, 2010. 9780312384357. (UK: Macmillan, 2010).

Perez has returned home to Fair Isle to introduce Fran to his parents. While they are there, warden Angela Moore's body is found in the island's bird observatory, with feathers in her hair. Left to his own resources by serious weather, Perez must deal with this murder alone.

Birds • Scotland, Shelter Islands, Fair Isle

Crombie, Deborah ✍

Duncan Kincaid/Gemma James

In contemporary times, it is not unusual to find American authors writing about English detectives. Deborah Crombie lived in England and Scotland for a time, but now lives in Texas. Detective Superintendent Kincaid comes from the upper class, and within the series he develops a professional and personal relationship with Sergeant Gemma James, who is not from his class. See the author's Web site at http://www. deborahcrombie.com/welcome/welcome.html. Readers may also enjoy Elizabeth George, Martha Grimes, and Anne Perry. **TR** Series subjects: **Teams**

A Share in Death. Scribner, 1993.

All Shall Be Well. Scribner, 1994.

Leave the Grave Green. Scribner, 1995.

Mourn Not Your Dead. Scribner, 1996.

Dreaming of the Bones. Scribner, 1997.

Kissed a Sad Goodbye. Bantam, 1999.

A Finer End. Bantam, 2001.

And Justice There Is None. Bantam, 2002.

Now May You Weep. William Morrow, 2003. 0060525231.

James has been promoted to detective inspector, and she joins her friend Hazel Cavendish for an outing in Scotland. Cavendish's former lover, distillery owner Donald Brodie, is murdered, and James finds herself dancing around the local authorities as she tries to help out her friend. Luckily, she is joined in the investigation by Kincaid.

Alcohol • Cooking • Scotland, Innesfree

In a Dark House. William Morrow, 2004. 0060525258.

Firefighter Rose Kearny discovers a dead female in a burning building, and the police discover that the victim was murdered before the fire. While Kearny works independently of the police to establish a theory that a serial arsonist is at work, the Detective Superintendent Kincaid is searching for a missing child named Harriet Novak, and Detective Inspector James is searching for a missing hospital administrator. When the kidnapping cases begin to blend with the arson cases, Kincaid realizes they are racing against time.

Arson • Children in jeopardy • England, London • Kidnapping

Water Like a Stone. William Morrow, 2007. 9780060525279.

With Kincaid at Scotland Yard and Gemma James with the Notting Hill Metropolitan Police, the family has to escape to the countryside at Christmastime. However, there is no peace at the holidays for these detectives; Juliet Newcombe, Kincaid's sister, finds the mummified body of a child in the walls of a dairy barn she is remodeling. When this discovery leads to the death of former social worker Annie Lebow and suspicion is cast on Juliet's husband, the detectives scramble to discover the truth.

Children in jeopardy • England, Cheshire, Nantwich

Where Memories Lie. Morrow, 2008. 9780061287510.

Detective Inspector James's friend Dr. Erika Rosenthal asks for her help when a diamond brooch she owned turns up for auction in London. When a clerk in the auction house is murdered in a hit and run, James knows she is on the scent of a major crime. With ties to an old murder surrounding Erika's husband David's death in 1952 while investigating Nazi sympathizers, the story moves from past to present to find a killer.

England, London • Jewels • Nazi Germany

Necessary as Blood. Morrow, 2009. 9780061287534.

In London's East End, detectives James and Kincaid are called upon to explain the disappearance of a young woman named Sandra Gilles and the subsequent murder of her Pakistani lawyer husband, Naz Malik. When it is discovered that the couple's child, Charlotte, may be the key to the whole case, the team cranks up its efforts to save a life before it is taken.

Children in jeopardy • England, London

Fossum, Karin ✍

Inspector Konrad Sejer

Inspector Konrad Sejer works the quiet streets of the small Norwegian town Elvestad. The middle-aged widower is often teamed with his younger colleague, Inspector Jakob Skarre. Despite its passive exterior, rural Norway provides fertile ground for criminal behavior and murder. Fossum can write a police procedural, but her strength is in the area of psychological suspense. Readers may also enjoy other Scandinavian writers, such as Henning Mankell, Ruth Rendell, and Minette Walters. **TR** Series subjects: **Norway, Elvestad**

*Evas Øye. Norway: J. W. Cappelen, 1995.

Don't Look Back. Harcourt, 2002. 0151010323. (Norway: *Se Deg Ikke Tilbake!* J. W. Cappelen, 1995).

Kollen Mountain dominates the town, and when the body of teenager Annie Holland is found floating in a lake on the slopes, the case becomes the concern of Sejer. Why did a missing six-year-old find the body before returning to the village? Why would this popular resident be murdered? In a close-knit community where everyone knows each other's business, it becomes evident that there are still many dark secrets to be discovered.

Drowning • Missing persons • Teenagers at risk

He Who Fears the Wolf. Harcourt, 2003. 9780151010912. (Norway: *Den Som Frykter Ulven*. J. W. Cappelen, 1997).

Deep in the woods an elderly woman is murdered, and the only witness, a twelve-year-old boy, points a finger at Errki Johrman. Johrman is a likely suspect because he is an escaped schizophrenic, but the witness may be as psychologically damaged as the suspect he accuses. Then a bank robbery occurs, and Sejer's chief suspect is being held hostage.

Hostages • Robbery • Schizophrenia

When the Devil Holds the Candle. Harcourt, 2004. 9780151011889. (Norway: *Djevelen Holder Lyset*. J. W. Cappelen, 1998).

Two teenagers named Zipp and Andreas are causing a minor crime wave in town, until one night Andreas elevates his game to home invasion. He chooses an elderly recluse named Irma Funder as his victim, but when he fails to come out of the house, his friend Zipp becomes curious, and the town begins a search for the missing boy. Sejer and Skarre are on the hunt but are unaware that the missing boy is trapped in a situation he cannot escape.

Hostages • Recluses • Teenagers at risk

The Indian Bride. Harcourt, 2007. 9780151011827. (Norway: *Elskede Poona*. J. W. Cappelen, 2000; UK: *Calling Out for You*. Vintage, 2005).

Gunder Jomann leaves the village of Elvestad for India; when he returns, he announces that in a few weeks his new Indian bride, Poona, will be joining him. On that fateful day, delayed by circumstances, Gunder is unable to meet his bride at the airport, and she is killed. It falls to Sejer and Skarre to find out who harbors such intense fear of the unknown that they would resort to murder.

Race relations

Black Seconds. Harcourt, 2007. 9780151015276. (Norway: *Svarte Sekunder*. J. W. Cappelen, 2000).

When almost-ten-year-old Ida Joner goes missing while taking a short bicycle ride into town, her case falls to Inspector Sejer. It is easy for the local townsfolk to blame Emil Mork, a local character who has not spoken since childhood. While Sejer worries he may not have enough information to solve this case, Emil's mother worries that she may be harboring a murderer, and Ida's cousin worries that a secret might be revealed.

Children in jeopardy • Missing persons • Mothers and daughters • Mothers and sons

*Drapet På Harriet Krohn. Norway: J. W. Cappelen, 2004.

The Water's Edge. Houghton Mifflin Harcourt, 2009. 9780151014217. (Norway: *Den Som Elsker Noe Annet.* J. W. Cappelen, 2007).

> After a couple out for a stroll discover the body of a seven-year-old boy and witness a man leaving the scene, Sejer and Skarre come to the scene. Their investigation reveals that others in the town fear a pedophile may be trolling in their town. Then another boy goes missing.
>
> *Children in jeopardy* • *Norway, Huseby* • *Pedophilia*

French, Tana ✍

Dublin Murder Squad

Tana French grew up in Ireland, Italy, the United States, and Malawi. She has lived in Dublin since 1990 and trained as a professional actress at Trinity College. She has worked in theater, film and voice over and is the liaison officer for the Purple Heart Theatre Company in Dublin. Her Web site is at http://www.tanafrench.com. Readers may also enjoy Minette Walters. **TR** Series subjects: **Ireland, Dublin**

In the Woods. Viking, 2007. 9780670038602. (UK: Hodder & Stoughton, 2007).

> Rob Ryan and Cassie Maddox catch their first big case as partners when a twelve-year-old girl's body is found in the woods near an archaeological dig. For Ryan, it is a startling coincidence. Twenty years earlier, two of his playmates disappeared in the woods, and he was the only witness. Unable to tell anyone what happened, he has grown up with a need to solve crimes, which will be put to the test on this one.
>
> *Archaeology* • *Children in jeopardy* • *Memory* • *Teams*

The Likeness. Viking, 2008. 9780670018864. (UK: Hodder & Stoughton, 2008).

> After the results of her first case, Cassie Maddox has been removed from the homicide squad. When her new boyfriend, Detective Sam O'Neill, asks for her help on a murder case, a startling coincidence is revealed. The victim is Lexie Madison, the very name Cassie used earlier in her career as an alias. Even odder, the two women look exactly alike. Cassie moves into Lexie's life at Whitethorn House to try to find the answers.
>
> *Ireland, Glenskehy* • *Mistaken identity*

Faithful Place. Viking, 2010. 9780670021871. (UK: Hodder & Stoughton, 2010).

> Undercover squad leader Frank Mackey is drawn into his own past when the contents of a suitcase, hidden for twenty-five years, reveal that his old girlfriend, Rosie Daly, never left town as he thought. Supposedly the two young lovers were to run away together, but Rosie did not show up at the rendezvous, and now Mackey wants to know why.
>
> *Memory*

Garcia-Roza, Luiz Alfredo ✍

Inspector Espinosa

World-weary Rio de Janeiro police Inspector Espinosa thinks like a philosopher and a romantic at the same time. In a world where the police are corrupt, Espinosa tries to bring a balance to the way crimes are solved by being the only honest cop on the force. Eventually he is promoted to Chief Inspector out of respect for his detective skills. Readers may also enjoy Georges Simenon, Colin Cotterill, and Janwillem van de Wetering. **TR** Series subjects: **Brazil, Rio de Janeiro**

The Silence of the Rain. Henry Holt, 2002. 0805068899. (Brazil: *O Siléncio da Chuva.* Companhia das Letras, 1996).

> Inspector Espinosa is assigned the case of murdered business executive Ricardo Carvalho, found shot in the head in his car in a parking garage, his briefcase missing. When Carvalho's secretary Rose disappears next, Espinosa begins to follow a trail that leads to two more bodies. The pressure mounts on the detective to explain these deaths and find the killer.

December Heat. Henry Holt, 2002. 0805068902. (Brazil: *Achados e Perdidos.* Companhia das Letras, 1998).

> When retired police officer Vieira's prostitute girlfriend Maglia is murdered, he calls on his old friend Inspector Espinosa to investigate. Though the facts point in only one direction, Espinosa is pulled in a second when additional victims begin to appear. Where is Vieira's missing wallet? To complicate matters, Espinosa must also deal with his own affairs of the heart when he meets an artist named Kika.
>
> *Prostitutes*

Southwesterly Wind. Henry Holt, 2004. 0805068910. (Brazil: *Vento Sudoeste.* Companhia das Letras, 1999).

> What should be done with a young man named Gabriel, who believes a psychic's prediction that he will commit murder will come true? Then two deaths occur that seem related to the man, and Inspector Espinosa must launch an investigation that deals both with the facts and the fate of a man predestined to crime.
>
> *Psychics*

A Window in Copacabana. Heny Holt, 2005. 978080507438. (Brazil: *Uma Janela em Copacabana.* Companhia das Letras, 2001).

> Three Rio police officers have been assassinated by a killer who leaves no trace. When Espinosa works the cases, he finds the officers were unpopular and corrupt. When Celeste, the mistress of one of the dead cops, is flung ten stories to her death, Espinosa is led to the witness: the beautiful and seductive Serena. With a task force under his control and a witness out of control, Espinosa feels the pressure of the city while trying to solve these cop killings.
>
> *Assassinations*

Pursuit. Henry Holt, 2006. 9780805074390. (Brazil: *Perseguido*. Companhia das Letras, 2003).

1

> Espinosa receives a complaint from psychiatrist Artur Nesse, who believes a patient has kidnapped his daughter. However, the patient is found murdered, and soon there are more deaths. To find the murderer, Espinosa must decide who has been telling the truth and who has not.
>
> *Psychiatrists*

Blackout. Henry Holt, 2008. 9780805079609. (Brazil: *Espinosa Sem Saida*. Companhia das Letras, 2006).

2

> When a one-legged homeless man is murdered for no apparent reason, the case haunts Chief Inspector Espinosa. Because the crime occurred near some of Rio's wealthiest residents, Espinosa concentrates on the deception that is key to maintaining the façade of wealth.
>
> *Homeless*

Alone in the Crowd. Henry Holt, 2009. 9780805079593. (Brazil: *Na Multidão*. Companhia das Letras, 2007).

> When the elderly Doña Laureta tries to visit Chief Inspector Espinosa, she is told he is unavailable. Two hours later, when she is hit by a bus, the question becomes, was she pushed? When he focuses on a suspect named Hugo Breno, Espinosa finds himself connected to both the suspect and an old murder that may provide the motive for the modern one.
>
> *Elderly • Memory*

3

George, Elizabeth ✍

Thomas Lynley/Barbara Havers

An American writing about English detectives, George has created an ensemble of characters in a similar fashion to McBain. Scotland Yard Inspector Lynley is another upper class detective à la Ngaio Marsh's Roderick Alleyn, being the Earl of Asherton. His team, which includes Sergeant Barbara Havers, pathologist Simon Allcourt-St. James, and Lady Helen Clyde, is an interesting ensemble. Readers may also enjoy Deborah Crombie and Martha Grimes. See the author's Web site at http://www.elizabethgeorgeonline.com. **TR** Series subjects: **Teams**

> *A Great Deliverance*. Bantam, 1989.
>
> *Payment in Blood*. Bantam, 1989.
>
> *Well-Schooled in Murder*. Bantam, 1990.
>
> *A Suitable Vengeance*. Bantam, 1991.
>
> *For the Sake of Elena*. Bantam, 1992.

Missing Joseph. Bantam, 1993.

Playing for the Ashes. Bantam, 1994.

In the Presence of the Enemy. Bantam, 1996.

Deception on His Mind. Bantam, 1997.

In Pursuit of the Proper Sinner. Bantam, 1999.

A Traitor to Memory. Bantam, 2001.

A Place of Hiding. Bantam, 2003. 0553801309. (UK: Hodder & Stoughton, 2003).

Guy Brouard is building a museum to honor those who resisted the German occupation of the island of Guernsey, when he is found murdered. Although some clues point to the past, there are plenty of suspects alive and related to the dead man to provide any detective with a puzzling case, as Simon St. James and his wife Deborah find when they choose to investigate.

England, Guernsey Islands

With No One as a Witness. HarperCollins, 2005. 0060545607.

A serial killer is at work, with the deaths of four children to his credit. When the case is assigned to Acting Superintendent Lynley and Detective Constable Barbara Havers, they must deal with the issue of three of the victims being from mixed marriages. While Lynley tries to fend off accusations of police prejudice, he must keep one eye on the recently demoted Havers to try to keep her from further damaging her career on the force.

Children in jeopardy • England, London • Serial killer

Careless in Red. Harper, 2008. 9780061160875.

Retired after his personal tragedy, Lynley is walking the cliffs of Cornwall when he discovers the body of Santo Kerne, who has fallen to his death. The officer on the case, Detective Inspector Bea Hannaford, thinks Lindley might be the one who tampered with Santo's climbing gear and caused his death. Having to fight his own despair, Lynley finds aid and comfort from his old colleague, Barbara Havers.

England, Cornwall, Casveyln • Rock climbing

This Body of Death. HarperCollins, 2010. 9780061160882.

Lynley is on leave, recovering from the consequences of events decsribed in a previous book, when Scotland Yard calls him back into service. A woman named Jemima Hastings has been found stabbed to death in a cemetery in London, and Lynley's replacement, Isabelle Ardery, needs his help when pressure is put on the department for results. Meanwhile, Lynley's former teammates, Barbara Havers and Winston Nkata, have their own issues to deal with when their beloved boss returns, but their new boss is not making their lives easy. Eventually the trail leads to New Forest, where Jemima's ex becomes suspect number one.

England, Hampshire, New Forest • Horses

Grimes, Martha ✍

Richard Jury/Melrose Plant

Written by an American, these English mysteries are reminiscent of Dorothy L. Sayers. Named for English pubs, each title features Grimes's well-developed supporting cast. Inspector Jury is supported by two major cohorts: the slightly potty professor, Melrose Plant, and Jury's intrusive Aunt Agatha. Grimes's breezy tone and use of humor add a lightness to the books that will appeal to readers who enjoy this kind of mystery. Her style echoes the traditional Golden Age writers. Over the course of the series Jury will be promoted to Superintendent. Readers may also enjoy Deborah Crombie and Elizabeth George. See the author's Web site at http://www.marthagrimes.com. **SB** **TR** Series subjects: **Teams**

The Man with a Load of Mischief. Little, Brown, 1981.

The Old Fox Deceiv'd. Little, Brown, 1982.

The Anodyne Necklace. Little, Brown, 1983.

The Dirty Duck. Little, Brown, 1984.

Jerusalem Inn. Little, Brown, 1984.

The Deer Leap. Little, Brown, 1985.

Help the Poor Struggler. Little, Brown, 1985.

I Am the Only Running Footman. Little, Brown, 1986.

The Five Bells and Bladebone. Little, Brown, 1987.

The Old Silent. Little, Brown, 1989.

The Old Contemptibles. Little, Brown, 1991.

The Horse You Came in On. Knopf, 1993.

Rainbow's End. Knopf, 1995.

The Case Has Altered. Henry Holt, 1997.

Stargazey. Henry Holt, 1998.

The Lamorna Wink. Viking, 1999.

The Blue Last. Viking, 2001.

The Grave Maurice. Viking, 2002.

The Winds of Change. Viking, 2004. 0670033278.

When a five-year-old is shot to death, the investigation leads to sad evidence of child abuse and pedophilia. The new case connects to the three-year-old abduction case surrounding businessman Viktor Baumann and a missing girl named Flora, the stepdaughter of Police Commander Brian Macalvie. With Melrose undercover as a gardener, Superintendent

Jury pushes forward his first case after his recovery from hospitalization, while Macalvie pursues his personal demons.

Children in jeopardy • *England, London* • *Pedophilia*

The Old Wine Shades. Viking, 2006. 9780670034796.

On suspension as a consequence of his actions in the last book, Jury does a little private enquiry when he meets Harry Johnson, a physicist, in a pub. Over a three-day period, Johnson's story of a missing mother and her autistic son, as well as the faithful family dog, intrigues Jury, but not as much as the fact of the dog's return nine months after his disappearance.

Autism • *Dogs* • *England, London* • *England, Surrey* • *Missing persons* • *Physics*

Dust. Viking, 2007. 9780670037865.

Wealthy and eligible bachelor Billy Maples has been found dead in a seedy London hotel, and Jury is assigned the case. As Jury probes into Maples's life, he discovers that the man's grandfather was a code breaker during World War II. Though he gets welcome assistance from pal Plant, who is assigned to investigate Henry James's Lamb House, Jury's love life is complicated by his continuing relations with pathologist Phyllis Nancy and a new attraction, Detective Inspector Lu Aguilar.

Code breakers • *England, London* • *James, Henry* • *World War II*

The Black Cat. Viking, 2010. 9780670021604.

Outside the pub The Black Cat, a black cat is the only witness to the shooting of an escort. Despite being off his turf, Jury is on the job while more escorts fall victim to the killer in London. Fighting local politics, hangover issues from previous cases, and animal witnesses, he manages to make some headway while worrying about the health of his lover, Detective Lu Aguilar.

Cats • *Dogs* • *England, Buckinghamshire, High Wycombe* • *Prostitutes*

Harrod-Eagles, Cynthia ✍

Bill Slider

Bill Slider is a Detective Inspector for London's Metropolitan Police whose home life is not pleasant. He and his crew normally cover the Shepherd's Bush district. Not unwilling to dally with his lover Joanna, he relies on the support of his best friend Sergeant Jim Atherton, who can be quite the ladies' man himself. Eventually Slider must deal with a change in leadership at work, when Detective Superintendent Fred "The Syrup" Porsons comes on board, and with a change in his situation at home when his relationship with his wife comes to an end. Readers may also enjoy M. C. Beaton for the lighter aspects and John Harvey or Ian Rankin for the darker aspects. See the author's Web site at http://www.cynthiaharrodeagles.com/cynthia_harrod_eagles. **TR**
Series subjects: **England, London**

Orchestrated Death. Scribners, 1991. 0684193884. (UK: Little, Brown, 1991).

> Slider is called in when the naked body of a beautiful violinist is discovered. With his home life in tatters, he finds himself attracted to his key witness. With the help of his sergeant, who thinks Slider is "menopausal," he plugs away at the case and finds himself interested in a very old and valuable Stradivarius.
>
> *Affairs • England, West Midlands, Birmingham • Violinists*

Death Watch. Scribner, 1993. 0684195194. (UK: Little, Brown, 1992).

> When a philandering salesman is found burnt to death under an assumed name at a motel, the initial investigation assumes suicide because of his many affairs, his failing business, and his debt. But Slider suspects murder. While investigating, Slider is disturbed to see patterns in the victim's behavior that mirror his own.
>
> *Affairs • Arson • Salesmen • Serial killer*

Death to Go. Scribner, 1994. 0684196506. (UK: *Necrochip*. Little, Brown, 1993).

> Initially Slider complains about being called to a fish and chips shop over a public health issue, until he realizes that the severed finger among the food belongs to the body discovered later in the dumpster behind the restaurant. When other body parts begin to appear around London and drag Slider into the lives of a varied cast of characters, it falls to him to decode the messages that are being sent. And what does all this have to do with his former Detective Sergeant, George Dickson?
>
> *Serial killer*

Grave Music. Scribner, 1995. 0684800462. (UK: *Dead End*. Little, Brown, 1994).

> When the much hated Stefan Radek, conductor of the Royal London Philharmonic, is murdered, Slider and Atherton discover that there is no end to the list of potential suspects. More disturbing to Slider is the fact that his lover Joanna is one of the chief violinists in the pit.
>
> *Affairs • Conductors • Orchestras*

Blood Lines. Scribner, 1996. 0684800470. (UK: Little, Brown, 1996).

> When a famous art critic's throat is slit in the men's room at a TV station just prior to his scheduled appearance, Slider looks at all the potential suspects who wished him silenced. To his great surprise, the clues lead back to the department and an officer of the law with something to hide.
>
> *Critics • Police corruption*

Killing Time. Scribner, 1998. 0684837765. (UK: Little, Brown, 1996).

> Slider is working with a young black female detective partner named Tony Hart while Atherton is recovering, and he is not happy. Initially he is unable to investigate the threats to exotic dancer Jay Paloma, which leads to the man's death. Seeking answers with his new partner, Slider finds

himself trying to decide if an attack on another officer has anything to do with the blackmail, drugs, politics, and prostitution that surrounded Paloma's life.

Blackmail • Drugs • Exotic dancers • Homosexuality • Politicians • Prostitutes

Shallow Grave. Scribner, 1999. 0684837773. (UK: Little, Brown, 1998).

An exclusive West London suburb is rocked by murder when contractor Edward Andrews's wife is found dead on a worksite. Slider is reunited with Atherton, and the two find that there may be more to discover in the famous historian's home that is being restored than there is in Edward's world. Both officers are struggling with their personal lives while trying to conduct a thorough investigation.

Affairs

Blood Sinister. St. Martin's Minotaur, 2001. 0312274858. (UK: Little, Brown, 1999).

When a female journalist named Phoebe Agnew is murdered, the case takes on extra significance because she was a vocal critic of the police. To make matters even worse, her lover is a high-ranking government official, and the police are wary about treading in that direction. Slider assembles his crew, but he needs to keep one eye on Atherton, who appears to be struggling to do his job.

Journalists

Gone Tomorrow. St. Martin's Minotaur, 2002. 0312300468. (UK: Little, Brown, 2001).

In an almost Golden Age setup, the murder victim in this story is found sitting on a swing on a playground in London, stabbed through the heart. Slider is soon investigating a man whose debts and drug use may lead to a crime lord who will stop at nothing. The problem is that no one wants to give up the name.

Drugs • Loan sharks • Missing persons • Organized crime • Pregnancy

Dear Departed. St. Martin's Minotaur, 2005. 9780312347680. (UK: Little, Brown, 2004).

Now engaged to his lover Joanna, who is pregnant with his child, Slider is happy at home. At work, he and his team are dealing with The Park Killer, a serial murderer leaving victims in public parks. Things become complicated when the latest victim's death appears to be a copycat killing. Rather than look at the perpetrator, the team finds the best clues may lie in the victim's world.

Copycat killers • Serial killer • Sisters

Game Over. UK: Severn House, 2008. 9780727866158.

A former BBC correspondent named Ed Stonax has been found murdered. His research had involved possible reasons for his death, but Slider's team is not having an easy time locating what it needs. Atherton has fallen in love with Stonax's daughter, and Slider is trying to find the time to marry Joanna before they become parents. On top of all this, Trevor "The Needle" Bates is on the loose and interested in getting revenge on Slider.

Journalists • Serial killer

Fell Purpose. UK: Severn House, 2009. 9780727868428.

> When seventeen-year-old Zellah Wilding, a successful student, is founded murdered in a London park. the team is confused. She had lied to her parents about her whereabouts and her relationships, and Slider eventually discovers she had ties to a boy from the wrong side of the tracks and that her father is a recently released rapist.
>
> *Ex-convicts • Teenagers at risk*

Hayder, Mo ✍

Jack Caffery

Detective Inspector Jack Caffery and his partners Paul Essex and Phoebe "Flea" Marley work out of London, England, in the Area Major Investigation Pool under Detective Chief Inspector Danniella Souness. Caffery is famous for his stoic nature, but these cases would trouble anyone. What few know is that Caffery is obsessed with the loss of his brother and still seeks retribution for that crime. Readers may also enjoy Thomas Harris and John Sandford. See the author's Web site at http://www.mohayder.net. **HB**

Birdman. Doubleday, 1999. 038549694X.

> When the mutilated corpse of a young woman is found dumped in the garbage near the Millennium Dome in Greenwich, the case falls to the unflappable Detective Inspector Jack Caffery. Why would someone sew a live bird into the chest of the victim? When four more deaths of unknown women occur in the same manner, the police realize they have a serial killer on the loose, one who is sexually motivated. When the clues lead to someone with medical knowledge, the case begins to gather focus.
>
> *England, Greenwich • Forensics • Medical • Necrophilia • Serial killer*

The Treatment. Doubleday, 2001. 0385496958.

> When a couple is found near death, bound in their own house, the crime seems enough on its own. Then Caffery's team hears that the couple's eight-year-old son Rory is missing. This triggers Caffery's own personal demon, and he goes on a hunt for the killer. With an endless list of potential suspects, the police find themselves sifting among a number of characters while Caffery obsesses about the man he suspects of past crimes.
>
> *Children in jeopardy • England, London • Obsession • Pedophilia*

Ritual. Atlantic Monthly Press, 2008. 9780871139924. (UK: Bantam, 2008).

> When police diver Sergeant Phoebe Marley discovers two hands that have recently been amputated, the police find themselves on the trail of the reason. Recently shifted to the Major Crime Investigation Unit in Bristol, Caffery is assigned the case and a new partner. When clues lead the team to

drugs on the streets of Bristol and the lost souls who use them, they are surprised to hear of a connection to the occult.

Diving • Drugs • England, Bristol • Muti • Witchcraft

Skin. Grove, 2010. 9780802119308. (UK: Bantam, 2009).

Caffery and "Flea" Marley are busy. Caffrey catches a case in which a suicide appears to have a connection to the muti mutilations they discovered on their last case. Then another suicide occurs, and he begins to have doubts. Meanwhile, Flea is diving into quarries looking for a missing woman while worrying about the connection to her own brother. While the two detectives work these cases and deal with their own personal demons, their attraction to each other continues to challenge them.

Diving • England, Bristol • Muti • Romance

Hess, Joan ✍

Arly Hanks

Maggody, Arkansas, is the location of this series of novels about female Police Chief Arly Hanks. Arly's adventures in rural Arkansas have a soft-boiled approach to crime. Hess has surrounded her detective with a nutty supporting cast, making these regional cop novels very enjoyable. They can be recommended to readers who enjoy the soft-boiled and traditional styles. Readers may also enjoy M. C. Beaton (Hamish Macbeth) and H. R. F. Keating. See the author's Web site at http://www.maggody. com. **SB TR** Series subjects: **Arkansas, Maggody • Humor**

Malice in Maggody. St. Martin's, 1987.

Mischief in Maggody. St. Martin's, 1988.

Much Ado in Maggody. St. Martin's, 1989.

Madness in Maggody. St. Martin's, 1991.

Mortal Remains in Maggody. Dutton, 1991.

Maggody in Manhattan. Dutton, 1992.

O Little Town of Maggody. Dutton, 1993.

Martians in Maggody. Dutton, 1994.

Miracles in Maggody. Dutton, 1995.

The Maggody Militia. Dutton, 1997.

Misery Loves Maggody. Simon & Schuster, 1999.

Murder@maggody.com. Simon & Schuster, 2000.

Maggody and the Moonbeams. Simon & Schuster, 2001.

Muletrain to Maggody. Simon & Schuster, 2004. 0743226380.

The Stump County Historical Society has decided to promote a documentary film and reenactment of the Civil War battle known as The Skirmish at Cotter's Ridge. Hanks has enough to do with all the reenactors descending on the town and the arrival of a famous author of Civil War romances, but when it is rumored that there is Confederate gold hidden in them there hills, even the locals become frenzied. Then the Historical Society's treasurer, Wendell Streek, is murdered, and an investigation must be launched.

Civil War • Reenactments

Malpractice in Maggody. Simon & Schuster, 2006. 9780743226394.

The Stonebridge Foundation has replaced Maggody's old folks' home, and the residents are leery of the new walled facility and its guards. Hanks is called behind the walls when a young female receptionist is found drowned in a pond, and her investigation may quell the rumors that Stonebridge is an asylum for the insane. However, it may also reveal that the murder of a local girl means one of the town's residents may be the guilty party.

Insane asylum

The Merry Wives of Maggody. Minotaur, 2010. 9780312363611.

The community hopes to reap the economic benefits of its first Maggody Charity Golf Tournament, but plans go awry when the winner is Tommy Ridner. When his corpse is found the next day in the bass boat he won, Sheriff Hanks is convinced she just has to find a jealous murderer who used a golf club as a deadly weapon. But then a second murder by club occurs, and the pregnant sheriff finds this one will not be easy to solve.

Golf

Hill, Reginald ✍

Andy Dalziel/Peter Pascoe

Yorkshire, England, is the setting for British writer Hill's long-running series. Dalziel's acerbic personality contrasts with Pascoe's brooding moodiness. The two cops' personalities are the yin and yang of these books, but as the series progresses the novels become rich in the depth of their plots and the increased reliance on psychological insight. Readers may also enjoy Colin Dexter and Peter Robinson. See the author's Web site at http://www.randomhouse.com/features/reghill. **TR HB** Series subjects: **England, Yorkshire • Teams**

A Clubbable Woman. UK: Collins, 1970 (US: Foul Play, 1984).

An Advancement of Learning. UK: Collins, 1971 (US: Foul Play, 1985).

Ruling Passion. UK: Collins, 1973 (US: Harper, 1977).

An April Shroud. UK: Collins, 1975 (US: Foul Play, 1986).

A Pinch of Snuff. UK: Collins, 1978 (US: Harper and Row, 1978).

A Killing Kindness. UK: Collins, 1980 (US: Pantheon, 1981).

Deadheads. UK: Collins, 1983 (US: Macmillan, 1984).

Exit Lines. UK: Collins, 1984 (US: Macmillan, 1985).

Child's Play. UK: Collins, 1987 (US: Macmillan, 1987).

Underworld. UK: Collins, 1988 (US: Scribner, 1988).

Bones and Silence. UK: Collins 1990 (US: Delacorte, 1990).

One Small Step. UK: Collins, 1990.

Recalled to Life. UK: Collins, 1992 (US: Delacorte, 1992).

Asking for the Moon. UK: Collins, 1994 (US: Norton, 1996).

Pictures of Perfection. UK: Collins, 1994 (US: Delacorte, 1994).

The Wood Beyond. UK: Collins, 1996 (US: Delacorte, 1996).

On Beulah Height. UK: Collins, 1998 (US: Delacorte, 1998).

Arms and the Women. UK: Collins, 1999 (US: Delacorte, 1999).

Dialogues of the Dead. UK: Collins, 2001. (U.S.: Delacorte, 2002).

Death's Jest-Book. HarperCollins, 2003. 0060528052. (UK: HarperCollins, 2003).

Franny Roote has been put away for murder by Pascoe, but now Roote has been released. Roote is taunting Pascoe with thanks for making him famous, sending veiled threats against Pascoe's family, and hinting about new murders. Then, while Roote is delivering an academic paper, a fire at Cambridge leaves an arson victim, and Pascoe believes Roote is back in action.

Arson • Cambridge • Serial killer

Good Morning, Midnight. HarperCollins, 2004. 0060528079. (UK: HarperCollins, 2004).

Businessman Pal Maciver has committed suicide in a locked-room situation that should make the case cut and dried for Dalziel and Pascoe. However, Pal's death echoes his father's suicide to the day, a case investigated by a younger Dalziel. But Pal has left a cassette tape with chilling evidence, and a book of Emily Dickinson's poetry may be a clue to a more complicated case. Suspicion falls on Kay Kafka, Pal's stepmother, who distracts the two detectives to the point where they appear to be in opposition to each other.

Locked room • Suicide

Death Comes for the Fat Man. HarperCollins, 2007. 9780060820824. (UK: HarperCollins, 2007).

> A bomb has put Dalziel in a coma. The only reason that Pascoe is alive to carry on the investigation is that the big man's body shielded him from most of the impact. Now, with a team of antiterrorist agents in tow, he is out to seek revenge for his partner. The path leads to the Knights Templar and those who use force to fight force.
>
> *Bombs* • *Coma* • *England, Manchester* • *Knights Templar* • *Terrorism*

The Price of Butcher's Meat. HarperCollins, 2008. 9780061451935. (UK: HarperCollins, 2008).

> Recuperating at Avalon Clinic from injuries received on the last case, Dalziel should be taking it easy. But when Chief Inspector Pascoe arrives because Lady Daphne Denham has been charred to death in a pig roaster cage, the two find themselves united again. Taking different paths, each detective moves toward a perpetrator from a list that includes a shady psychiatrist, some greedy landowners, and a man from Dalziel's past.

Hillerman, Tony ✍

Joe Leaphorn/Jim Chee

Originally characters in two separate series, these two Native American detectives eventually find themselves working together in the same books. Joe Leaphorn is the experienced detective who has established his way in the world. Jim Chee is the brash, young man who tries to maintain his contact with his spirituality while acting as a detective. Besides creating great characters and plots, Hillerman's strength is his ability to sympathetically depict the Navajo culture without distracting from the pace of the mystery, creating works that are as much literature as genre writing. Tony Hillerman passed away in 2008. Readers may also enjoy Nevada Barr, Jean Hager, J. A. Jance (Joanna Brady), Reginald Hill, and Abigail Padgett. See a fan's Web site at http://www.umsl.edu/~smueller. **TR HB** Series subjects: **Native Americans** • **New Mexico** • **Teams**

> *The Blessing Way.* Harper & Row, 1970.
>
> *Dance Hall of the Dead.* Harper & Row, 1973.
>
> *Listening Woman.* Harper & Row, 1978.
>
> *People of Darkness.* Harper & Row, 1980.
>
> *The Dark Wind.* Harper & Row, 1982.
>
> *The Ghostway.* Harper & Row, 1984.
>
> *Skinwalkers.* Harper & Row, 1987.
>
> *A Thief of Time.* Harper & Row, 1988.

Talking God. Harper & Row, 1989.

Coyote Waits. Harper & Row, 1990.

Sacred Clowns. Harper & Row, 1993.

The Fallen Man. HarperCollins, 1996.

The First Eagle. HarperCollins, 1998.

Hunting Badger. HarperCollins, 1999.

The Wailing Wind. HarperCollins, 2002.

Sinister Pig. HarperCollins, 2003. 006019443X.

The FBI steals a case from Chee when a body is discovered at the edges of a natural gas field within his jurisdiction. Chee teams with Hopi Federal Bureau of Land Management cop Cowboy Dashee, and the pair believe the truth might be connected to some missing money from the Tribal Trust Fund, so they investigate anyway. Officer Bernadette Manuelito now works for the Customs Service, and the danger she finds herself in troubles her silent admirer, Chee. Meanwhile, Leaphorn is also doing some investigating, and the three separate probes find themselves melding into one.

Skeleton Man. HarperCollins, 2004. 0060563443.

Leaphorn is called back to work as a consultant when his replacement wants to know how a diamond came into the possession of Billy Tuye, a young Hopi boy. When the diamond leads to the revelation of a fifty-year-old plane crash in the Grand Canyon, a relative of one of the victims wants to use DNA to prove her right to the diamonds. Chee and his fiancée, ex-cop Bernie Manuelito, find themselves drawn into the investigation while struggling with their relationship. Others are after additional diamonds at the crash site, and a race is on to reveal what has been buried under water for five decades, protected by an old Hopi sacred site.

Diamonds

The Shape Shifter. HarperCollins, 2006. 9780060563455.

With too much time on his hands, Leaphorn is troubled by an old case that did not get solved before he retired. When his former colleague Mel Bork sends him a picture of a Navajo rug that might be evidence from an old arson and murder case, Leaphorn decides to do a little digging to unearth the truth. Then Bork is murdered. With Jimmy Chee freshly returned from his honeymoon, Leaphorn finds a willing partner and another cop who will not rest until all the crimes are solved.

Rugs

Arnaldur Indriðason ✍

Erlendur Sveinsson

Detective Erlendur Sveinsson is an Icelandic detective working the mean streets of Reykjavik. He is in his fifties, divorced, and still dealing with his troubled daughters. More important, he is haunted by the death of his brother and his own survival in the same incident. He, his partner Sigurdur Oli, and their female colleague Elinborg find that life on an island is no less complicated than in any other major city in the world. Readers may also enjoy Karin Fossum, Mo Hayder, Henning Mankell, Georges Simenon, or Per Wahloo and Maj Sjowall. **TR** Series subjects: **Fathers and daughters** • **Iceland, Reykjavik**

*Synir Duftsins. Vaka-Helgafell, 1997.

*Dauðarósir. Vaka-Helgafell, 1998.

Jar City. Thomas Dunne, 2005. 9780312340704. (Iceland: Myrin. Vaka-Helgafell, 2000; UK: Tainted Blood. Harvill, 2004).

> Sveinsson lands a case in which the only clues to the death of an old man named Holberg are a photo of a young girl's grave and a written clue. When it is revealed that the victim was never convicted of the crime of which he was accused, the police wonder if they have a case of revenge.
>
> *Genetics • Rape • Revenge*

🎗 *Silence of the Grave.* St. Martin's Minotaur, 2006. 9780312427320. (Iceland: Grafarþögn. Vaka-Helgafell, 2001; UK: Picador, 2002).

> Sveinsson is dealing with a body found on the outskirts of town that may have rested there for fifty years. Is this death important to today's generation, or should Sveinsson be dealing with the current realities of his daughter? Secrets from World War II that are revealed lead to prominent citizens of the city and a startling confession.
>
> **DA**
>
> *World War II*

Voices. St. Martin's Minotaur, 2007. 9780312358716. (Iceland: Röddin. Vaka-Helgafell, 2002; UK: Harvill Press, 2006).

> Not even Christmas gives Sveinsson and his team a rest, when a Santa Claus at a local hotel is murdered. The police are surprised by the details of the slightly sordid death of this seemingly loveable character named Gudlaugur, a former childhood singing sensation. It is only when the team begins to dig into the man's life that his darker secrets are revealed.
>
> *Christmas • Santa Claus*

Arctic Chill. Minotaur, 2009. 9780312381035. (Iceland: Vetrarborgin. Vaka-Helgafell, 2005; UK: Harvill, 2008).

> When a young Asian boy is found frozen in a puddle of his own blood in the dead of winter, the case falls to Sveinsson. Immediately he knows he must deal with the racism in Icelandic society, but over the long term the case begins to open doors in his own personal life that he would prefer to not walk through. With the death of his mentor, the memory of his own dead brother, and a missing woman to worry about, his stress level begins to rise.
>
> *Children in jeopardy • Immigration*

 The Draining Lake. St. Martin's Minotaur, 2008. 9780312358730. (Iceland: Kleifarvatn. Vaka-Helgafell, 2004; UK: Harvill Secker, 2007).

> When an earthquake causes the level of Lake Kleifarvatn to fall and reveal a dead body, it is up to Sveinsson's team to determine if murder has been committed. The remains are bound by a Russian transmitter, which may mean this is a leftover from the Cold War days. When Sveinsson discovers that some young Icelandic students were educated in Communist East Germany, his job becomes determining who is still alive to tell the tale.
>
> **BA**
>
> *Academia • Cold War • Communism • Germany, East • Lakes*

Hypothermia. Minotaur, 2010. 9780312569914. (Iceland: Harðskafi. Vaka-Helgafell, 2007; UK: Harvill Secker, 2009).

> A suicide is not normally a police matter, but Sveinsson cannot let go of the death of Maria, found hanging in her summer cottage. Her death by this means seems so unlikely. As Sveinsson begins to dig, he discovers that there is as much in his own life that troubles him as in the life of the woman he is investigating. In his spare time, he is also still obsessed with a missing persons case that calls out to him to solve it.
>
> *Suicide*

James, P. D. 🖉

Adam Dalgliesh

British writer James's series about Inspector (later Chief Superintendent) Dagliesh combines dramatic stories, literate writing, and most of the classic traditional elements from the best of the Golden Age. With a subdued personality that separates him from the great thinking or eccentric detectives, Dalgliesh brings a solemn dignity to his investigation that places him in the forefront of the books yet keeps his personality distant even from the reader. Dalgliesh can also claim to be a published poet! Readers may also enjoy Ngaio Marsh, Colin Dexter, Ruth Rendell, and Peter Robinson. **TR**

> *Cover Her Face.* UK: Faber & Faber, 1962 (US: Scribner, 1966).
>
> *A Mind to Murder.* UK: Faber & Faber, 1963 (US: Scribner, 1967).

Unnatural Causes. UK: Faber & Faber, 1967 (US: Scribner, 1967).

Shroud for a Nightingale. UK: Faber & Faber, 1971 (US: Scribner, 1971).

The Black Tower. UK: Faber & Faber, 1975 (US: Scribner, 1975).

Death of an Expert Witness. UK: Faber & Faber, 1977 (US: Scribner, 1977).

A Taste for Death. UK: Faber & Faber, 1986 (US: Knopf, 1986).

Devices and Desires. UK: Faber & Faber, 1989 (US: Knopf, 1990).

Original Sin. UK: Faber & Faber, 1994 (US: Knopf, 1995).

A Certain Justice. UK: Faber & Faber, 1997 (US: Knopf, 1997).

Death in Holy Orders. UK: Faber & Faber, 2001 (US: Knopf, 2001).

Murder Room. Knopf, 2003. 1400041414. (UK: Faber & Faber, 2003).
When Neville Dupayne decides to campaign to close the Dupayne Museum, his decision affects his siblings and everyone who works at the museum. The museum's mission was to present England between the wars, including its homicides, which were exhibited in the Murder Room, and Neville is murdered in the style of one of the famous murders the museum presented. Dalgleish is called in to solve the case, and he is on site when a second murder occurs. He still has time to romance Cambridge professor Emma Lavenaham.
England, London • Museums

The Lighthouse. Knopf, 2005. 9780307262912. (UK: Faber & Faber, 2005).
The remote island of Combe, located off the Cornish coast of England, is a refuge for the rich and powerful who need a place to rest. When murder occurs, Commander Dalgliesh and his team of Detective Inspector Kate Miskin and Sergeant Francis Benton-Smith are sent to the island to solve the crime. Author Nathan Oliver has been murdered, and the cause might lie with the residents of the island, or trouble may have followed these people on their retreat.
England, Combe Island • Islands

The Private Patient. Knopf, 2008. 9780307270771. (UK: Faber & Faber, 2008).
Journalist Rhoda Gradwyn has been murdered shortly after surgery for removal of an old scar under the hands of surgeon George Chandler-Powell. Commander Dalgliesh is called in and journeys to the private clinic at Cheverell Manor in Dorset to seek the truth. With Dalgliesh feeling that his time is running out at the Yard but interested in getting married, he concentrates on whether aging had anything to do with the murder or if it was the dogged determination to find the truth that got the journalist murdered.
Aging • England, Dorset • Journalists

Jance, J. A. ✍

J. P. Beaumont

Beaumont is a heroic figure in the Seattle Police force, with a reputation for being a wild card. His battles with alcohol and the demons in his personal life add richness to the texture of modern Seattle, a city with its own troubles. Readers may also enjoy Thomas Adcock, Lawrence Block (Matthew Scudder), Michael Connelly, and John Sandford. **TR** **HB** Series subjects: **Washington, Seattle**

Until Proven Guilty. Avon, 1985.

Injustice for All. Avon, 1986.

Trial by Fury. Avon, 1986.

Taking the Fifth. Avon, 1987.

Improbable Cause. Avon, 1988.

A More Perfect Union. Avon, 1988.

Dismissed with Prejudice. Avon, 1989.

Minor in Possession. Avon, 1990.

Payment in Kind. Avon, 1991.

Without Due Process. Morrow, 1992.

Failure to Appear. Morrow, 1993.

Lying in Wait. Morrow, 1994.

Name Withheld. Morrow, 1996.

Breach of Duty. Avon, 1999.

Birds of Prey. Morrow, 2001.

Partner in Crime. Morrow, 2002.

Long Time Gone. Morrow, 2005. 9780688138240.

Beaumont is now working for the Washington State Attorney's Special Homicide Investigation Team as an investigator out of the Seattle office. When Sister Mary Katherine's repressed memories cause her to dream of a long-forgotten murder case, Beaumont is given the assignment. However, when his ex-partner and best friend Ron Peter's ex-wife is murdered, Beaumont must choose between his day job and his personal demons when deciding what to investigate.

Cold case • Religion

Justice Denied. Morrow, 2007. 9780060540920.

Everyone is disappearing in the Northwest. While Beaumont works the case of an ex-con who has been murdered after being released from prison, he also looks for a missing whistleblower who disappeared when Mount Saint Helens exploded. His girlfriend, Mel Soames, is investigating the deaths of sex offenders who have been set free and searching for the missing father of her childhood friend. As all these threads begin to weave a pattern, the two special investigators find a conspiracy that proves threatening to them.

Missing persons • Sex crimes • Wrongful convictions

Fire and Ice. Morrow, 2009. 9780061239229.

Beaumont has a case in Seattle in which six young women have been burnt to death. Meanwhile, in Cochise County Brady is dealing with the death of an elderly ATV park caretaker who was run over and left to die. When it turns out that one of the Seattle victims is related to Brady's detective Jaime Carbajal, a link is made between the two investigations that will lead to another murder.

Serial killer

Joanna Brady

Successful in performing as an investigator on her first case, Brady becomes the sheriff of Cochise County in Arizona. As the widow of the previous sheriff, she finds herself on a mission to educate herself in the ways of crime and to face down all opposition to her attempts to prove herself worthy. Although not quite as troubled as Jance's previously created character Beaumont, Brady is still a troubled woman making a challenging career change. These novels can be recommended to traditional mystery readers. Readers may also enjoy Nevada Barr, Jean Hager, Tony Hillerman, and Abigail Padgett. **TR** Series subjects: **Arizona, Cochise County**

Desert Heat. Avon, 1993.

Tombstone Courage. Morrow, 1994.

Shoot, Don't Shoot. Morrow, 1995.

Dead to Rights. Avon, 1996.

Skeleton Canyon. Avon, 1997.

Rattlesnake Crossing. Avon, 1998.

Outlaw Mountain. Avon, 1999.

Devil's Claw. Morrow, 2000.

Paradise Lost. Morrow, 2001.

Partner in Crime. Morrow, 2002.

Exit Wounds. Morrow, 2003. 0380977311.

A murder with eighty-five-year-old bullets would be unusual enough; Carol Mossman and her seventeen dead stray dogs are found in a trailer during a blistering heat wave. But when two more women are found murdered on remote ranch land with the same antique bullets, Brady knows she has a serial killer on the loose.

Dogs • Serial killer

Dead Wrong. Morrow, 2006. 9780060540906.

While pregnant with her second child, Brady must investigate the death of an ex-con who was connected to a prominent judge in her county and the murderer of a pregnant woman. When animal control officer Jeannine Phillips is beaten, it opens a second case that finds Brady battling an establishment rancher who may have issues with illegal immigration. As she races against the clock to solve the crime before giving birth, Brady must deal with connections to one of her father's famous cases.

Alcoholism • Dysfunctional families • Immigration • Pregnancy

Damage Control. Morrow, 2008. 9780060746780.

This novel features the complicated life of a sheriff trying to raise her new son and protect her mother from the challenges of aging. While husband Butch can help on the domestic front, at work Sheriff Brady is confronted by multiple cases that confound and challenge her department. An apparent suicide by an elderly couple looks suspicious, and a care facility is losing its residents, one of whom is found dead. Brady must decide if all these issues have a common denominator.

Aging

Fire and Ice. Morrow, 2009. 9780061239229.

Beaumont has a case in Seattle in which six young women have been burnt to death. Meanwhile, in Cochise County Brady is dealing with the death of an elderly ATV park caretaker who was run over and left to die. When it turns out that one of the Seattle victims is related to Brady's detective Jaime Carbajal, a link is made between the two investigations that will lead to another murder.

Serial killer

Kaminsky, Stuart ✍

Porfiry Rostnikov

American writer Kaminsky started his series set in the Soviet Union about the time that things were beginning to unravel there. The books reveal what life was like under the Communists and then how life has changed for Russian citizens. Rostnikov has his physical and political problems, but he manages to keep a solid team around him, consisting of Sasha Tkach and Emil Krapo. Stuart Kaminsky passed away in the fall of 2009. Readers may also enjoy H. R. F. Keating, William Marshall, and Janwillem Van de Wetering. **TR** **HB**

> *Death of a Dissident.* Charter, 1981. (UK: *Rostnikov's Corpse.* Macmillan, 1981).
>
> *Black Knight in Red Square.* Charter, 1984.
>
> *Red Chameleon.* Scribner, 1985.
>
> *A Fine Red Rain.* Scribner, 1987.
>
> *A Cold Red Sunrise.* Scribner, 1988.
>
> *The Man Who Walked Like a Bear.* Scribner, 1990.
>
> *Rostnikov's Vacation.* Scribner, 1991.
>
> *Death of a Russian Priest.* Columbine, 1992.
>
> *Hard Currency.* Fawcett Columbine, 1995.
>
> *Blood and Rubles.* Fawcett Columbine, 1996.
>
> *Tarnished Icons.* Ivy, 1997.
>
> *The Dog Who Bit a Policeman.* Mysterious, 1998.
>
> *Fall of a Cosmonaut.* Mysterious, 2000.
>
> *Murder on the Trans-Siberian Express.* Mysterious, 2001.

People Who Walk in Darkness. Forge, 2008. 9780765318862.

Rostnikov is off to Siberia when a Canadian geologist named Luc O'Neil is murdered at a diamond mine. Meanwhile, other offices from his unit are in Kiev looking for some smugglers. When two murders occur back home, it becomes obvious to Rostnikov and his compatriots that this is not an isolated problem and that someone is pulling the strings behind a national conspiracy.

Diamonds • Jewels • Russia, Siberia

A Whisper to the Living. Forge, 2009. 9780765318886.

The Office of Special Investigations is searching for the Bitsevsky maniac, a serial killer responsible for over forty deaths. As Rostnikov sets out to find the killer, his team also must deal with a British investigative journalist who has the Russian mob stirred up by his investigation into prostitution in the country and a famous boxer who may also be a murderer. When the investigation begins to reach for the untouchable, Rostnikov has to decide between his own personal safety and the pursuit of justice.

Journalists • Prostitutes • Russia, Moscow • Serial killer

Keating, H. R. F. ✍

Ganesh Ghote

Taking advantage of the widening horizons of mystery fiction, Keating chose to create a series of novels featuring a Bombay Criminal Investigation Division officer. Ganesh Ghote, naïve by nature but not to be underestimated, provides a fascinating look at a fresh location for the mystery. It would be easy to compare Ghote to Charlie Chan, but these novels are less dependent on the traditional than those by Biggers. Readers may also enjoy Stuart Kaminsky, William Marshall, and Janwillem Van de Wetering. **SB TR** Series subjects: **India, Bombay**

The Perfect Murder. UK: Collins, 1964. (US: Dutton, 1965).

Inspector Ghote's Good Crusade. UK: Collins, 1966. (US: Dutton, 1966).

Inspector Ghote Caught in Meshes. UK: Collins, 1967. (US: Dutton, 1968).

Inspector Ghote Hunts the Peacock. UK: Collins, 1968. (US: Dutton, 1968).

Inspector Ghote Plays a Joker. UK: Collins, 1969. (US: Dutton, 1969).

Inspector Ghote Breaks an Egg. UK: Collins, 1970. (US: Doubleday, 1971).

Inspector Ghote Goes by Train. UK: Collins, 1971. (US: Doubleday, 1972).

Inspector Ghote Trusts the Heart. UK: Collins, 1972. (US: Doubleday, 1973).

Bats Fly Up for Inspector Ghote. UK: Collins, 1974. (US: Doubleday, 1974).

Filmi, Filmi, Inspector Ghote. UK: Collins, 1976. (US: Doubleday, 1977).

Inspector Ghote Draws a Line. UK: Collins, 1979. (US: Doubleday, 1979).

Go West, Inspector Ghote. UK: Collins, 1981. (US: Doubleday, 1981).

The Sheriff of Bombay. UK: Collins, 1984. (US: Doubleday, 1984).

Under a Monsoon Cloud. UK: Hutchinson, 1986. (US: Viking, 1986).

The Body in the Billiard Room. UK: Hutchinson, 1987. (US: Viking, 1987).

Dead on Time. UK: Hutchinson, 1988. (US: Mysterious Press, 1989).

Inspector Ghote. His Life and Crimes. UK: Hutchinson, 1989.

The Iciest Sin. UK: Hutchinson, 1990. (US: Mysterious Press, 1990).

Cheating Death. UK: Hutchinson, 1992. (US: Mysterious, 1994).

Doing Wrong. UK: Macmillan, 1994. (US: Otto Penzler, 1994).

Asking Questions. St. Martin's, 1997.

Bribery, Corruption Also. St. Martin's Press, 1999.

Breaking and Entering. UK: Macmillan, 2000. (US: St. Martin's Minotaur, 2001).

Inspector Ghote's First Case. St. Martin's Minotaur, 2009. 9780312384043. (UK: Allison & Busby, 2008).

> This prequel to all of the other books in this series finds the fresh Ghote promoted to the rank of inspector within the Bombay police. He has asked for a little leave to take care of his pregnant wife Protema, but is pulled into the mysterious circumstances around the suicide of Iris Dawkins by the former police commissioner, Sir Rustom Engineer. Finding himself in opposition to the lead investigator, Darrani, Ghote finds that homicide investigation is not easier than walking a beat.
>
> *Suicide*

Kellerman, Faye ✍

Peter Decker/Rina Lazarus

Working for the Los Angeles Police Department, Lt. Peter Decker embarks on a path of discovery that leads back to his Jewish roots. Along the way, he begins a relationship with Rina Lazarus, adding depth to the series as she explores their Jewish heritage and beliefs. Readers may also enjoy Deborah Crombie, Elizabeth George, and Anne Perry. **TR** Series subjects: **California, Los Angeles** • **Husbands and wives** • **Teams**

> *The Ritual Bath*. Arbor House, 1986.
>
> *Sacred and Profane*. Arbor House, 1987.
>
> *Milk and Honey*. Morrow, 1990.
>
> *Day of Atonement*. Morrow, 1991.
>
> *False Prophet*. Morrow, 1992.
>
> *Grievous Sin*. Morrow, 1993.
>
> *Sanctuary*. Headline, 1994.
>
> *Justice*. Morrow, 1995.
>
> *Prayers for the Dead*. Morrow, 1996.
>
> *A Serpent's Tooth*. Morrow, 1997.
>
> *Jupiter's Bones*. Morrow, 1999.
>
> *Stalker*. Morrow, 2000.
>
> *The Forgotten*. Morrow, 2001.
>
> *Stone Kiss*. Warner, 2002.

Street Dreams. Warner, 2003. 0446531316.

> Peter's daughter Cindy is an LAPD officer. One night she finds an abandoned baby in a dumpster. Her attempt to track down the mother leads to danger

and brings her father into her life as an investigator. A developmentally disabled teenager is the mother, and the possibility that she has been raped leads Cindy into areas of the heart from both the past and the present.

Handicapped • Rape

The Burnt House. Morrow, 2007. 9780061227325.

When a small commuter plane crashes after taking off from Burbank Airport, Decker investigates for hints of terrorism. What he does not expect to find is the bodies of four victims not on the plane's roster. Unaccountably, the body of stewardess Roseanna Dresden is missing. After time passes, Decker begins to believe that Roseanna may not have been on the airplane but instead may be the victim of her husband's need to raise cash quickly.

Aircraft accidents • Missing persons

The Mercedes Coffin. Morrow, 2008. 9780061227332.

Music industry producer Primo Ekerling has been found dead in the trunk of his Mercedes. The crime echoes an unsolved fifteen-year-old murder of music teacher Ben Little, which still interests Genoa Greeves, a wealthy tech industry figure, who decides to fund an investigation into both crimes. When the case is assigned to Decker, he is shocked when one of the cops on the old case commits suicide before testifying. Will he be able to use old clues to solve a contemporary murder?

Music business

Blindman's Bluff. Morrow, 2009. 9780061702327.

When shopping mall developer Guy Kaffey, his wife, and two bodyguards are all killed inside their mansion at Coyote Ranch, their son Gil is the only survivor. For Lt. Decker, the only clue the son can provide is that his attackers spoke Spanish. When a blind courtroom translator needs help identifying whom he overheard discussing the crime, Decker asks Rita for help and before he knows it, his wife is in the middle of his case and in danger.

Real estate development

Hangman. Morrow, 2010. 9780061702563.

Decker is disturbed when an old friend, Dr. Terry McLaughlin, goes missing after a meeting with her abusive husband. Left behind is fourteen-year-old Gabe, a piano prodigy, who is now a ward of Peter and Rina. When a death at a construction site seems to tie into the case, it opens a door that Decker is afraid to walk through.

Abuse • Nurses • Wards

Leon, Donna ✍

Guido Brunetti

Guido Brunetti is a detective who lives with his wife Paola, a professor of English literature, daughter Chiara, and son Raffi. Part of the pleasure of these books is the dynamic conversations around the dinner table among the family members. Brunetti approaches his case intellectually, not unlike a Golden Age detective, which often infuriates his boss, Patta. But time is Brunetti's ally, and eventually he is able to solve all the puzzles that are put before him, despite having to live in a world of bureaucratic confusion and corruption. Readers may also enjoy some of the Golden Age writers, some of the Scandinavian writers, and Alexander McCall Smith. See the author's Web site at http://www.groveatlantic.com/leon/author.htm. **TR** Series subjects: **Families • Fathers and daughters • Fathers and sons • Husbands and wives • Italy, Venice**

Death at La Fenice. HarperCollins, 1992. 0060168714.

> World-famous German conductor Helmut Wellauer has been found dead backstage at the Venetian opera house, La Fenice. Called to the scene for his first case is police commissario Guido Brunetti. Clues abound as the detective discovers the conductor was not a nice man, his wife is indifferent to his death, and the homosexuals who work in his profession often faced his scorn. While Brunetti attacks this case intellectually, his irritating supervisor calls for action.
>
> *Conductors • Homosexuality • Music*

Death in a Strange Country. HarperCollins, 1993. 0060170085.

> When an American soldier is found floating in one of the canals, the case occupies Brunetti's team's time. While Patta puts pressure on Brunetti to end the international scandal and restore the tourists' faith in Venice, Brunetti knows that other elements may be afloat in the case besides the dead body.
>
> *Corruption • Environment • Tourism*

Dressed for Death. HarperCollins, 1994. 0060177950.

> When a man's body is found in an area known to be the prostitutes' trolling ground, with shaved legs and wearing high heels, the immediate conclusion of the police is that they are working on the death of a transvestite. Brunetti's investigation reveals that the clues were clumsy, and instead the police may now be on the lookout for a killer who is preying on the vulnerable.
>
> *Transvestites*

Death and Judgment. HarperCollins, 1995. 0060177969.

> A series of seemingly unrelated deaths begin to come together once they fall under the watchful eye of Brunetti. When an accountant is murdered and it is found that his telephone calls match those of a dead attorney, he begins to tie the two together in a conspiracy that will reveal the dark side of corruption in Italy.
>
> *Drugs • Prostitutes*

Acqua Alta. HarperCollins, 1996. 0060186518.

> An American archaeologist named Brett Lynch is beaten, and Brunetti wonders if it is a homophobic reaction to her being the lover of famous opera diva Flavia Petrelli. When it is revealed that Lynch and museum director Francesco Semenzato were on the same dig in China, whose relics may now contain very clever forgeries, Brunetti knows he is on the trail of the real reason for the attack. Then someone is murdered while the city of Venice begins to flood.
>
> *Antiquities • Archaeology • Floods • Lesbians*

Quietly in Their Sleep. Penguin, 2007. 9780143112204. (UK: *The Death of Faith.* Macmillan, 1997).

> When the nursing sister who cared for Brunetti's mother appears at his door for help, she is using a new name and claiming that she had to flee the convent because of the suspicious deaths of five patients. As Brunetti begins to investigate, he finds he has nothing to examine. Has Maria Testa been lying to him, or does he need to search even deeper into the mysteries of the convent to get to the truth?
>
> *Convents • Hospitals • Medical • Nuns*

A Noble Radiance. Penguin, 2003. 0142003190. (UK: Heinemann, 1998).

> An excavation on some farmland near Venice uncovers the body of Roberto Lorenzoni, a kidnapping victim who has been missing for two years. He was snatched because he was a member of one of Venice's richest families, and the case seems like an open and shut ransom failure. But Brunetti knows the family's history, including how they got their money, and he knows there is more to this death than he originally thought.
>
> *Kidnapping*

Fatal Remedies. Penguin, 2007. 9780143112426. (UK: Heinemann, 1999).

> When Paola decides to take on the sex trade and its abuse of children, she begins by smashing the windows of a tourist agency known for sex tours. Her arrest puts Brunetti on the spot, as he is caught between the loyalty he has to his family and the love of his own children versus the pressures he is under at work to solve a crime connected to this incident that may reveal more than some want.
>
> *Prostitutes*

Friends in High Places. Penguin, 2008. 9780143114147. (UK: Heinemann, 2000).

> While trapped in a bureaucratic nightmare involving improvements in the apartment where he lives, Brunetti is shocked when Rossi, the official who approached him with information only Brunetti was to hear, is found dead at the bottom of some scaffolding.
>
> *Bureaucracy • Corruption • Graft*

A Sea of Troubles. Penguin, 2009. 9780143116202. (UK: Heinemann, 2001).

> Pellestrina is an island near Venice where fisherman ply their trade. One day a fire on a boat leaves two men missing. Forced to rely on Patta's secretary, Signorina

Elettra, because of the closed nature of the fishing community, Brunetti not only takes advantage of her knowledge, but finds himself attracted to her as well.

Affairs • Fishing

Wilful Behaviour. Penguin, 2010. 9780143117582. (UK: Heinemann, 2002).

Claudia Leonardo is Paola's student, but she approaches Brunetti one day with the story of her grandfather and a crime he may have committed. When Leonardo is found dead, Brunetti knows that someone is trying to keep the past in the past.

Art • Grandfathers and granddaughters

Uniform Justice. Atlantic Monthly, 2003. 0871139030. (UK: Heinemann, 2003).

Venice's elite San Martino Military Academy is rocked when one of the young cadets, Ernesto Moro, commits suicide. When Brunetti believes that it may be murder, his investigation is met with resistance because the academy wishes to protect its reputation, and the boy's father refuses to cooperate.

Military cadets

Doctored Evidence. Atlantic Monthly, 2004. 0871139189. (UK: Heinemann, 2004).

When everyone else is willing to assume that the Romanian housekeeper is guilty of murdering her elderly employer, Maria Grazie Battestini, it leads to her death. Only Brunetti and his sense of justice keep the investigation open.

Maids

Blood from a Stone. Atlantic Monthly, 2005. 9780871138873. (UK: Heinemann, 2005).

When an illegal immigrant street vendor is murdered, it falls to Brunetti to find the reason for this crime. Is this a reaction to the competition of the local businesses, the smuggling and selling of illegal goods, or are there larger issues at stake here? When he finds convincing evidence for a large scope to the case, Brunetti quickly finds himself pulled in several directions and has to use his personal resources to solve this one.

Immigration • Race relations

Through a Glass Darkly. Atlantic Monthly, 2006. 9780871139375. (UK: Heinemann, 2006).

Vianello, assistant to Brunetti, has a friend named Marco Ribetti, who has been arrested during an environmental protest. With Brunetti's help, Marco is released, to the public disappointment of Marco's father-in-law, Giovanni De Cal, owner of a glass factory on the island of Murano. When death strikes at the factory, Brunetti must decides which side of the issue has elevated the game to murder.

Environment • Glass making • Italy, Murano

Suffer the Little Children. Atlantic Monthly, 2007. 9780871139603. (UK: Heinemann, 2007).

Brunetti is left to explain why three policemen have invaded the home of a pediatrician and kidnapped the man's eighteen-month-old son. The doctor is left mute by the attack, but Brunetti discovers that the son was illegally adopted from Albania. Is this the reason for the attack, or are there more sinister desires at play?

Adoption • Children in jeopardy • Kidnapping

The Girl of His Dreams. Atlantic Monthly, 2008. 9780871139801. (UK: Heinemann, 2008).

Two cases occupy Brunetti's time in this book. The first involves a religious charlatan who might be using the church for profit. The second involves a Gypsy girl found floating in a canal with her clothes full of stolen goods. Each case opens different doors for Brunetti, and it is his sense of justice and his use of time that lead him to the answers he seeks.

Children in jeopardy • Gypsies • Religion

About Face. Atlantic Monthly, 2009. 9780802118967. (UK: Heinemann, 2009).

Brunetti is asked by the police to investigate the death of a truck driver who may have been doing some illegal hauling of waste. At the same time he is asked by his father-in-law, Maurizio Cataldo, to look into his business partner, while Brunetti is more fascinated by the partner's wife's botched face-lift.

Environment • Face lifts

A Question of Belief. Atlantic Monthly, 2009. 9780802119421. (UK: Heinemann, 2009).

The head of the employment records for the Commune has brought the odd case of a judge's behavior to Brunetti's office, and he is intrigued. As he opens the investigation into the judge, Brunetti finds new levels of corruption that so often makes up the Italian way of doing business. Meanwhile, Inspector Vianello wants help when his aunt seems to have fallen under the spell of a religious snake charmer.

Corruption • Judges • Religion

Mayor, Archer ✍

Joe Gunther

Joe Gunther has an interesting career as a law enforcement agent working for local authorities, until he establishes the Vermont Bureau of Investigation with his team of Sammie Martens and Willy Kunkle. A widower with a girlfriend named Gail

Zigman (later new girlfriend Lyn Silva), his troubled personal life is balanced against his dedication to the job. For readers interested in setting, the state of Vermont is displayed in all its natural glory and its unfortunate dark side. For readers who enjoy the exploration of social issues, each book takes on a different challenge to Vermont's residents. Readers may also enjoy K. C. Constantine, Steve Hamilton, and William Kent Krueger. See the author's Web site at http://www.archermayor.com. **TR** Series subjects: **Vermont, Brattleboro**

Open Season. Putnam, 1988. 0399133984.

Police lieutenant Gunther is quick to discover that the victims of assault are all connected to an old court case in which a Vietnam veteran was convicted of murder. Is the ski-mask-covered perpetrator trying to tell the police they have the wrong man in jail? Gunther races against time when he realizes that the attacker may be trying to reach the real murderer before the police do and that his own life is at risk.

Courtroom drama • Vigilantism

Borderlines. Putnam, 1988. 0399135537.

Now the temporary chief for Brattleboro, Gunther finds himself in the sleepy town of Gannett on temporary assignment with the state's attorney. A suspicious fire nearly engulfs him and kills five members of the back-to-nature cult Natural Order. The Order has been buying land in the area and has created fear among the local residents. When other victims begin to be killed, Gunther comes to the realization that the small town he remembers as a boy has changed into a cauldron of emotions.

Arson • Cults • Vermont, Gannett

Scent of Evil. Mysterious, 1992. 0892964715.

A connection between the dead stockbroker Charlie Jardin and a police officer named John Woll, whose wife had been stepping out with Jardin, makes Gunther's life miserable. When a potential witness, local drug dealer Milly Crawford, is eliminated before he can be interviewed, Gunther becomes aware that the conspiracy involved in this case may be wider than he thought.

Drugs • Police corruption

The Skeleton's Knee. Mysterious, 1992. 0892964707.

When Abraham Fuller's orthopedic surgery leads to an aneurysm, the doctors discover a twenty-year-old bullet in his body. When Gunther investigates, he discovers the old recluse lived on a plot of land with a corpse who had a replacement knee. Following the trail to Chicago and back again, Gunther discovers that the tendrils of some crimes never fall away, no matter how much time passes.

Illinois, Chicago

Fruits of the Poisonous Tree. Mysterious, 1994. 0892965576.

When Gunther's girlfriend Gail Zigman is raped, the policeman embarks on a vendetta against Bob Vogel, a local who is believed to have raped and escaped punishment before. But despite his personal involvement, eventually Gunther's hunter instincts kick in, and he realizes he may be being led down the wrong path. Is it possible a copycat rapist is at work? Meanwhile Gail, the media, and the town are making a public spectacle of his inability to find the man.

Rape

The Dark Root. Mysterious, 1994. 0892965584.

When a home invasion occurs and the victims are among the few Asian American residents of this small town, Gunther finds himself up against a wall of silence. As he pushes the investigation, he discovers that an Asian gang may be trying to decide who gets to operate on his turf. Turning to his large law enforcement agencies and his allies across the border, Gunther decides to take a stand against the gang.

Asian Americans • Canada, Quebec, Montreal • Organized crime

The Ragman's Memory. Mysterious, 1996. 089296636X.

Some members of the town elite have decided that Brattleboro needs a convention center, and construction is under way. Meanwhile, Gunther has a series of random murders to solve, including those of a troubled teenager named Shawna Davis, a nursing home patient, and a homeless man. As if that were not enough, the deaths seem connected to an activist who has gone missing, while a local selectman is pressuring Gunther to bury the case. Do The Ragman's shattered memories really hold the key to the case?

Construction • Homeless • Post-traumatic stress disorder • World War II

Bellows Falls. Mysterious, 1997. 0892966378.

Sent to the town of Vermont Falls to investigate a fellow officer named Brian Padgett, who has been charged with sexual harassment, Gunther finds himself up against small town eagerness to duck and cover on the big issues. The charge comes from Jan Bouch, the wife of local drug lord Norm Bouch, who appears to be able to conduct his business at will. The problem is that his network of young drug dealers keeps losing members, who cannot be accounted for.

Drugs • Vermont, Bellows Falls

The Disposable Man. Mysterious, 1998. 0892966858.

When a garroted body, strangled with piano wire, is found to have links to Russia, Gunther believes he may be dealing with a leftover from the Cold War. But when modern Russian mafiosos and the CIA take an interest in Vermont's doings, Gunther finds himself on the run in a desperate attempt to clear his reputation.

Central Intelligence Agency • Organized crime • Russian Mafia

Occam's Razor. Mysterious, 1998. 0892966823.

Gunther has two seemingly unrelated cases to investigate. A murdered man has been found on the local railroad tracks; he was left there so that the local train would obliterate his identity. A woman who is known to the police for various activities is found knifed. Then an anonymous phone call comes in, and Gunther begins to be led down a path that will link the two crimes and lead him to bigger tragedy. His chief suspect is a legislator who is interested in reforming the police in the state.

Police reform • Toxic waste

The Marble Mask. Mysterious, 1998. 0892967234.

When a body is found frozen on Mansfield Mountain, Gunther finds a series of puzzling things about the corpse, from its broken limbs to the ice pick wound in its heart. Perhaps most intriguing is the discovery that the corpse is over fifty years old, and it is identified as Jean Deschamps, a World War II smuggler whose son Michel is now the local crime boss. Will this disrupt the peace between the Canadian gang and the Sherbrooke Hell's Angels? This puzzle will challenge the members of Gunther's team, now organized as the Vermont Bureau of Investigation.

Canada, Quebec, Sherbrooke • Organized crime • Vermont, Stowe Mountain • World War II

Tucker Peak. Mysterious, 2001. 0892967242.

Tucker Peak, an exclusive ski resort area, has suffered from condo break-ins, and Gunther's crew is asked to investigate. They lose their chief suspect when he goes missing and his girlfriend is murdered. Going undercover with Sammie Martens, Gunther discovers that the condo owners may be in financial difficulties. Meanwhile, an environmental group called the Tucker Protection League may be guilty of more than sabotage.

Environment • Ski resorts • Undercover operations • Vermont, Stowe Mountain • Vermont, Tucker Peak

The Sniper's Wife. Mysterious, 2002. 0892967676.

When Willy Kunkle's ex-wife is found dead in New York, with a heroin overdose the most likely cause, it is only Willy's cop instincts that keep the case from ending right there. He launches a private investigation that will reveal as much about the current death as it does about who Willy really is.

Alcoholism • Drugs • New York, New York • Vietnamese War, 1961–1975

Gatekeeper. Mysterious, 2003. 0892967668.

When a Rutland drug dealer is strung up from a railroad trestle, the governor makes it Gunther's business to clean up the drug trade in Vermont. The plan is to have Sammie Martens go undercover as Greta Novak and try to set up her own drug network to replace the dead man. Meanwhile, other people in Gunther's life discover that drug use is affecting people near and dear to them.

Drugs • Massachusetts, Holyoke • Undercover operations • Vermont, Rutland

The Surrogate Thief. Mysterious, 2004. 089296815X.

Long ago, when his wife was dying of cancer, a distracted police officer named Joe Gunther slipped up on an investigation. Now, thirty-two years later, Gunther is handed a case wherein the murder weapon is the same one used in that cold case. As he begins to examine the evidence, he also examines himself when it is discovered that the opponent in Gail's run for the state senate may also tie into the past.

Cold case • Elections

St. Alban's Fire. Mysterious, 2005. 9780892968169.

A string of arson fires in barns in the St. Albans area culminates in the death of teenager Bobby Cutts. When it appears that local real estate agents may be profiting and that the clues point out of state, Gunther and Willy Kunkle find themselves walking the mean streets of Newark.

Arson • Barns • New Jersey, Newark • Vermont, St. Albans

The Second Mouse. Mysterious, 2006. 9780892960729.

When the body of Michelle Fisher is found, her death appears to be unaccountable. While Gunther needs help determining whether it is natural, suicide, or murder, he cannot get help from medical examiner Beverly Hillstrom, because her department is under attack. Believing his cop instincts, Gunther suspects murder. Meanwhile, Mel Martin is interested in growing his criminal enterprises, while his wife and friend are carrying on an affair behind his back. Eventually these two cases will come together, and Gunther will be tested once again.

Medical examiners • Vermont, Bennington

Chat. Grand Central, 2007. 9780446582582.

When his mother and brother are seriously hurt in a car accident, Gunther quickly believes that their injuries can be tied to him. He helps the local police with their investigation, which begins to look at some local Brattleboro people who hold a grudge against him, discovering along the way that his fellow officers are very willing to help. Meanwhile, the VBI is investigating a case with multiple bodies that has led them to the Internet and to chat rooms where young people are pulled in for sexual activity.

Internet • Mothers and sons • New Hampshire, Dartmouth • Teenagers at risk • World Wide Web

The Catch. St. Martin's Minotaur, 2008. 9780312381912.

When a deputy sheriff is murdered during a routine traffic stop, the VBI goes into action on behalf of a fellow officer. The evidence points to drug runners connected to Alan Budney, a member of the lobster fishing community who is believed to be a drug lord.

> *Drugs • Fishing • Lobster fishing • Maine, Rockland*

The Price of Malice. Minotaur, 2009. 9780312381929.

When Gunther's new girlfriend Lyn Silva's father and brother are thought to be missing on their boat, Gunther is distracted from his job. At work, the team is investigating the murder of Wayne Castine, who may have been a pedophile. But he has to set that investigation aside when evidence begins to show that Lyn's relatives were dealing with some smugglers and may have been taken care of, and Lyn may be in danger.

> *Fishing • Maine • Pedophilia • Smugglers*

Red Herring. Minotaur, 2010. 9780312381936.

With a single drop of the wrong blood at the crime scene the only major clue, Gunther and the VBI begin an investigation into one death, only to find that this will be the same clue at multiple murders. The odd thing is that the drop of blood at each scene is not from the same source. With Gail running for governor and the spotlight on the VBI, Gunther feels pressure to solve this big case.

> *Forensics • Serial killer*

McBain, Ed (pseud. of Evan Hunter) ✍

The 87th Precinct/Steve Carella

Ed McBain is credited with putting the procedure in the police procedural. His long-running series about the cops who work with Steve Carella in the 87th Precinct of Isola (read: Manhattan) are considered the best examples of integrating real police procedure into the mystery. One of the strengths of these novels is the ensemble cast that populates the stories. Ed McBain passed away in 2005. **SB TR HB** Series subjects: **State unknown, Isola • Teams**

> *Cop Hater*. Permabooks, 1956.
>
> *The Mugger*. Permabooks, 1956.
>
> *The Pusher*. Permabooks, 1956.
>
> *The Con Man*. Permabooks, 1957.
>
> *Killer's Choice*. Permabooks, 1958.
>
> *Killer's Payoff*. Permabooks, 1958.
>
> *Lady Killer*. Permabooks, 1958.
>
> *Killer's Wedge*. Simon & Schuster, 1959.
>
> *'Til Death*. Simon & Schuster, 1959.

Ransom. Simon & Schuster, 1959.

Give the Boys a Great Big Hand. Simon & Schuster, 1960.

The Heckler. Simon & Schuster, 1960.

See Them Die. Simon & Schuster, 1960.

Lady, Lady, I Did It! Simon & Schuster, 1961.

Like Love. Simon & Schuster, 1962.

The Empty Hours. Simon & Schuster, 1962.

Ten Plus One. Simon & Schuster, 1963.

Ax. Simon & Schuster, 1964.

He Who Hesitates. Delacorte, 1965.

Doll. Delacorte, 1965.

Eighty Million Eyes. Delacorte, 1966.

Fuzz. Doubleday, 1968.

Shotgun. Doubleday, 1969.

Jigsaw. Doubleday, 1970.

Hail, Hail, the Gang's All Here! Doubleday, 1971.

Sadie When She Died. Doubleday, 1972.

Let's Hear It for the Deaf Man. Doubleday, 1973.

Hail to the Chief. Random House, 1973.

Bread. Random House, 1974.

Blood Relatives. Random House, 1975.

So Long as You Both Shall Live. Random House, 1976.

Long Time No See. Random House, 1977.

Calypso. Viking, 1979.

Ghosts. Viking, 1980.

Heat. Viking, 1981.

Ice. Arbor House, 1983.

Lightning. Arbor House, 1984.

Eight Black Horses. Arbor House, 1985.

And All Through the House. Mystery Guild, 1986.

Poison. Arbor House, 1987.

Tricks. Arbor House, 1987.

Lullaby. Morrow, 1989.

Vespers. Morrow, 1990.

Widows. Morrow, 1991.

Kiss. Morrow, 1992.

Mischief. Morrow, 1993.

Romance. Warner, 1995.

Nocturne. Warner, 1997.

The Big Bad City. Simon & Schuster, 1999.

The Last Dance. Simon & Schuster, 2000.

Money, Money, Money. Simon & Schuster, 2001.

Fat Ollie's Book. Simon & Schuster, 2003. 0743202708.

Ollie Weeks of the 88th Precinct has been a thorn in the side of the 87th Precinct crew, but not more than when he decides to write a fictional account of the murder of the mayor of Isola. The difficulties start when the manuscript is stolen and the plot is believed to be real. The shooting of a councilman who lives in the 87th Precinct keeps the cops focused on the real as well as the surreal.

Authors

The Frumious Bandersnatch. Simon & Schuster, 2004. 0743250346.

When kidnappers dressed as terrorist leaders snatch rising hip-hop star Tamar Valparaiso from a yacht while she is performing her first video, the case falls to the 87th Precinct crew. Meanwhile, the always challenging Fat Ollie Weeks continues his romance with new love Detective Patricia Gomez, who interesting activities while on a federal task force makes Carella's life difficult.

Kidnapping • Musicians

Hark! Simon & Schuster, 2004. 0743250354.

The Deaf Man returns from the dead to taunt the 87th Precinct cops, and he begins his quest for revenge by taking out the woman who betrayed him in *Mischief*. His challenges to the cops about his new crimes are clues in the form of Shakespearean quotes and anagrams. For the third straight book in this series, Fat Ollie's book is a subplot that adds humor to the tale.

Shakespeare, William

Fiddlers. Simon & Schuster, 2005. 9780151012169.

A serial killer is shooting people in the face at close range, his first victim a blind violinist. As the killings spread across greater Isola, the 87th Precinct detectives are stretched to the limit.

Serial killer

McCrumb, Sharyn ✍

Spencer Arrowood (<u>The Ballad Novels</u>)

Set in the rural areas of the Appalachian Mountains of Tennessee, McCrumb's *Ballad Novels*, which all take their titles from folk ballads, are dark and humorless looks at the effects of crime on this rural community. Based on her own family history and the stories she heard as a child, McCrumb weaves a tapestry that includes character, setting, and plot. By the time *The Songcatcher* and *Ghost Riders* (2003) was published, McCrumb's writing had become more mainstream and less crime related. Readers may also enjoy K. C. Constantine. See the author's Web site at http://www.sharynmccrumb. com. **TR** Series subjects: **Appalachia**

> *If Ever I Return, Pretty Peggy-O.* Scribner, 1990.
>
> *The Hangman's Beautiful Daughter.* Scribner, 1992.
>
> *She Walks These Hills.* Scribner, 1994.
>
> *The Rosewood Casket.* Dutton, 1996.
>
> *The Ballad of Frankie Silver.* Dutton, 1998.

The Songcatcher. Dutton, 2001. 0525944885.
> Country star Lark McCourry is heading home to Tennessee, where her estranged father, John Walker, is dying. When the plane she is flying in crashes in the mountains, she struggles to survive. Contrasted with the story of Lark's ancestor, Malcolm McCourry, who began his life as an indentured sailor and ended up in the Appalachian Mountains, Lark and her forefather are connected by the songs they sang.
> *Music*

The Devil Amongst the Lawyers. St. Martin's, 2010. 9780312558161.
> When teacher Emma Morton is accused of murdering her father in their rural Virginia town, the media decide to make her the next big thing of 1935. It takes Tennessee reporter Carl Jennings to see the town in the harsh light of reality. While he sees one vision of the town of Wise, Carl finds everyone else is only willing to believe the myths, like those told by national reporter Henry Jemigan. He turns to his cousin Nora Bonesteel, gifted with second sight, to aid him in revealing the truth.
> *Historical (1900–1999)* • *Second sight* • *Teachers* • *Virginia, Wise*

McGarrity, Michael ✍

Kevin Kerney

The Southwest has become an increasingly popular place for mystery stories, and McGarrity's New Mexico settings certainly are one of the significant attractions of this series. When Kerney is forced to step aside as Chief of Detectives in Santa Fe, his desire to provide a sense of justice to the cases that cross his path keeps him coming back for more. Eventually he returns to the force as the Deputy Chief of the State Police. This series can be recommended to traditional and hard-boiled mystery novel readers. Readers may also enjoy Tony Hillerman. See the author's Web site at http://michaelmcgarrity.tripod.com/default.htm. **TR** **HB**

> *Tularosa.* Norton, 1996.
>
> *Mexican Hat.* Norton, 1997.
>
> *Serpent Gate.* Scribner, 1998.
>
> *Hermit's Peak.* Scribner, 1999.
>
> *The Judas Judge.* Dutton, 2000.
>
> *Under the Color of the Law.* Dutton, 2001.
>
> *The Big Gamble.* Dutton, 2002.

Everyone Dies. Dutton, 2003. 0525947612.

> Stalked by a cunning killer who has announced that "everyone dies," Kerney and his pregnant wife, Lieutenant Colonel Sara Brannon, find that the deaths of a number of people lead back to them. Then the clues begin to indicate that they are being stalked.
>
> *New Mexico, Santa Fe • Serial killer*

Slow Kill. Dutton, 2004. 052594799X.

> Vacations are never restful for police detectives, so when Kerney arrives in Paso Robles at the Double J Horse Ranch to buy horses, he should expect trouble. Listed as one of the suspects when hotel magnate Clifford Spalding dies of poisoning, Kerney finds he must clear up the case to defend his reputation. Once he is free to return to Santa Fe, he discovers the effects of the case follow him there and as far as Virginia, where his wife, Sara, is stationed.
>
> *California, Paso Robles • Horses • New Mexico, Santa Fe*

Nothing But Trouble. Dutton, 2006. 9780451412287.

> Taking some time off from homicide, Santa Fe Police Chief Kerney accepts a job working with his childhood friend Johnny Jordan as a technical adviser on a Western film. With his wife, Army Lt. Col. Sara Brannon, and his son Patrick, he heads to Bootheel. But when an undercover Border Patrol officer is murdered near the film site, Kerney finds he cannot hide from homicide, while Sara is called away to Ireland to hunt an international smuggler first met in the previous novel. Her series of adventures overseas separate her from her husband and son and strain the long-distance relationships once again.
>
> *Arizona, Bootheel • Immigration • Ireland*

Death Song. Dutton, 2008. 9780525950363.

When Deputy Sheriff Tim Riley and his wife Denise are murdered in separate locations, it forces Police Chief Kerney to stop thinking about retiring to England with his wife Sara and to start an investigation. Teamed with his Mescalero son Sergeant Clayton Istee, the two find themselves on the trail of drugs infiltrating their area. Their efforts focus on the eighteen-year-old son of the murdered officer and force the two men to try to understand their own troubled relationship.

Drugs • Fathers and sons • New Mexico, Lincoln County • New Mexico, Santa Fe

Dead or Alive. Dutton, 2009. 9780525950813.

Living in London with his wife Sara after his retirement, Kerney returns to Santa Fe when his old neighbor Riley Burke is murdered by escaped convict Craig Larson. Partnered with his son Clayton Istee, he acts as a special investigator as they hunt Larson across the American Southwest, while Larson conducts a murder spree that terrorizes the area.

New Mexico, Santa Fe

Penny, Louise

Chief Inspector Armand Gamache

Chief Inspector Armand Gamache of the Surete du Québec is a traditional police officer who follows clues to discover the perpetrator with his team in the traditional style of mystery puzzlers. However, do not be deceived by the quiet pace of these Canadian tales. The intelligence shown by both the character and the author will be appreciated by readers who like to take their time and savor a good clue-driven tale. Readers may also enjoy Donna Leon, P. D. James, and Elizabeth George. See the author's Web site at http://www.louisepenny.com. **TR** Series subjects: **Canada, Québec, Three Pines**

 Still Life. St. Martin's Minotaur, 2006. 9780312352554. (UK: Headline, 2005).

When an artist named Jane Neal is found shot through the heart by an arrow in the village of Three Pines on Thanksgiving Sunday, the case falls to Chief Inspector Armand Gamache of the Surete du Québec. While this is good hunting territory, which could mean her death is an accident, Gamache discovers that some of the villagers have both the means and the motive to kill. This is especially true after he discovers the rancor caused by a painting, recently completed before Neal's death, that she placed in a local show.

DI

Artists

A Fatal Grace. St. Martin's Minotaur, 2007. 9780312352561. (UK: *Dead Cold.* Headline, 2006).

C. C. de Poitiers is the head of a business called "Be Calm," a self-help guidance method that she herself was unable to apply. Known in the small town of Three

Pines as a ruthless socialite, her death by electrocution while watching a curling match is not mourned. Her husband and daughter are suspects. When Gamache comes to town, he must determine whether her death had anything to do with the recent death of a homeless person.

Christmas • Curling • Holidays

The Cruelest Month. St. Martin's Minotaur, 2008. 9780312352578. (UK: Headline, 2007).

With the best intentions, some residents of Three Pines decide it is time to have a séance to drive out the evil spirits from their plagued town. Then Madeleine Favreau dies of fright at the haunted Old Hadley House. Back on the spot is Chief Inspector Gamache to try to determine whether the death was a result of natural causes, or a nefarious human intervened with the spirits.

Easter • Haunted houses • Holidays • Séances

A Rule Against Murder. Minotaur, 2009. 9780312377021. (UK: *The Murder Stone*. Headline, 2008).

One of the rules of mystery fiction should be never go on vacation with a Chief Inspector; when Reine-Marie joins her husband for their annual holiday at Manoir-Bellechasse, no one should be surprised that it leads to murder. When a statue of one of Irene Finney's many husbands falls and kills a daughter at a family reunion, the Chief Inspector cannot resist an investigation.

Resorts • Vacations • Wedding anniversaries

The Brutal Telling. Minotaur, 2009. 9780312377038. (UK: Headline, 2009).

When the sanctity of a local bistro is shattered by the discovery of the dead body of a stranger in Three Pines, Chief Inspector Gamache and his team are called to the scene. In the remote woods, the team discovers that the dead man may be tied to some impressive antiques, including some rare books. Then he is led right back to Three Pines. Could the problem be the secrets held by Olivier, the owner of the bistro?

AG **AN**

Antiques • Bistro • Coffee house

Bury Your Dead. Minotaur, 2010. 9780312377045. (UK: Sphere, 2010).

Gamache is on leave from his job and recuperating in Québec City from the trauma of a previous case. Drawn back into reality from his depressed state, he finds himself investigating the death of Augustin Renaud, a man obsessed with finding the remains of Samuel de Champlain, founder of Québec. Even with this distraction, he cannot help but communicate with Three Pines and contemplate what went wrong on the last case.

AG

Canada, Québec, Québec City • Champlain, Samuel de • Depression • Historians

Perry, Anne ✍

Thomas Pitt/Charlotte Pitt

Perry's command of the Victorian period is evident in this series. Thomas Pitt struggles with the fact that he is often unable to deal with the upper classes. His contact in that world is Charlotte Ellison. As the series progresses, Pitt marries Charlotte, their love allowing her to marry outside her class. Eventually, Thomas graduates to the Special Branch, where he still deals with murder in a society gone wrong. The novels not only provide fine mysteries, but they also dissect the ills of Victorian society. They can be recommended to traditional mystery readers. Readers may also enjoy Elizabeth Peters (Amelia Peabody), Deborah Crombie, Elizabeth George, and Martha Grimes. See the author's Web site at http://www.anneperry.net. **TR** **Historical.** Series subjects: **England, London • Historical (1800–1899) • Teams • Victorian England**

> *The Cater Street Hangman.* UK: Hale, 1979. (US: St. Martin's, 1979).
>
> *Callander Square.* UK: Hale, 1980. (US: St. Martin's, 1980).
>
> *Paragon Walk.* St. Martin's, 1981.
>
> *Resurrection Row.* St. Martin's, 1981.
>
> *Rutland Place.* St. Martin's, 1983.
>
> *Bluegate Fields.* St. Martin's, 1984.
>
> *Death in the Devil's Acre.* St. Martin's, 1985.
>
> *Cardington Crescent.* St. Martin's, 1987.
>
> *Silence in Hanover Close.* St. Martin's, 1988.
>
> *Bethlehem Road.* St. Martin's, 1990.
>
> *Highgate Rise.* Fawcett Columbine, 1991.
>
> *Belgrave Square.* Fawcett Columbine, 1992.
>
> *Farrier's Lane.* Fawcett Columbine, 1993.
>
> *The Hyde Park Headsman.* Fawcett Columbine, 1994.
>
> *Traitor's Gate.* Fawcett Columbine, 1995.
>
> *Pentecost Alley.* Fawcett Columbine, 1996.
>
> *Ashworth Hall.* Fawcett, 1997.
>
> *Brunswick Gardens.* Fawcett, 1998.
>
> *Bedford Square.* Ballantine, 1999.
>
> *Half Moon Street.* Ballantine, 2000.
>
> *The Whitechapel Conspiracy.* Ballantine, 2001.
>
> *Southampton Row.* Ballantine, 2002.

Seven Dials. Ballantine, 2003. 0345440072.

Lovat, a junior diplomat, has been found murdered in the garden of an Egyptian woman named Ayesha Zakhari. She has ties to a senior Cabinet minister, Saville Ryerson, who is negotiating a deal between Egyptian cotton growers and England's textile industry. Pitt must travel to Egypt for Her Majesty's Special Branch to investigate, while Charlotte stays home to search for the reason a valet known to her maid has gone missing. Before this book is over, the two cases will blend into one.

Egypt, Alexandria

Long Spoon Lane. Ballantine, 2005. 0345469275.

Special Branch Investigator Pitt is assigned the case of an anarchist bomber who is upset with police corruption in working-class neighborhoods. When his investigation leads him to Long Spoon Lane and the body of Magnus Landsborough, the son of a lord, the two Pitts must try to decide who shot the young man and how involved he was in the terrorism. Thomas also must deal with police corruption leading back to an old nemesis on Bow Street.

Anarchists • Police corruption • Terrorism

Buckingham Palace Gardens. Ballantine, 2008. 9780345469311.

A prostitute has been murdered at Buckingham Palace, and Thomas Pitt is called in to solve the crime. It is believed that the dead woman was brought to the palace to entertain one of the four financial wizards brought there by the Prince of Wales when he decided to build a railroad across the African continent. When it appears that Thomas's career may hang in the balance, he recruits his own maid to spy among the palace elite.

Prostitutes • Railroads

Rendell, Ruth ✍

Reginald Wexford

A master of psychological suspense, Rendell applies her talents to a series about Reginald Wexford, the police inspector for the town of Kingmarkham. Partnered with Mike Burden, Wexford's cases often follow the patterns of the Golden Age but are enhanced with modern sensibilities and themes that enrich her books in comparison to those that came before her. These novels can be recommended to readers of the traditional mystery. Readers may also enjoy Colin Dexter, Reginald Hill, and P. D. James (Adam Dalgliesh). **TR** Series subjects: **England, Sussex, Kingmarkham**

From Doon with Death. UK: Long 1964. (US: Doubleday, 1965).

A New Lease of Death. UK: Long, 1967. (US: Doubleday, 1967; also published as *Sins of the Fathers.* Ballantine, 1970).

Wolf to the Slaughter. UK: Long, 1967. (US: Doubleday, 1968).

The Best Man to Die. UK: Long, 1969. (US: Doubleday, 1970).

A Guilty Thing Surprised. UK: Hutchinson, 1970. (US: Doubleday, 1970).

No More Dying Then. UK: Hutchinson, 1971. (US: Doubleday, 1972).

Murder Being Once Done. UK: Hutchinson, 1972. (US: Doubleday, 1972).

Some Lie and Some Die. UK: Hutchinson, 1973. (US: Doubleday, 1973).

Shake Hands for Ever. UK: Hutchinson, 1975. (US: Doubleday, 1975).

A Sleeping Life. UK: Hutchinson, 1978. (US: Doubleday, 1978).

Put on by Cunning. UK: Hutchinson, 1981. (US: *Death Notes.* Pantheon, 1981).

The Speaker of Mandarin. UK: Hutchinson, 1983. (US: Pantheon, 1983).

An Unkindness of Ravens. UK: Hutchinson, 1985. (US: Pantheon, 1985).

The Veiled One. UK: Hutchinson, 1988. (US: Pantheon, 1988).

The Gunner's Daughter. UK: Hutchinson, 1992. (US: Mysterious Press, 1992).

Simisola. UK: Hutchinson, 1994. (US: Crown, 1995).

Road Rage. UK: Hutchinson, 1997. (US: Crown, 1997).

Harm Done. UK: Hutchinson, 1999. (US: Crown, 1999).

The Babes in the Woods. Crown, 2003. 140004930X. (UK: Hutchinson, 2002).

The two children of Katrina and Roger Dale, and their babysitter Joanna Troy, are missing. The case is assigned to Wexford and Mike Burden while Kingsmarkham is suffering a flood. When Troy is found dead in the woods, the kidnapping case becomes a murder. Suspicion falls on a religious cult, while clues also point to a neighbor, a family friend, and the babysitter herself.

Children in jeopardy

End in Tears. Crown, 2005. 9780307339768. (UK: Hutchinson, 2005).

A stone is dropped from a bridge and kills a person. Teenage mother Amber Marshalson's head has been stoved in by a brick, and her pregnant girlfriend Megan Bartlow was murdered in an old housing project. The cases are handed to Wexford and his young aide, Burden. While the pair search for someone with a motive to kill women, Wexford must deal with his own daughter Sylvia's pregnancy.

Surrogate mothers • Teenage pregnancy

Not in the Flesh. Crown, 2007. 9780307406811. (UK: Hutchinson, 2007).

When a man hunting mushrooms on vacant land discovers a buried hand, an eleven-year-old case is handed to Chief Inspector Wexford. Unfortunately, the DNA available does not tell the police which of the eighty-four people who went missing over that period has now been uncovered. Then a second body is uncovered in an abandoned house near the first corpse, and Wexford is on the trail of a double murderer.

The Monster in the Box*. Scribner, 2009. 9781439150337. (UK: Hutchinson, 2009).

> Police officers never forget, and Wexford has always had his doubts about the innocence of one Kingsmarkham resident, Eric Tango. Tango was a suspect in the very first case Wexford ever worked, but he could never gather enough evidence for a conviction. Additional unsolved crimes only added to Wexford's discomfort, especially because Tango knew of Wexford's suspicions and taunted the officer to press charges. Now, Tango has returned.
>
> *Serial killer*

Robinson, Peter ✎

Alan Banks

Canadian author Robinson has written a series of novels set in Yorkshire, England, where he grew up. Banks, a displaced big city cop, incorporates some big-city sensibilities when he works the more genteel countryside murders of this area. He is often teamed with Constable Susan Gay. The vistas and themes of Robinson's books have earned him award nominations. Readers may also enjoy Colin Dexter and Reginald Hill. See the author's Web site at http://www.inspectorbanks.com/index.html. **TR** **HB** Series subjects: **England, Yorkshire, Eastvale**

> *Gallows View.* Canada: Viking, 1987. (US: Scribner, 1990).
>
> *A Dedicated Man.* UK: Viking, 1989. (US: Scribner, 1991).
>
> *The Hanging Valley.* Canada: Penguin, 1989. (US: Scribner, 1992).
>
> *A Necessary End.* U, K,: Viking, 1989. (US: Scribner, 1992).
>
> *Past Reason Hated.* UK: Viking, 1991. (US: Scribner, 1993).
>
> *Wednesday's Child.* UK: Viking, 1992. (US: Scribner, 1994).
>
> *Final Account.* Viking, 1994. (US: Berkley, 1995).
>
> *Innocent Graves.* Berkley Prime Crime, 1996.
>
> *Blood at the Root.* Avon, 1997.
>
> *Not Safe After Dark & Other Stories.* Crippen & Landru, 1998.
>
> *In a Dry Season.* Avon, 1999.
>
> *Cold Is the Grave.* Morrow, 2000.
>
> *Aftermath.* Morrow, 2001.

Close to Home. Morrow, 2003. 0060198788.

When the remains of his childhood friend Graham Marshall are unearthed, Banks is haunted by the memory of Graham's disappearance in 1965, and he returns to England from a vacation to help in the investigation. Without Banks present in Yorkshire, Anne Cabbot has to work alone on the disappearance of the teenage son of a famous rock star, a man who traumatized his family by committing suicide when his son Luke Armitage was only a young boy.

Children in jeopardy • England, Cambridgeshire, Petersborough

Playing with Fire. Morrow, 2004. 006019877X.

When the homeless artist Thomas McMahon and a drug addicted Tina Aspern are immolated when the barges they squat on are burned, Detective Chief Inspector Banks and Detective Inspector Annie Cabbot get the case. With a former boyfriend or a peeping tom as suspects, the cops focus on other issues that may broaden the case, including the value of an old painting held by another victim of fire.

Arson • Art

Strange Affair. Morrow, 2005. 0060544333.

Healing from the disastrous consequences of his previous case, Banks is contacted by his younger brother Roy, who needs his help. Roy is a successful businessman who has been estranged from his brother. When Banks finds Roy's quarters deserted in London, he does not have to wait too long to discover his brother may be a kidnapping victim. Detective Inspector Cabbot meanwhile is investigating Banks's connections to a shooting victim who had Banks's address on a note in her pocket.

England, London • Kidnapping

Piece of My Heart. Morrow, 2006. 9780060544355.

A freelance writer named Nicholas Barber, working on a piece about the classic rock band the Mad Hatters, is found murdered, and the case is given to Detective Chief Inspector Alan Banks and Annie Cabbot. The Mad Hatters fell under suspicion in 1969 for the murder of a woman found dead after a Woodstock-like concert, and that case was investigated by Detective Inspector Stanley Chadwick. After a series of mishaps, the band is now willing to get back on the road, and the only thing standing in their way is suspicion of murder. Told in chapters that alternate between the present and 1969, the two detectives work on their separate cases with a common goal.

Rock music

Friend of the Devil. Morrow, 2007. 9780060544379.

Detective Inspector Annie Cabbot is working in a nearby precinct on a case involving a dead paraplegic named Karen Drew, who was found outside her home on a cliff, her throat slashed. Newly minted Detective Chief Inspector Robinson is working a case in Eastvale, the rape and murder of a nineteen-year-old named Harley Daniels, who was found in a rough area called the Maze. Cabbot's victim may be connected to killings committed prior to her accident. When these two cases merge, they lead to a serial killing duo responsible for deaths in a previous case.

Serial killer

All the Colors of Darkness. Morrow, 2009. 9780061362934.

Mark Hardcastle's body is found hanging from a tree in Eastvale, and the investigation of his suicide falls to Detective Inspector Annie Cabbot. The case takes a twist when Hardcastle's boyfriend, Laurence Silbert, is found dead in his home from a vicious attack. When Banks returns from a holiday to take an interest in the case, he discovers that MI6 may be involved in the deaths.

MI6 • Spies

Bad Boy. Morrow, 2010. 9780061362958.

With Banks on vacation, it falls to Annie Cabbot to deal with a mother who wants to report that her daughter, Erin Doyle, has a loaded gun in her possession. When the police invade Erin's bedroom to retrieve the weapon, it turns out that it belongs to Jaff McCready, who happens to be Tracy Banks's new bad boy friend. When the two disappear, it means Banks must return to Eastvale to search for his daughter, whose situation has turned from adventure to being a hostage.

Fathers and daughters • Gun control • Hostages

Sandford, John (pseud. of John Camp) ✍

Lucas Davenport

At times it is difficult to distinguish between the thriller and the detective novel. Davenport's constant battles against serial killers could be categorized as thrillers, because we know who is committing the murders, but he is a hard-working Minneapolis cop either way. As the series progresses, Davenport takes a job as Minnesota's number one criminal troubleshooter at the State Bureau of Criminal Apprehension. These novels can be recommended to readers who like hard-boiled detectives. Readers may also enjoy Lawrence Block (Matthew Scudder) and J. A. Jance (Joanna Brady). See the author's Web site at http://www.johnsandford.org. **HB** Series subjects: **Minnesota, Minneapolis • Serial killer.**

Rules of Prey. Putnam, 1989.

Shadow Prey. Putnam, 1990.

Eyes of Prey. Putnam, 1991.

Silent Prey. Putnam, 1992.

Winter Prey. Putnam, 1993.

Night Prey. Putnam, 1994.

Mind Prey. Putnam, 1995.

Sudden Prey. Putnam, 1996.

Secret Prey. Putnam, ,1998.

Certain Prey. Putnam, 1999.

Easy Prey. Putnam, 2000.

Chosen Prey. Putnam, 2001.

Mortal Prey. Putnam, 2002.

Naked Prey. Putnam, 2003. 0399150439.

Lucas Davenport has moved to the state for a new job as a troubleshooter in the Bureau of Criminal Apprehension, bringing along his family. His new partner is Del Capslock. When a black man and a white woman are found hung together in the woods in northern Minnesota, his first case appears to be a racial powder keg. Led through the case by a twelve-year-old named Letty West, the two discover that there is more in the woods than just racial hatred.

Lynching • Minnesota, Armstrong • Minnesota, Broderick • Race relations

Hidden Prey. Putnam, 2004. 039915180X.

When a Russian sailor named Vladimir Orslov is found murdered in Duluth, the case falls into the lap of Davenport. Though initially it seems a routine professional hit, the explanation escapes Davenport, and he is joined on the investigation by a female Russian cop, Nadya Kalin. Does this mean there is more to this death than he realized? The answer is yes, when the bullet that did the deed appears to be fifty years old.

Minnesota, Duluth • Russian policemen • Sailors

Broken Prey. Putnam, 2005. 0399152725.

Davenport, a Minnesota State Bureau of Criminal Apprehension investigator, sets aside his political work for the governor and takes on a serial killer again. This series of killings has sexual overtones, and the focus is on Charlie Pope, a recently released sex offender. But when it becomes obvious that Pope may not have what it takes to pull off these sophisticated copycat murders, Davenport and his partner begin to look elsewhere.

Minnesota, Mankato

Invisible Prey. Putnam, 2007. 9780399154218.

When Minnesota State Senator Burt Kline is accused of having sex with a minor, the governor expects Davenport to handle this sensitive case. At the same time, he is investigating the murder of Constance Bucher and her maid, who were killed among a vast collection of antiques, which might have been the motive.

When more murders occur, it surprises Davenport that these two separate events may have a common thread.

Antiques • Sex with a minor

1

Phantom Prey. Putnam, 2008. 9780399155000.

The first person to disappear, Frances Austin, is a member of the Twin Cities' Goth community, and when her case lands in Davenport's lap, he does not expect there will be more. But when other young Goths go missing, he begins to believe that he is dealing with a serial killer.

Goths

Wicked Prey. Putnam, 2009. 9780399155673.

2

With the Republican Convention in town, Davenport has plenty of distractions at work to keep him busy. Rumors of an assassination plot against the main candidate and a caper set on taking down the bag men for the Republicans make for interesting days. But crime comes home when a small-time operator named Randy Whitcomb, who is paralyzed, decides to work out his issues by taking on Davenport. The method will be to shoot Letty, but not if she can stop Whitcomb first.

Assassinations • Republican National Convention

3

Storm Prey. Putnam, 2010. 9780399156496.

Early one morning, Davenport's surgeon wife Weather Karkinnen sees three men leaving the hospital garage where she works. She is surprised to then discover the pharmacy has been robbed. The robbers killed one of the pharmacy workers and now begin to stalk Weather with the intent of eliminating the only witness to their crime.

Eyewitnesses • Hospitals • Pharmacies

Virgil Flowers

Virgil Flowers was brought into the Minnesota State Bureau of Criminal Apprehension as an investigator by Lucas Davenport. As the one that gets all the tough cases, Flowers proves himself worthy of having his own series. Readers may also enjoy Michael Connelly's Harry Bosch series. See the author's Web site at http://www.johnsandford.org. **HB**

Dark of the Moon. Putnam, 2007. 9780399154775.

Flowers is in the sleepy town of Bluestem because a doctor and his wife were murdered, he with his eyes shot out of his head. While Flowers is there, a third murder takes place when Bill Judd, hated by many residents in Bluestem for a pyramid scheme he ran years ago, has his house burned to the ground with him in it. The question for Flowers is whether the two cases are related.

Arson • Medical • Minnesota, Bluestem

Heat Lightning. Putnam, 2008. 9780399155277.

> Flowers gets the call when a second body is found murdered with the same signature: a lemon left in the mouth of the victim, posted at a veterans' memorial. As Flowers begins to try to connect the dots, he discovers that each of the victims served in Vietnam, where the signature was used by Vietnamese firing squads. Fearful that someone from the past is trying to right a wrong, Flowers begins to look to the Vietnamese community for a clue.
>
> *Minnesota, Stillwater • Vietnamese War, 1961–1975*

Rough Country. Putnam, 2009. 9780399155987.

> When Erica McDill, an advertising executive and a Democratic Party supporter of the governor, is murdered at the Eagle Nest Lodge, Flowers gets the call because he is fishing in the area. Surprised to discover that the resort caters to a lesbian clientele, he also discovers that men are also available for casual sex. Then a murder from the past proves of interest, and the clues begin to point to a number of possible perpetrators.
>
> *Homosexuality • Lesbians • Minnesota, Grand Rapids • Resorts*

Bad Blood. Putnam, 2010. 9780399156908.

> Initially Bob Tripp tries to cover up his murder of soybean farmer Jacob Flood, whom he has hit over the head with a bat and dumped in a grain bin. But when Flowers breaks down Tripp's story, the young man admits his guilt by hanging himself in his cell. When the local sheriff indicates to Flowers that he has suspicions about what happened, Flowers keeps at the case and discovers it might connect to an earlier murder and a local church with controlling interests in its congregation.
>
> *Farmers • Religion • Suicide*

Wambaugh, Joseph ✍

"Hollywood" Nate Weiss

Joseph Wambaugh is considered one of the major innovators in police procedurals. As a former police officer, he understands how officers react when crimes are committed. He also understands how police communicate. After writing many seminal works of crime fiction, he took a hiatus but returned to print with the three novels in a series set in the famed Hollywood district of Los Angeles. His books will appeal to readers of crime fiction and the police procedural writers Ed McBain, Michael Connelly, Stephen Cannell, and James Ellroy. See the author's Web site at http://www.josephwambaugh.net. **HB** Series subjects: **California, Hollywood • California, Los Angeles**

Hollywood Station. Little, Brown, 2006. 9780316066143.

> This novel attempts to show what a stressed, underfunded, and understaffed police district looks like in contemporary California. While the peculiarities

of officers such as Flotsam and Jetsam or the appropriately nicknamed "Hollywood" Nate Weiss could be enough, they find themselves on the streets up against the cranked-up antics of a citizenry high on crack. More of a character study and a slice of life at the Hollywood Station, this novel is Wambaugh's version of a police reality show.

Drugs • Hollywood • Russian Mafia

Hollywood Crows. Little, Brown, 2008. 9780316025287.

When Hollywood and his partner Bix Rumstead are made crows, or cops on the Community Relations Office staff, they think their ship has come in when they are assigned to the attractive Margo Aziz. Because she is caught in an ugly divorce proceeding with her nightclub owning husband Ali, Margo decides she needs a fall guy. Or fall guys, as she ensnares the two cops in her plot to murder her husband and walk away from the crime.

Matricide

Hollywood Moon. Little, Brown, 2009. 9780316045186.

Hollywood and his partner Dana Vaughn get involved in the case of a young man named Malcolm Rojas, who has been attacking women. At the same time, Flotsam and Jetsam are dealing with two other lowlifes who are carrying on and attracting their attention on a constant basis. Eventually even these stressed and challenged cops figure out that the three are tied into a bigger high-tech scam.

Computers

Wilson, Robert ✍

Jefe Javier Falcón

Jefe Javier Falcón is a Spanish detective inspector with the Grupo de Homicidios de Sevilla whose personal life is a mess. In a state of chronic depression, he finds work a salvation. Readers who enjoy this series may also like Henning Mankell and Jo Nesbø. The author's Web site can be found at http://www.robert-wilson.eu. **TR** Series subjects: **Spain, Seville**

The Blind Man of Seville. Harcourt, 2003. 0151008353. (UK: HarperCollins, 2003).

During Easter Week in Seville, Detective Inspector Falcón is handed the case of a restaurateur whose corpse has been decorated with the dead man's eyelids. Initially it appears to be a case of infidelity gone mad. When a clue at the scene of the crime leads Falcón to the diaries of his father, a famous artist, what he reads shatters his own world. As more victims fall to the serial killer and Falcón continues to read, he begins to understand how he will be pulled into this case on a personal level.

Artists • Fathers and sons • Serial killer

The Vanished Hands. Harcourt, 2004. 9780156032827. (UK: *The Silent and the Damned*. Houghton Mifflin Harcourt, 2003).

> Falcón is assigned the double suicide of construction businessman Rafael Vega and his wife Lucia. Initially, it looks like Rafael smothered Lucia and then killed himself. The cryptic note left at the scene, plus two more suicides, including a police officer in the sex crimes unit, have Falcón trying to link all the deaths into one case.
>
> *Organized crime* • *Prostitutes* • *Russian Mafia* • *Suicide*

The Hidden Assassins. Harcourt, 2006. 9780151012398. (UK: HarperCollins, 2006).

> When a massive bomb explodes and it is discovered that a mosque was located in the basement of the building that was flattened, all of Seville is on terrorist alert. Falcón finds he must deal with a larger issue than an individual's death as he struggles with whether Muslims mishandled their explosives or were the victims of the attack.
>
> *Terrorism*

The Ignorance of Blood. UK: HarperCollins, 2009. (US: Houghton Mifflin Harcourt, 2009. 9780151012459).

> When Seville is hit by a terrorist attack, Inspector Falcón is set on the path of the perpetrators when an automobile accident dumps evidence in his lap. It appears that some Russian mobsters were blackmailing a local politician, with a turf war over prostitution and drugs the ultimate result. When a close friend reveals a dark secret involving Islamic extremists, the circle begins to close on the investigation.
>
> *Organized crime* • *Russian Mafia* • *Terrorism*

Lone Wolf Police

The police who are categorized as lone wolves are actually holdovers from the great detective style. Through circumstances often out of their control, they are forced to live within the institution but act outside it. The appeal of their solo act can be their heroism, as they step outside the safety net that an institution can provide. Lone wolf police are very similar to the detectives found in the private detectives section, where it is standard that the detective is a lone wolf, and the exceptions are detectives who work inside an institution. Readers who are attracted to the private detectives should find these lone wolves appealing as well.

The Modern Practitioners

Billingham, Mark ✍

Tom Thorne

Detective Inspector Tom Thorne is a flawed man. Working in the greater London area for the Metropolitan Police Service, he is a middle-aged man with an attitude. Not always satisfied to let police procedure reach its inevitable goal, he will often push the envelope to make investigations personal. Billingham often employs the point of view of the killer to enhance the tension in his books, but also to create a more believable antagonist. Readers who enjoy this series will also enjoy Ian Rankin, Michael Connelly, or Henning Mankell. See the author's Web site at http://www.markbillingham.com. **HB** Series subjects: **England, London**

Sleepyhead. Morrow, 2002. 0066212995. (UK: Little, Brown, 2001).

Three victims have left the police believing they are dealing with a serial killer. When the fourth victim, Alison Willetts, is left in a locked-in syndrome coma, the work of Detective Inspector Tom Thorne begins to point to a more insidious idea. Thorne's downfall is that he begins to believe a vigilante's attitude will get him to the solution. Or maybe it is that he begins to fall for the victim's doctor, Anne Coburn, who he just happens to believe is the perpetrator's girlfriend.

Coma • Doctors • Locked-in syndrome • Medical • Serial killer

Scaredy Cat. Morrow, 2002. 0066213002. (UK: Little, Brown, 2002).

A serial killer is stalking the tube, viciously strangling his female victims in a repetitive pattern that is the cop's only clue. Thorne, while dealing with his own personal demons, begins a methodical police investigation that leads nowhere. Then the breakthrough comes, and Thorne fears that he may have a unique serial killer situation to deal with. Now he knows he is going to have to push some buttons in order to get justice done, especially when he discovers the killer may be manipulating the police.

Serial killer

Lazybones. Morrow, 2003. 0060560851. (UK: Little, Brown, 2003).

Douglas Remfry, a rapist, has just been released from prison when his bound body is found in a North London hotel room. At first it is assumed to be a revenge case, but the police shift their focus when a second released prisoner is found murdered in the same fashion. Thorne needs to discover who is tricking these ex-cons into coming to an arranged killing field.

Rape • Serial killer • Vigilantism

The Burning Girl. Morrow, 2004. 9780060745264. (UK: Little, Brown, 2004).

> When a war breaks out between two North London gangs, the backstory leads Thorne to a gang leader named Billy Ryan and the strange circumstances that led to his marriage. Thorne may be looking for someone seeking revenge or a copycat, whose victims are marked with an X on their bodies. Either way, the perpetrator has made it personal, and Thorne is going to need to sort this one out to save himself.
>
> *Copycat killers • Organized crime*

Lifeless. Morrow, 2005. 9780060841669. (UK: Little, Brown, 2005).

> On leave for general misconduct and depressed about the death of his father, Thorne is at the bottom. When London is plagued with a serial killer preying on the homeless and leaving £20 notes pinned to the victims, Thorne is brought back and sent underground. Living on the streets, Thorne is able to discover that the cause of the crime lies in the past and at the doorstep of the agency he works for.
>
> *Homeless*

Buried. HarperCollins, 2007. 9780061255694. (UK: Little, Brown, 2006).

> The force is going full force after the kidnappers of Luke Mullen, the son of a retired fellow officer. When the kidnappers end up dead and it looks like their murderer is the missing teen, the case is handed to Thorne, on special assignment to the kidnap squad. Not taking the easy path, Thorne decides to investigate the past life of former DCS Muller to see who might want to exact revenge.
>
> *Fathers and sons • Kidnapping • Revenge*

Death Message. HarperCollins, 2009. 9780061432750. (UK: Little, Brown, 2007).

> First the image of one dead man appears on Thorne's cell phone. Then a second. As the images continue to arrive, Thorne makes a connection to a man named Marcus Brooks. Brooks served time for the murder of a Black Dog biker and then lost his own family just after his release. Now the questions are, who really did the first murder, and how involved were his fellow officers?
>
> *Bikers • Cell phones • Revenge*

Burke, James Lee ✍

Dave Robicheaux

Former homicide cop Robicheaux has retired to a bait shop in New Iberia, Louisiana, where he tries to repair a life ripped apart by violence and alcoholism. In the tradition of Travis McGee, Robicheaux is motivated the most when people close to him are in danger. Eventually he joins the New Iberia sheriff's staff and returns to the saddle as a professional. Among Burke's many talents is his use of words, which makes his novels read like fine literature. The books will also appeal to readers looking for a unique setting. Readers may also enjoy Kent Anderson, Lawrence Block (Matthew

Scudder), Michael Connelly, and James Crumley. See the author's Web site at http://www.jamesleeburke.com. **HB** Series subjects: **Louisiana, New Iberia**

The Neon Rain. Holt, 1987.

Heaven's Prisoners. Holt, 1988.

Black Cherry Blues. Little, Brown, 1989.

A Morning for Flamingos. Little, Brown, 1990.

A Stained White Radiance. Hyperion, 1992.

In the Electric Mist with Confederate Dead. Hyperion, 1993.

Dixie City Jam. Hyperion, 1994.

Burning Angel. Hyperion, 1995.

Cadillac Jukebox. Hyperion, 1996.

Sunset Limited. Doubleday, 1998.

Purple Cane Road. Bantam, 2000.

Jolie Blon's Bounce. Simon & Schuster, 2002.

Last Car to Elysian Fields. Simon & Schuster, 2003. 0743245423.

In the 1950s, singer Junior Crudup was sent to Angola Penitentiary and became a lost legend of blues music. In the present, Father Jimmie Dolan is being hunted by a hit man named Max Coll, Clete Purcel goes to jail, and three underaged teenagers are killed while driving drunk. The three separate stories come together during New Iberia sheriff Robicheaux's attempts to connect the sins of the past with the dangers of the present.

Blues • Hit men • Louisiana, New Orleans • Music

Crusader's Cross. Simon & Schuster, 2005. 9780743277198.

A prostitute named Ira Durbin, who was a paramour of Robicheaux's half-brother Jimmie in 1958, disappeared before any long-term arrangements could be made. In the present, Robicheaux hears a deathbed confession that leads him to probe into her disappearance and her connections to the mob. While his attempts to reveal what has happened in the past anger the mob, Robicheaux must also deal with a string of current murders that leads him to Valentine Chalons and his scary sister, Honoria.

Organized crime • Prostitutes • Serial killer

Pegasus Descending. Simon & Schuster, 2006. 9780743277723.

Robicheaux still carries the emotional scars of having been too hammered to save the life of Dallas Klein when the two were cops twenty-five years ago and Klein was killed during a robbery. So when Dallas's daughter, Trish, crosses paths with Whitey Bruxal in New Iberia, Robicheaux considers revenge. The suicide of a college student named Yvonne Darbonne provides a distraction at first, until that case seems to be connected to the first.

Revenge

The Tin Roof Blowdown. Simon & Schuster, 2007. 9781416548485.

> In the aftermath of Hurricane Katrina and deployment to the troubled New Orleans, Robicheaux is investigating the shooting of two looters outside Otis Baylor's home. He is also trying to find a priest who is missing from the Ninth Ward. While he leaves his own New Iberia behind, he must confront the new New Orleans: a city in utter chaos where a vigilante may be the most effective enforcer in town.
>
> *Hurricane Katrina*

Swan Peak. Simon & Schuster, 2008. 9781416548522.

> When Robicheaux and Clete Purcel take a fishing vacation to Montana, they encounter the same violence they are used to in their own home state. After fishing in the wrong spot and losing his equipment to mean-spirited security men for a Texas oil man protecting their boss's land, Clete realizes that there are connections in this incident to the past. Then two young people are murdered, while a prison guard shows up from Texas looking for an escaped con. As all the plotlines begin to merge, the level of violence continues to rise as these two ex-partners try to restore order.
>
> *Escaped prisoners • Fishing • Montana • Organized Crime*

The Glass Rainbow. Simon & Schuster, 2010. 9781439128299.

> Several women have been murdered in Jefferson Davis Parish, and Robicheaux and Purcel believe they can catch the serial killer. Clues point to best-selling author Robert Weingart, a man with a criminal past. Robicheaux must also deal with the developing relationship between his adopted daughter Alafiar and novelist Kermit Abelard, whose family has plagued New Iberia for years. When Clete's reputation is tarnished by his violent actions, it puts their friendship to the test once again, and it is up to Robicheaux to decide if the Abelards are as evil as he believes they are.
>
> *Authors • Fathers and daughters • Serial killer*

Cain, Chelsea ✍

Archie Sheridan

In the Portland, Oregon, that is more remembered for the Green River Killer than for any of its good graces, Cain has set two individuals in conflict: one is a police officer damaged by the capture of a serial killer, and the other is the beautiful serial killer who still seduces him long after her capture and eventual escape. This bizarre relationship is key to the impact of these books. Readers who enjoy these books may also enjoy Thomas Harris and Jeffry P. Lindsay. See the author's Web site at http://www.chelseacain.com. **HB** Series subjects: **Journalists • Oregon, Portland • Serial killer**

Heartsick. St. Martin's Minotaur, 2007. 9780312368463.

> When a serial killer begins to kill teenagers in Portland, the case is assigned to Archie Sheridan. Sheridan was tortured by serial killer Gretchen Lowell years ago, but that does not keep him from visiting her in prison to use her as an ally. Add in the punked-up journalist Susan Ward, and Sheridan has enough help to find the killer, as long as he can trust Lowell.

Sweetheart. St. Martin's Minotaur, 2008. 9780312368470.

> Sheridan is trying to get off the pain pills he is addicted to and to stop obsessively visiting Lowell in prison, when dead people begin to show up in Portland park at the spot where Lowell left her first victim many years ago. Reporter Ward's investigation of a U.S. senator's relationship with a babysitter may connect to Sheridan's new case. Then Lowell escapes from prison, and all hell breaks loose as she tries to integrate herself into her old nemesis for the last time.

Evil at Heart. Minotaur, 2009. 9780312368487.

> With Archie in the hospital after his last attempt to catch serial killer Gretchen Lowell, the merry murderess has been growing into a cult fan favorite while trying to keep a low profile. But when Portland begins to discover new bodies with her trademark signature at the scene, the Portland police return to Archie for help. Journalist Susan Ward also maintains her vigilance on this case as she tries to discover clues from the friends of Gretchen Lowell.

Connelly, Michael ✍

Harry Bosch

In a contemporary Los Angeles that echoes Raymond Chandler, Harry Bosch struggles against a system that places him outside its safety net. Bosch, a Vietnam veteran, is haunted by his sad childhood. He is also a dedicated cop, but his contrary nature means he can be his own worst enemy when dealing with the system. Complex plots and a noirish atmosphere highlight these rogue cop tales in which the past has as great an effect on the characters as the present. Readers may also enjoy Kent Anderson, Lawrence Block (Matthew Scudder), Robert Crais, and Ian Rankin. See the author's Web site at http://www.michaelconnelly.com. **HB** Series subjects: **California, Los Angeles**

> *The Black Echo.* Little, Brown, 1992.
>
> *The Black Ice.* Little, Brown, 1993.
>
> *The Concrete Blonde.* Little, Brown, 1994.
>
> *The Last Coyote.* Little, Brown, 1995.
>
> *Trunk Music.* Little, Brown, 1997.

Angels Flight. Little, Brown, 1999.

A Darkness More Than Night. Little, Brown, 2001.

City of Bones. Little, Brown, 2002.

Lost Light. Little, Brown, 2003. 0316154601.

Having hung up his badge, Harry is finding little stimulation in retirement and gets a private investigator's license to help solve one of his own cold cases. Four years earlier, Harry had been investigating the murder of a film land production assistant named Angella Benton, whose death is linked to a real heist of an armored car that took place on a movie set. Harry is not the only one affected by this case, as he finds the FBI, Homeland Security, and the wounded LAPD officer who brings him back into thea case he was removed from.

Films • Homeland Security • Hollywood

The Narrows. Little, Brown, 2004. 0316155306.

Bosch has retired from the LAPD and set up a private investigation business. Hired by the widow of FBI agent Terry McCaleb to determine the reason behind his death, Bosch finds himself on the trail once again of the serial killer known as The Poet. Add one more ghost when the trail leads to Rachel Walling.

Nevada, Las Vegas • Private investigator • Serial killers

The Closers. Little, Brown, 2005. 0316734942.

Hearing the siren call of the LAPD, Bosch takes advantage of a need for experience and trusted officers to return to the saddle in the Open Unsolved Unit. When DNA on a gun ties it to the seventeen-year-old murder of a teenage schoolgirl, Bosch and partner Kiz Rider delve into the case. As the gun is connected to a white supremacist named Roland Mackey, the old case will not prove an easy one to close.

Cold case • Supremacists

Echo Park. Little, Brown, 2006. 9780316734950.

Working the Open Unsolved division has its advantages if you have a twenty-year-old case you did not solve. Bosch is revisiting the Marie Gesto disappearance, which he could not crack in 1993, because the D.A. has found a man willing to plea bargain to the murder. When it turns out that the man may have been on a rampage for years because Bosch did not rein him in, this is a nightmare for the cop. He turns to his partner, Kiz Rider, and an old flame, Rachel Walling, to help him get over his guilt.

Missing persons • Serial killer

The Overlook. Little, Brown, 2007. 9780316018951.

Back on the Homicide Squad, Bosch gets the call when a Dr. Stanley Kent, who has clearance to handle radioactive material, is found assassinated near Mullholland

Drive. When the FBI steps in because of national security concerns, Bosch finds himself once again in the vicinity of Rachel Walling.

Doctors • Homeland Security • Hospitals • Terrorism

 The Brass Verdict. Little, Brown, 2008. 9780316166294.

When fellow Hollywood defense attorney Jerry Vincent is murdered, it falls to Haller to defend his client Walter Elliott, a studio executive, against murder charges. Accused of killing his wife and her lover, Elliott's case was built by Bosch. Haller is frightened when he discovers evidence that may indicate who killed Vincent and who might want to kill him. As Haller and Bosch see the weakness in each other's cases, it falls to the two to begin to work together to discover the truth.

Brothers • California, Hollywood • Hollywood

9 Dragons. Little, Brown, 2009. 9780316166317.

When investigating the homicide of a Chinese American liquor store owner named John Li, Bosch crosses paths with a Hong Kong triad. Then he gets the worst call a parent can get: your daughter has been kidnapped. On a plane to Hong Kong to find her, Bosch realizes he will be a fish out of water.

China, Hong Kong • Gangs • Kidnapping • Triads

The Reversal. Little, Brown, 2010. 9780316069489.

Reversing roles, Haller is hired to retry Jason Jessup, a man who has served twenty-four years in prison for a murder that new DNA evidence shows he did not do. Teamed with his ex-wife, D.A. Maggie McPherson, Haller insists that he will only take the case if Bosch will do the legwork. With the half-brothers feuding, his ex-wife sitting next to him at the prosecutor's table, most of the witnesses dead, and the whole world watching, Haller finds himself under enormous pressure to get this right.

DNA • Retrials

Harvey, John ✍

Charlie Resnick

Divorced and lonely, Charlie Resnick has all the classic symptoms of the loner cop. British author Harvey sets his series in Nottingham and features jazz as one of the underlying themes. The themes of these novels are very dark. Readers may also enjoy Bill James, Ian Rankin, and Peter Robinson. See a Web site about this author at http://www.mellotone.co.uk. **HB** Series subjects: **England, East Midlands, Nottingham**

Lonely Hearts. UK: Viking, 1989. (US: Henry Holt, 1989).

Rough Treatment. UK: Viking, 1990. (US: Henry Holt, 1990).

> *Cutting Edge.* UK: Viking, 1991. (US: Henry Holt, 1991).
>
> *Off Minor.* UK: Viking, 1992. (US: Henry Holt, 1992).
>
> *Wasted Years.* UK: Viking, 1993. (US: Henry Holt, 1993).
>
> *Cold Light.* UK: Heinemann, 1994. (US: Henry Holt, 1994).
>
> *Living Proof.* UK: Heinemann, 1995. (US: Henry Holt, 1995).
>
> *Easy Meat.* UK: Heinemann, 1996. (US: Henry Holt, 1996).
>
> *Still Waters.* UK: Heinemann, 1997. (Henry Holt, 1997).
>
> *Last Rites.* UK: Heinemann, 1998. (US: Henry Holt, 1999).

Cold in Hand. Harcourt, 2008. 9780151014620. (UK: Heinemann, 2008).

As Detective Inspector Resnick is contemplating retirement, he is asked to lead an investigation into a dispute between two gangs that has led to the death of a teenage girl. When his lover and partner, Detective Inspector Lynn Kellogg is accused of actually committing the deed, it appears to be tied to a murder case Kellogg is investigating that involves human trafficking for sex.

Gangs • Holidays • Prostitutes • Valentine's Day

James, Bill (pseud. of James Tucker) ✍

Desmond Iles/Colin Harpur

Paired together, these two British cops are world weary and cynical. With Desmond Iles leading the investigations under the scrutiny of his boss, Colin Harpur, their cases combine police procedure with suspense. The key is the truce that Iles tries to maintain among the various drug lords. The cops' personal lives are equally dysfunctional, and the triumphs and tragedies within their families make up a significant part of the books. These novels can be recommended to hard-boiled readers. Readers may also like John Harvey and Ian Rankin. **HB** Series subjects: **Drugs • England • Organized crime • Teams**

> *You'd Better Believe It.* UK: Constable, 1985. (US: St. Martin's, 1986).
>
> *The Lolita Man.* UK: Constable, 1986. (US: Foul Play, 1991).
>
> *Halo Parade.* UK: Constable, 1987. (US: Foul Play, 1992).
>
> *Protection.* UK: Constable, 1988. (US: Foul Play, 1992).
>
> *Come Clean.* UK: Constable, 1989. (US: Foul Play Press, 1993).
>
> *Take.* UK: Macmillan, 1990. (US : Countryman Press, 1994).
>
> *Club.* UK: Macmillan, 1991. (US: Countryman Press, 1995).
>
> *Astride a Grave.* UK: Macmillan, 1991. (US: Foul Play Press, 1996).
>
> *Gospel.* UK: Macmillan, 1992. (US: Foul Play Press, 1997).
>
> *Roses, Roses.* UK: Macmillan, 1993. (US: Foul Play Press, 1998).

In Good Hands. UK: Macmillan, 1994. (US: Norton, 2000).

The Detective Is Dead. UK: Macmillan, 1995. (US: Norton, 2001).

Top Banana. UK: Macmillan, 1996. (US: Foul Play, 1999).

Lovely Mover. UK: Macmillan, 1998. (US: Foul Play Press, 1999).

Panicking Ralph. UK: Macmillan, 1998. (US: Norton, 2001) .

Lovely Mover. Foul Play, 1999. 0393047636. (UK: Macmillan, 1998).

Harpur decides it is time for him to try a little undercover work in the drug community. When drug kingpin Keith Vine decides he needs to remove Eleri ap Vaughan from his list of pushers, Harpur has to balance his ability to gather information against his ability to arrest a murderer.

Undercover operations

Eton Crop. UK: Macmillan, 1999. (US: Foul Play Press, 1999).

Kill Me. UK: Macmillan, 2000. (US: Norton, 2000).

Pay Days. UK: Constable, 2001. (US: Norton, 2001).

Naked at the Window. Norton, 2002. 0393051986. (UK: Constable, 2002).

When Panicking Ralph Ember and his partner Beau Derek wander into the murder scene of their supplier Barney Cross, it leads to Derek's death and Ember being on the run. When the London mobsters who are responsible for Derek's death start ending up dead as well, Harpur and Iles are dragged into the action.

Revenge

The Girl with the Long Back. Norton, 2004. 0393058557. (UK: Constable, 2003).

While Iles tries to maintain a balance in the constant drug wars that he fights, a change in status, such as the transfer of Chief Mark Lane, can upset the apple cart. Then Harpur, again unhappy with what he sees, decides to use a teenage daughter of one of his informers as an undercover agent, and all hell breaks loose when three people are killed.

Easy Streets. Norton, 2005. 9780393060423. (UK: Constable, 2004).

Iles's alliances with Mansel Shale and Panicking Ralph Ember are in tatters when a new chief constable changes the rules. When a bombing kills a small-time drug dealer, it sets off a long-anticipated and unpreventable turf war that leaves dead bodies on the streets and provides cases for Harpur to solve. Meanwhile, Iles has to figure out exactly who is trying to capture all the drug business in his district.

Wolves of Memory. Norton, 2006. 9780393061888. (UK: Constable, 2005).

When a caper by London's top organized crime gang goes awry because the police are tipped off, blame falls on Ian Ballion. To protect him and his family, the powers that be relocate him to the city where Harpur and Iles live. Now the two cops find themselves as bodyguards matched against the best hit men the crime lords have.

Informers • Revenge

Girls. Countrymen, 2007. 9780881507805. (UK: Constable, 2006).

While the occasional truce that Iles is able to broker among the local drug lords has been challenged from inside the county, it now faces a challenge from Albanian dealers moving into Panicking Ralph and Mansel Shale's territory. With these gangs comes another problem: sex trafficking.

Prostitutes

The Sixth Man and Other Stories. Severn House, 2006. 9780727864383.

A collection of the following Harpur and Iles stories: "The Sixth Man," "For Information Only," "Free Enterprise," "Rendezvous One," "Like an Arrangement," and "Night Light." The collection also contains the following stories: "Going Straight," "Elsewhere," "War Crimes," "Body Language," "Fancy," "Big City," "At Home," "A Bit of Eternity," and "Emergency Services."

Short stories

Pix. Countryman, 2009. 9780881508826. (UK: Constable and Robinson, 2008).

When the drug war flares up in their district again, Detective Constable Inspector Harpur and Constable Iles find themselves balancing their illegally collected evidence against their boss Iles's erratic behavior. This time they have to deal with an intruder into the drug business named Chandor, who leaves the dead body of Graham Trove in drug lord Mansel Shale's house while helping himself to Shale's fine art.

Art

In the Absence of Iles. Countryman, 2009. 9780881508833. (UK: Constable, 2008).

This novel is a departure in the series by James. The officer at the center of the investigation is Assistant Chief Constable Esther Davidson. The basic plot involves her decision to undertake an undercover investigation of an organized crime operation called the Cormax Turton Guild. This leads to the murder of an officer and a trial. The author also uses the narrative to divulge how a police department carries out an operation of this nature.

Undercover operations

Lovesey, Peter ✍

Peter Diamond

British writer Lovesey's Peter Diamond faces the ultimate lone wolf punishment: exclusion. Booted from the force, he needs to redeem himself in the eyes of the very authority he fails to understand or respect. Whether inside or outside, Diamond is not a team player, and his cases test his personal abilities to carry out his mission. Readers may also enjoy John Harvey and Ian Rankin. **TR HB** Series subjects: **England, Somerset, Bath**

> *The Last Detective.* UK: Scribner, 1991. (US: Doubleday, 1991).
>
> *Diamond Solitaire.* UK: Little, 1992. (US: Mysterious, 1993).
>
> *The Summons.* UK: Little, 1995. (US: Mysterious, 1995).
>
> *Bloodhounds.* UK: Little, 1996. (US: Mysterious Press, 1996).
>
> *Upon a Dark Night.* UK: Little, 1997. (US: Mysterious Press, 1997).
>
> *The Vault.* UK: Little, 1999. (US: Soho, 2000).
>
> *Diamond Dust.* Little Brown, 2002. (US: Soho, 2002).

The House Sitter. Soho, 2003. 1569473269. (UK: Little, Brown, 2003).

How could a woman be murdered on a public beach in full view of all the other sunbathers? That is the puzzle handed to the police when Emma Tysoe is found dead on a Sussex beach. Locking horns with the original Sussex investigating officer, Henrietta Mallin, when it is discovered that Tysoe lived in Bath, Diamond's first job is to connect her profiler job to her death. He then finds himself up against a serial killer known as The Mariner, who leaves quotes from the Coleridge poem to taunt the police.

Coleridge, Samuel Taylor • England, Sussex • Locked room • Serial killer

The Secret Hangman. Soho, 2007. 9781569474570. (UK: Sphere, 2007).

When Diamond wants to alter the decision that a woman and her former partner both committed suicide, he finds himself up against his boss, Assistant Chief Constable Georgina Dallymore. Meanwhile, in his personal life, where he still grieves for his dead wife, a woman begins to send him anonymous love letters.

Hangings • Serial killer • Suicide

Skeleton Hill. Soho, 2009. 9781569475980. (UK: Sphere, 2009).

An English Civil War reenactment goes awry when the bones of a twenty-year-old victim are discovered on the refreshed battlefield. The case is assigned to Diamond to investigate the past, until professor Rupert Hope, a Cavalier reenactor, is murdered in the present. When it turns out that Diamond's superior is a part of an interest group with an interest in his case, things rapidly begin to unravel.

Reenactments

Mankell, Henning ✍

Kurt Wallander

Sweden's troubled Inspector Kurt Wallander is damaged by the effects of his job and alcohol abuse. His relationship with his family, both his father and daughter, are strained by his inability to deal with his own emotions. His daughter Linda eventually will become a policewoman with cases of her own. Despite all his difficulties and his weary worldview, Wallander remains a dogged detective in Ystad, with cases that often involve major social issues troubling his country. Readers can find the author's Web site at http://www.henningmankell.com. Readers may also enjoy John Harvey, Steig Larsson, Jo Nesbø, Ian Rankin, or Maj Sjowall and Per Wahloo. **HB** Series subjects: **Alcoholism • Fathers and daughters • Sweden, Skåne, Ystad**

Faceless Killers. New Press, 1997. 156584341X. (Sweden: *Mördare Utan Ansikte*. Ordfront, 1991).

> In the frozen province of Skåne, Sweden, an elderly farmer is murdered in his farmhouse. Inspector Kurt Wallander is assigned to the case. His first and only clue is the dying word spoken by the farmer's wife, "foreigner." As racial tension builds in the region and another death occurs, pressure is put on Wallander to solve the crime. Rejected by his father, wife, and daughter, Wallander lives a lonely and isolated life, not unlike the landscape across which he is chasing a killer.
>
> *Hate groups • Race relations • Sweden, Skåne, Lunnarp Village*

The Dogs of Riga. New Press, 2003. 1565847873. (Sweden: *Hundarna i Riga*. Ordfront, 1991).

> When two corpses float ashore in a rubber life raft, the case is handed to Wallander. He determines that the dead men were Eastern European criminals and that their voyage originated in Latvia. With Latvia moving toward freeing itself from Russian dominance, Wallander finds that other elements are quite willing to fill any power gaps.
>
> *Corruption • Latvia, Riga • Organized crime • Russian mafia*

The White Lioness. Norton, 2008. 1565844246. (*Den Vita Lejoninnan*. Ordfront, 1993.

> Wallander knows he has a missing persons and murder case in his hometown involving real estate agent Louise Akerblom. How does this all tie to the recent release of Nelson Mandela from prison in South Africa? And, why does the KGB care? When these elements start to come together, Wallander knows he is racing against the clock to prevent an international tragedy.
>
> *KGB • Mandela, Nelson • South Africa*

The Man Who Smiled. Norton, 2006. 9781565849938. (Sweden: *Mannen Som Log*. Ordfront, 1994).

> After shooting a man in the line of duty, Wallander falls into an alcoholic depression that leads him to thinking about leaving the force. Ignoring pleas for

help from a lawyer who believes his father has been murdered, Wallander is shocked out of his doldrums when the lawyer, Sten Torstensson, is also murdered. Returning to the force after a one-year absence, he teams up with a rookie officer to lead an investigation of double murder.

Fathers and sons • Lawyers • Sweden, Malmö

Sidetracked. Norton, 1999. 9781565845077. (Sweden: Villospår. Ordfront, 1995).

Wallander's life is torn apart when he witnesses a young woman dousing herself with gasoline and setting herself on fire. With no rest, he is then called to the murder site of a former minister of justice, who has been scalped. With a serial killer on the loose, all the efforts of the force are focused on the hunt, but Wallander keeps thinking about the young girl in the field.

Serial killer • Suicide

The Fifth Woman. Norton, 2000. 1565845471. (Sweden: *Den Femte Kvinnan.* Ordfront, 1996).

Still depressed by the death of his father, Wallander must investigate the reasons for an especially cruel murder: a man has been impaled on bamboo stakes in a very carefully set trap. Then a second body appears, and Wallander realizes he has a serial killer on the loose who wants his victims to suffer a slow, painful death. What he does not realize immediately is the tie among all these men and why they are being killed.

Revenge • Serial killer

Step Behind. Norton, 2002. 1565846524. (Sweden: *Steget Efter.* Ordfront, 1997).

During the annual Midsummer's Eve celebration, three college students disappear. While Wallander begins a search for the missing students, detective Svedberg is murdered. Then, after the bodies of the three are found, a fourth student who missed the party is also murdered. Despite his continuing disillusionment with everything and his newfound diabetes, Wallander keeps plugging away.

College students • Holidays • Midsummer's Eve • Missing persons

Firewall. New Press, 2002. 1565847679. (Sweden: *Brandvägg.* Ordfront, 1998).

A series of random crimes and events strike Ystad: a man dies at an ATM, two teenagers murder a taxi driver, and the city suffers a blackout. It is up to Wallander to discover the link among these events and how it connects to an upcoming financial attack that will cripple the economy.

Blackouts

The Pyramid. Norton, 2008. 9781565849945. (Sweden: *Pyramiden.* Ordfront, 1999).

A collection of the following stories: "Wallander's First Case," "The Man with the Mask," "The Man on the Beach," "The Death of the Photographer," and "The Pyramid."

Short stories

Before the Frost. Norton, 2005. 1565848357. (Sweden: *Innan Frosten*. Leopard, 2002).

Linda Wallander has graduated from the academy and is ready to join the force that her father has served so faithfully but with sometimes devastating personal consequences. However, she needs to wait until the fall to officially come on board, so she is living with her father again. When a corpse is found posed in prayer next to a Bible with suggested improvements written in it, the police know they have a major crime to solve. While Wallander believes he can connect it to a series of strange events in the community, Linda begins to get involved in a dangerous way while searching for her missing friend Anna.

Cults • Missing persons • Religion

Nesbø, Jo ✍

Harry Hole

Inspector Harry Hole is a recovering alcoholic working for the Norwegian Security Service. Assigned to the more political cases of the NSS, he finds he must always balance the case against whatever is going on in his own personal life, including his relationship with his girlfriend, Rakel. Readers may also enjoy Lawrence Block's Matt Scudder, Henning Mankell, and Ian Rankin. See the author's Web site at http://www.jonesbo.com. **TR** Series subjects: **Alcoholism • Norway, Oslo**

Redbreast. HarperCollins, 2006. 9780061133992. (Norway: Rødstrupe. Aschehoug, 2000).

Recovering alcoholic Hole has been assigned to the Security Service and given the job of following Sverre Olsen, a neo-Nazi whom the police would like to put away forever. What he discovers is that the scars remaining from Norwegian service for the Nazis in Russia during World War II may now be driving a current effort to kill the one responsible for historical crimes.

Assassinations • Nazis • Neo-Nazis • Skinheads • World War II

Nemesis. Harper, 2008. 9780061655500. (Norway: *Sorgenfri*. Aschehoug, 2002).

When a series of savage bank robberies leave bodies behind, the case is assigned to Hole. While he is investigating, he gets an invitation from an old girlfriend, Anna Bethsen. Waking the next morning with no memory of what happened, he is informed that Anna is dead. As he ponders both crimes with the help of fellow officer Beate Lonn, it begins to appear that Anna's death and the bank robberies may be tied together.

Bank robberies • Memory loss

The Devil's Star. Harper, 2010. 9780061133978. (Norway: Marekors. Aschehoug, 2003).

Hole is desperate when he cannot make anyone else believe that his fellow cop Tom Waaler is very dirty. Despite being off the wagon again, he is assigned to catch a serial killer who is chopping off a finger of his victims and leaving a pentagram-shaped diamond on them. The problem is that his partner on the case is Waaler.

Police corruption • Serial killer

O'Connell, Carol ✍

Kathleen Mallory

Mentored by an experienced police officer, Mallory is saved from a life on the streets. However, the compelling question in this series is whether she be saved from herself. Her abilities with a computer save her from the streets and give her a place on the police force, but can she find a place for herself in society? Eventually Mallory gets her act together enough to make detective grade on the NYPD and is partnered with an interesting character named Riker. Readers may also enjoy Abigail Padgett and Steig Larsson. **TR HB** Series subjects: **New York, New York**

> *Mallory's Oracle.* Putnam, 1994.
>
> *The Man Who Cast Two Shadows.* Putnam, 1995.
>
> *Killing Critics.* Putnam, 1996.
>
> *Stone Angel.* Putnam, 1997.
>
> *Judas Child.* Putnam, 1998.
>
> *Shell Game.* Putnam, 1999.
>
> *Crime School.* Putnam, 2002.

Dead Famous. Putnam, 2003. 0399150846.

A trial in Chicago has generated so much controversy that a radio shock jock named Ian Zachary has taken up the cause. Unfortunately, so has a serial killer named The Reaper, who has begun to murder each of the jurors. How does this tie into the story of Riker, Mallory's wounded ex-partner, or the deformed crime scene cleaner, Johanna Apollo? Mallory wants to find out, with or without the FBI's help.

Federal Bureau of Investigation • Radio personalities • Serial killer • Trials

Winter House. Putnam, 2004. 0399152113.

When a burglar is murdered with an ice pick, the case seems to be one of self-defense. But when Mallory's investigation proves that the defender is none other than Nedda Winter, missing for over fifty years, the case turns ugly. Winter was the only member of an extended family that was brutally attacked long ago—by an ice-pick-wielding murderer.

Missing persons

Find Me. Putnam, 2006. 9780399153952.

> When it is revealed that Route 66 outside of Chicago may be the gravesite for many missing children, all victims of Mack the Knife, the families of these missing persons are drawn to it. Mallory also comes, ostensibly on vacation, but still in search of her own story. When the killer leaves clues to new graves, Mallory is energized to take on the case full time. Riker is left wondering about the dead body found in Mallory's New York apartment.
>
> *Illinois, Chicago • Missing persons • Serial killer • Vacations*

Parker, T. Jefferson ✍

Charlie Hood

Charlie Hood is an L.A. sheriff's deputy riding the Antelope Valley area near Los Angeles. He is the kind of man who does not always make the right choices, but whatever choice he makes, things are not always going to get better. Unlucky in love, he tries to do the right thing by mentoring Bradley Jones, a ward he feels responsible for because of his actions. Readers may also enjoy Michael Connelly, Henning Mankell, and Ian Rankin. See the author's Web site at http://www.tjeffersonparker.com. **HB**
Series subjects: **California, Los Angeles, Antelope Valley**

L.A. Outlaws. Dutton, 2008. 9780525950554.

> A legendary outlaw is stalking Los Angeles under the guise of Joaquin Murrita, a nineteenth-century California legendary tall tale. The modern-day Robin Hood is stealing from the rich and giving to the poor, but it is still Charlie Hood's job to track her down when one of her stunts goes wrong and ten gangsters are left dead at the scene of a $10 million dollar diamond rip-off. When Charlie falls for the eyewitness in the case, things really get complicated.
>
> *Capers • Murrita, Joaquin • Robin Hood*

The Renegades. Dutton, 2009. 9780525950950.

> While on a routine stop with his partner, Terry "Mr. Wonderful" Laws, Terry is killed. Hood is recruited in Internal Affairs to investigate the murder, and he agrees, in part because he feels the killer deliberately did not kill him. Almost immediately, the reader knows that Mr. Wonderful was not, and the book is paced by the race between a determined outlaw and the investigating cop. As the scene shifts from the dangerous streets of L.A. and the drug-maintained fortresses of Mexico, a sense of noir descends on the character, as he is still affected by incidents from the first book in this series.
>
> *Drugs • Mexico, Jacumba • Partners • Police corruption*

Iron River. Dutton, 2010. 9780525951490.

> Hood is on loan to the ATF when a shootout kills the son of Benjamin Armenta, a powerful leader of the smugglers who plague the border. Now bent on vengeance, Armenta declares war on the ATF, and the action gets gruesome. Little does Hood

know that his protégé, Bradley Jones, is involved in one of the deals that are about to go sour.

Bureau of Alcohol, Tobacco and Firearms • Gun control • Mexican–American border wars

The Border Lords. Dutton, 2011.

ATF agent Sean "Oz" Ozburn is Hood's friend. While on a stakeout, Hood sees his undercover buddy shoot four members of the North Baja Cartel, and he knows he has to be the one to bring in the rogue cop. While Ozburn pursues a Love 32 gun deal, it puts him closer to the main man but deeper into danger. Hood has to decide whether he must support his friend or end the masquerade while also keeping one eye on L. A. sheriff's deputy Bradley Jones as he tries his own sting.

Gun control

Perry, Anne ✍

William Monk

As if solving crimes in Victorian England were not tough enough, Perry handicaps her detective by taking away his memory. Struggling with his own fate and the various crimes of the times, Monk is a searcher after the truth on many fronts. He receives aid and comfort from his nurse, Hester Latterly, and their alliance helps him patch his life back together, eventually leading to marriage. Later, his connection to the crimes comes through counsel for the defense Oliver Rathbone, and Monk becomes a private inquiry agent. Readers may also enjoy Elizabeth Peters (Amelia Peabody) and Charles Todd. See the author's Web site at http://www.anneperry.net. **TR Historical**. Series subjects: **England, London • Historical (1800–1899) • Victorian England**

> *The Face of a Stranger.* Fawcett Columbine, 1990.
>
> *A Dangerous Mourning.* Fawcett Columbine, 1991.
>
> *Defend and Betray.* Fawcett Columbine, 1992.
>
> *A Sudden, Fearful Death.* Fawcett Columbine, 1993.
>
> *The Sins of the Wolf.* Fawcett Columbine, 1994.
>
> *Cain His Brother.* Fawcett Columbine, 1995.
>
> *Weighed in the Balance.* Fawcett Columbine, 1996.
>
> *The Silent Cry.* Fawcett Columbine, 1997.
>
> *A Breach of Promise.* Fawcett Columbine, 1998.
>
> *The Twisted Root.* Ballantine, 1999.
>
> *Slaves of Obsession.* Ballantine, 2000.
>
> *Funeral in Blue.* Ballantine, 2001.

Death of a Stranger. Ballantine, 2002. 0345440056.

Monk's latest client is a woman whose fiancé may be mixed up in some nefarious affairs at his railway firm. When railway magnate Nolan Baltimore's body is found in a brothel, it shocks society. Meanwhile Hester has to deal with prostitutes who are coming to her East End clinic damaged by their pimps, who are angry at business being shut down. Are the events related? As Monk tries to decide, he is stunned by memories that begin to return to his consciousness.

Memory • *Prostitutes* • *Railroads*

The Shifting Tide. Ballantine, 2004. 0345440099.

Monk's client is shipping kingpin Clement Louvain, who is missing a shipment of ivory from Africa sent on the ship *Maude Idris*. Keeping the facts from the police and trying to deal with the murder of one of the crewmen on the ship, Monk struggles on. Meanwhile, Hester is treating a woman who Louvain says is a mistress of an old friend and trying to figure out how she fits into the facts of Monk's case when the woman is killed.

Ivory • *Ships*

Dark Assassin. Ballantine, 2006. 0345469291.

When Monk gets appointed superintendent of the Thames River Police station during a time of crisis, he battles himself and his fellow officers to regain his confidence as an official detective. When two lovers fall off Waterloo bridge to their deaths, Monk is led into a war between their two houses. Was Mary Havilland trying to solve the murder of her father? Did Toby Argyll try to save her, or did he push her off the bridge and share her fate? With the aid of Hester, Monk is able to determine that a connection to a corrupt construction project and the typhoid epidemic may hold the key to solving both cases.

Construction • *Sewers* • *Suicide* • *Typhoid*

Execution Dock. Ballantine, 2009. 9780345469335.

Monk is now the commander of the Thames River Police, and his first case deals with the death of a thirteen-year-old boy dumped in the Thames. The facts lead Monk to a secret sex ring that uses young boys for their pleasure. The kingpin of the ring is Jericho Phillips, who becomes Monk's target for bringing about this tragedy. When Phillips walks away from court free, Monk must turn to the people around Hester's clinic, who will provide the operatives he needs to bring down the mastermind.

Pedophilia • *Pornography*

Rankin, Ian ✍

John Rebus

Following the tradition established by fellow Scotsman McIlvanney, Rankin created a masterfully crafted and very disturbed police officer in John Rebus. His drive to solve crimes is balanced against his personal struggles to remain in touch with the human spirit. This series displays the underbelly of Scotland, and these hard-boiled stories can be recommended to readers who enjoy a tough, gritty story. Readers may also enjoy John Harvey and Bill James. See the author's Web site at http://www.ianrankin.com. **HB** Series subjects: **Scotland, Edinburgh**

> *Knots and Crosses.* UK: Bodley Head, 1987. (US: Doubleday, 1987).
>
> *Hide and Seek.* UK: Barrie & Jenkins, 1991. (US: Otto Penzler, 1994).
>
> *Wolfman* (also published as *Tooth and Nail*). UK: Century, 1992.
>
> *A Good Hanging and Other Stories.* UK.: Century, 1992. (US: St. Martin's Minotaur, 2002).
>
> *Strip Jack.* UK: Orion, 1992. (US: St. Martin's, 1994).
>
> *The Black Book.* UK: Orion, 1993. (US: Otto Penzler, 1994).
>
> *Mortal Causes.* UK: Orion, 1994.
>
> *Let It Bleed.* UK: Orion, 1995. (US: Simon & Schuster, 1996).
>
> *Black and Blue.* UK: Orion, 1997. (US: St. Martin's, 1997).
>
> *The Hanging Garden.* UK: Orion, 1998. (US: St. Martin's, 1998).
>
> *Dead Souls.* UK: Orion, 1999. (US: St. Martin's Minotaur, 1999).
>
> *Death Is Not the End.* UK: Orion, 1998. (US: St. Martin's Minotaur, 2000).
>
> *Set in Darkness.* UK: Orion, 2000. (US: St. Martin's Minotaur, 2000).
>
> *The Falls.* UK: Orion, 2000. (US: St. Martin's Minotaur, 2001).

 Resurrection **Man.** Little, Brown, 2003. 0316766844. (UK: Orion, 2002).

Sent to the Scottish Police College for rehabilitation, Rebus finds himself working on an old case, first handled by the school's inspector, in which he might have been culpable. His actual assignment is to investigate the activities of the other bent cops sent to the school. At the same time, Detective Sergeant Siobhan Clarke is working the murder of an art dealer, which will bring Rebus up against an old nemesis and unite all three stories into one. **ED**

> *Police corruption*

A Question of Blood. Little, Brown, 2004. 0316095648. (UK: Orion, 2003).

Detective Sergeant Siobhan Clarke and Rebus are handed the case of a former member of an elite military unit named Lee Herdman, who has committed suicide after shooting three boys at a private school. Two of the boys are dead, but the survivor is James Bell, the son of a politician willing to use his son's injuries to campaign against the ownership of guns. When the investigators uncover that Herdman had a relationship with a fifteen-year-old Goth named Teri Cotter, who displays her life to the world via the Internet, they begin to unravel a situation with many layers. One layer finds Rebus related to one of the victims and under suspicion for the death of a criminal who has been stalking Siobhan.

Academia • Military

Fleshmarket Alley. Little, Brown, 2005. 0316095656. (UK: *Fleshmarket Close*. Orion, 2004).

Rebus is handed a case involving the murder of a Kurdish refugee, whose death reveals a contemporary underground for human smuggling as they try to seek asylum while dumped in detention housing run by for-profit companies. Siobhan Clarke has the other main case in the book: a rape victim commits suicide, and her sister goes missing when a recently paroled rapist is murdered.

Racism • Rape • Slavery

The Naming of the Dead. Little, Brown, 2007. 9780316057578. (UK: Orion, 2006).

There is a Group of Eight world summit meeting planned for Edinburgh. Ben Webster, the Scottish representative, falls to his death just prior to its start. Meanwhile, Rebus is pursuing the reason behind the murder of Cyril Colliar, henchman of crime boss Cafferty and a recently paroled sex offender. While all others focus on the security for the summit, Rebus's investigation of local crime leads him to cast doubt on the apparent suicide of Webster.

World Summit meetings

Exit Music. UK: Orion, 2007. (US: Little, Brown, 2008. 9780316057585).

While Rebus is dreaming of retirement, he is handed the case of the murder of Alexander Todorov, a Russian dissident poet. Initially the case looks like a mugging, but it is complicated by the presence of a group of Russian businessmen looking to expand their territory. Getting resistance from the local politicians, Rebus knows he will not be able to slip away quietly.

Poets • Retirement

Todd, Charles (pseud. of Caroline Todd and Charles Todd) ✍

Ian Rutledge

Ian Rutledge has returned from the First World War a damaged man, haunted by the voice of a Scotsman he had to execute on the battlefield. A brilliant investigator prior to the war, he now struggles to regain his skills and his sanity as an inspector for Scotland Yard. These novels are written by a mother-son team. Readers may also enjoy Anne Perry. **TB** Historical. Series subjects: **Historical (1900–1999) • World War I**

A Test of Wills. St. Martin's, 1996.

Wings of Fire. St. Martin's, 1998.

Search the Dark. St. Martin's, 1999.

Legacy of the Dead. Bantam, 2000.

Watchers of Time. Bantam, 2001.

A Fearsome Doubt. Bantam, 2002.

A Cold Treachery. Bantam, 2005. 0553803492.

> Rutledge is sent to the Lake District town of Urskdale when five members of the Elcott family are murdered during a severe blizzard. When one young member of the family named Josh remains missing, Rutledge focuses on that puzzle to lead him to the solution of this brutal crime.
>
> *England, Lake District, Urskdale*

A Long Shadow. Morrow, 2006. 9780060786717.

> When the local constable is shot with an arrow while searching Firth Woods, Rutledge is assigned the job of discovering why. When Rutledge makes a connection between this crime and a missing girl, he finds himself in danger as well. He is used to being haunted by Hamish, but now he finds himself stalked by a mysterious stranger who leaves shell casings to taunt him.
>
> *England, East Midlands, Dudlington*

A False Mirror. Morrow, 2007. 9780060786731.

> Stephen Mallory, who served with Rutledge in World War I, has taken his former girlfriend and her housekeeper hostage in the small village of Hampton Regis. Now Rutledge has to negotiate their release while trying to prove that Mallory is innocent of assaulting Matthew Hamilton, the original charge that caused Mallory to act. Rutledge has his doubts, as he knows that Mallory was not an ideal soldier.
>
> *England, Hampton Regis • Hostages*

A Pale Horse. Morrow, 2008. 9780061233562.

> Fountain Abbey lies in ruins, and within it lies the corpse of an unidentified man whose face is covered by a gas mask. Rutledge has been charged by the British War Office with locating a missing man whose service to the country is so secret even the detective cannot know what it was. Is this man the one Rutledge seeks? Have the local police identified the correct suspect? Rutledge's search takes him to Uffington Castle and its magnificent 400-foot-tall chalk statue, White Horse, carved into the hill above it. It also takes him deep within the closed community of residents of this small town, from whom he hopes to receive the clues he needs to find a killer and to put to rest the effects of an illicit affair.
>
> *England, Berkshire • England, Yorkshire, Fountains Abbey • Small towns*

A Matter of Justice. Morrow, 2009. 9780061233593.

> Financier Harold Quarles has been murdered in Somerset, and the case is given to Ian Rutledge. As he begins to investigate, he discovers that the

man was hated by everyone near his estate. Even more sinister, Quarles appears to have had a secret buried in the war, not unlike Rutledge himself.

England, Somerset

The Red Door. Morrow, 2010. 9780061726163.

Walter Teller, a famous author of a pre–World War I book recounting his missionary life, is missing, and Rutledge gets the case. His disappearance sets members of his family against each other and leads Rutledge on a few wild goose chases, until a discovery clears the air. On a separate case, Rutledge must deal with the bludgeoning death of a Lancashire woman who died behind the red door of her house. Painted as a greeting for his return from the war, the door never served its purpose. Should something be made of the fact that the missing man is named Peter Teller?

England, Lancashire • Missing persons

Detectives Who Support the Police

As the police forces developed as legitimate practitioners of police procedure, they became surrounded by support forces geared to making their lives easier or by businesses willing to help the police for a profit. To aid in the administration of justice, police forces find themselves allied with the judicial system. From the ranks of each of these support groups, authors have selected detectives with particular skills to act as detectives on their own. The appeal of this type of detective is that he or she can sometimes function like the professional, the private, or the amateur, thus giving the reader a choice of a broad style of character to read.

Cornwell, Patricia ✍

Kay Scarpetta

Chief Medical Examiner Dr. Kay Scarpetta, working out of Richmond, Virginia, has proved to be one of the best-selling mystery characters. Often working with her niece Lucy Farinelli, an FBI agent, and police captain Peter Marino, Scarpetta uses her medical skills to play detective. Eventually she moves her operations from Florida, to South Carolina, to Massachusetts; marries forensic psychologist Benton Wesley; becomes a private forensic consultant for CNN; and becomes the chief of the Cambridge Forensic Center. Readers may also enjoy Aaron Elkins, Sharyn McCrumb (Elizabeth MacPherson), and John Sandford. See the author's Web site at http://www. patriciacornwell.com. **HB** Series subjects: **Forensics • Massachusetts, Cambridge • Medical • Virginia, Richmond**

Postmortem. Scribner, 1990.

Body of Evidence. Scribner, 1991.

All That Remains. Scribner, 1992.

Cruel and Unusual. Scribner, 1993.

The Body Farm. Scribner, 1994.

From Potter's Field. Scribner, 1995.

Cause of Death. Putnam, 1996.

Unnatural Exposure. Putnam, 1997.

Point of Origin. Putnam, 1998.

Black Notice. Putnam, 1999.

Scarpetta's Winter Table. Wyrick and Company, 1998.

The Last Precinct. Putnam, 2000.

Blow Fly. Putnam, 2003. 0399150897.

Having given up her job as Virginia's Chief Medical Examiner, Scarpetta has relocated to Florida as a private forensic consultant. When a puzzling death in Louisiana confounds her, she receives a message from her old nemesis, The Wolfman, who may have some information for her about her new case.

Florida, Delray Beach • Louisiana, East Baton Rouge • Serial killer

Trace. Putnam, 2004. 0399152199.

After a five-year hiatus, Scarpetta, with Pete Marino, returns to the Chief Medial Examiner's office in Virginia when her replacement, Dr. Joel Marcus, asks for her help on a case involving the death of a fourteen-year-old girl. Last Precinct P.I. agency head and Scarpetta's niece, Lucy, has a separate case in which she tries to determine who attempted to kill her best friend and housemate, Henrietta.

Predator. Putnam, 2005. 9780399152832.

Scarpetta is now an independent contractor working for the National Forensic Academy in Florida, teamed with Pete Marino, Benton Wesley, and Lucy Farinelli. The forensic specialists find themselves hunting a dangerous serial killer when four people go missing. Their research leads them to Basil Jenrette, a killer who is the subject of a study being done in Massachusetts and introduces the team to psychiatrist Dr. Marilyn Self.

Florida • Massachusetts, Boston • Serial killer

Book of the Dead. Putnam, 2007. 9780399153938.

Now living in Charleston, South Carolina, where she operates her own forensics lab, Scarpetta is hired to autopsy the body of sixteen-year-old Drew Martin, an international tennis star who was tortured and murdered in Rome. Other murders occur, including an abused child and a rich woman. Confused by the details that connect these murders, the team of Pat, Lucy, and Benton find themselves having to turn to their nemesis from the previous book, Dr. Self.

> *Italy, Rome • South Carolina, Charleston • Tennis*

Scarpetta. Putnam, 2008. 9780399155161.

Scarpetta accepts a job in New York City when the police ask her to investigate the claims of a man locked in the Bellevue Hospital psychiatric ward. Oscar Bane has requested that she investigate his claims that he is innocent of the murder of his girlfriend. While she wonders if he is guilty, more murders occur, and the case becomes one of wondering what the connection among all the victims is.

> *Serial killer • New York, New York*

The Scarpetta Factor. Putnam, 2009. 9780399156397.

Scarpetta has taken a job as the senior forensic analyst for CNN. When she begins an examination of the death of a Central Park jogger named Toni Darien, she finds eerie connections to missing financial planner Hannah Starr. Lucy is also studying the Darien case, along with other regular series characters. But the scariest part of the case involves the role of her husband Benton's past and the strange characters who keep reappearing in her life.

> *Journalists • Television*

Port Mortuary. Putnam, 2010. 9780399157219.

As the new chief of the Cambridge Forensic Center, Scarpetta discovers that a man appears to have died after he was brought to the morgue at the center. Eventually the body reveals more details that will set Scarpetta on the path of danger, revealing a time when she first was a member of the Air Force and had to deal with a hate crime that haunts her today. Using brand new 3D radiology, Scrapetta believes she has the key to a mass conspiracy that could lead to mass murder.

> *CT-assisted virtual autopsy • Delaware, Dover • Dover Air Force Base • 3D radiology*

Cotterill, Colin ✍

Dr. Siri Paiboun

In the People's Democratic Republic of Laos, the Communists are now in charge of this former French colony. Former Pathet Lao freedom fighter and Paris-trained Dr. Siri Paiboun is seventy-two years old. Appointed the nation's coroner, he finds he has little support to actually carry out his duties despite the help of two assistants, the mentally challenged Geung and Dtui the nurse. However, he does have magical visions of the dead to help him work through his cases. Later in the series, he even finds romance with Madame Daeng. Readers may also enjoy Alexander McCall Smith and Eliot Pattison. The author's Web site can be found at http://www.colincotterill.com. **TR**

Series subjects: **Aging** • **Autopsy** • **Communism** • **Coroners** • **Forensics** • **Historical (1900–1999)** • **Laos, Vientiane** • **Medical** • **People's Democratic Republic of Laos**

The Coroner's Lunch. Soho, 2004. 1569473765.

> Siri Paiboun must determine who killed a visiting Vietnamese delegation to prevent an international incident. Although the bodies were found in a reservoir, it does not appear that they drowned. His other major case involves determining whether an official's wife died of natural causes or from poison when she collapsed at a banquet.
>
> *Poisons* • *Vietnam*

 ***Thirty-Three Teeth***. Soho, 2005. 9781569473887.

> Times are very busy for the Laotian coroner, who must deal with identifying two burnt corpses for the government, which does not like his results. He ends up with a court date and must represent himself against charges. Meanwhile, a frightening creature is stalking the streets and mutilating people, and the royal family has been moved out of the city. When an attack threatens one of the coroner's staff, he is able to discover the truth.
>
> **DI**
>
> *Kings* • *Laos, Luang Prabang*

Disco for the Departed. Soho, 2006. 9781569474280.

> Paibourn and Dtui are sent to the Hiraphan Province when the new president of Laos discovers a corpse encased in cement on his property. Paibourn's understanding of the mystical helps when he must deal with clues from a Cuban relief worker's afterlife that tell a tale of soul transfers. With a national celebration looming and the pressure on, he must work fast to find a murderer.
>
> *Laos, Hiraphan Province, Vieng Xai*

Anarchy and Old Dogs. Soho, 2007. 9781569474631.

> When a blind, retired dentist named Dr. Buagaew is run over by a truck and his body is delivered to Paibourn's morgue, the coroner decides to investigate the reason for the letter in the old man's pocket. It is written with a code hidden by invisible ink and describes some moves in the game of chess. But there is a bigger game afoot, and before he knows it, Paibourn and his team are deep into an espionage adventure.
>
> *Dentists* • *Laos, Pakse*

Curse of the Pogo Stick. Soho, 2008. 9781569474853.

> With the doctor away in the north, Dtui is left in charge of the unit and must deal with a corpse that is booby trapped with explosives. While returning, Paiboun is kidnapped by some female Hmong and set to the task of performing an exorcism of a pogo stick.
>
> *Exorcism* • *Explosives* • *Hmong*

The Merry Misogynist. Soho, 2009. 9781569475560.

> The dear doctor has a new wife, Madame Daeng, and new digs above her noodle shop in Vientiane. When a young woman is strangled and left tied to a tree, her corpse comes to Paiboun to dissect, and he begins an investigation. But he must also deal with a crazy man, the spirit of his dead dog, and of course, his new wife.
>
> *Marriage*

Love Songs from a Shallow Grave. Soho, 2010. 9781569476277.

> When three women are pierced to death with a fencing sword, the mystery falls on Paiboun's morgue table. When his investigation finds him lured to Cambodia by a false offer, he is thrown in prison and accused of being a spy. Now he must face all the horrors of the Khmer Rouge to discover the truth and free himself.
>
> *Cambodia • Khmer Rouge • Prisoners*

Deaver, Jeffrey ✍

Lincoln Rhyme

Lincoln Rhyme was NYPD's head of forensics, but an accident left him a quadriplegic, only able to lift one finger. But what he lacks in physical movement is made up for by his mental facilities and his determination to continue apprehending criminals. Aided by Amelia Sachs, Rhyme continues to work from his bedside. Over time he assembles a team of investigators who turn to him like an oracle or do his bidding because of his track record. His cases can be recommended to hard-boiled mystery readers. Readers may also enjoy John Sandford and Mary Willis Walker. **HB** Series subjects: **African Americans • Forensics • New York, New York • Physically challenged • Quadriplegic • Serial killer**

> *The Bone Collector.* Viking, 1997.
>
> *The Coffin Dancer.* Simon & Schuster, 1998.
>
> *The Empty Chair.* Simon & Schuster, 2000.
>
> *The Stone Monkey.* Simon & Schuster, 2002.

The Vanished Man. Simon & Schuster, 2003. 0743222008.

> "The Conjurer" Malerick is a homicidal mastermind who manages to ckill without being caught by using an illusionist's techniques. He first comes to Rhyme's attention when, cornered in a classroom in a music school, he disappears from the locked room. Allied with Sachs, Rhyme decides he needs his own magician, named Kara, as an ally against this deadly enemy.
>
> *Locked room • Magic*

The Twelfth Card. Simon & Schuster, 2005. 0743260929.

> Amelia Sachs is drawn to the case of a young black girl named Geneva Settle, who was attacked at the library while researching her slave ancestor, Charles

Singleton. The central question is, what does a teenager know that would earn the interest of a white hit man named Thompson Boyd? Does it really relate to what happened in 1868, when Singleton was arrested?

Children in jeopardy • *New York, Harlem*

The Cold Moon. Simon & Schuster, 2006. 9780743260930.

A clock has been left at the scene of two murders, which sets Rhyme and Sachs on the trail of a serial killer known as The Watchmaker, who has threatened to murder eight more people. A second case, a suicide that might be tied to some crooked cops, finds Sachs doing her first lead on a murder case.

Police corruption • *Suicide*

The Broken Window. Simon & Schuster, 2008. 9781416549970.

When Rhyme's cousin Arthur is accused of murder, he is not interested in investigating because the case is airtight. Then some compelling pieces of evidence point Rhyme to a data mining operation whose intent may be more evil than predicting a person's next consumer interest: it may pinpoint how to falsely accuse people of murder. Revealing the killer becomes a race for Rhyme's team when the mysterious "522" turns his resources on the personal lives of the detectives.

Computers • *Data mining* • *Identity theft*

The Burning Wire. Simon & Schuster, 2010. 9781439156339.

When a city bus explodes in broad daylight, it reveals the existence of a new type of serial killer. By using the power that runs the city, the killer is able to create terror throughout the city by striking at will. Although Rhyme is willing to help, the revelation that his old nemesis The Watchmaker may be working in Mexico distracts him from the first case. Eventually, his own physical condition begins to deteriorate as he loses his ability to multitask on two separate investigations.

Electricity

Elkins, Aaron ✍

Gideon Oliver

Proving that the past has many secrets, Elkins created a forensic physical anthropologist named Gideon Oliver, who helps solve current mysteries by unraveling their histories. To add spice to the series, Oliver is a traveling consultant, visiting many foreign locations in his searches, echoing the career of Elkins. As the series progresses, his wife Julie helps give a "plucky couple" feeling to the cases. The series has drawn praise for its accuracy in presenting the anthropological aspects of the cases without taking anything away from the development of the character. Readers who enjoy Elkins may also enjoy Patricia

Cornwell, Sharyn McCrumb (Elizabeth MacPherson), and Elizabeth Peters (Jacqueline Kirby/Amelia Peabody). **TR** Series subjects: **Forensics**

> *Fellowship of Fear.* Walker, 1982.
>
> *The Dark Place.* Walker, 1983.
>
> *Murder in the Queen's Armes.* Walker, 1985.
>
> *Old Bones.* Mysterious Press, 1987.
>
> *Curses!* Mysterious Press, 1989.
>
> *Icy Clutches.* Mysterious Press, 1990.
>
> *Dead Men's Hearts.* Mysterious Press, 1994.
>
> *Twenty Blue Devils.* Mysterious, 1997.
>
> *Make No Bones.* Mysterious, 1999.
>
> *Skeleton Dance.* Morrow, 2000.

Good Blood. Berkley Prime Crime, 2003. 0425194116.

Vacations are never passive for detectives, and this trip to Italy with his wife Julie is no exception for Oliver. While vacationing in the village of Stresa on an island in Lake Maggiore, ostensibly to help their friend Phil run a tour, they are present when Achille, the only child of Vincenzo de Grazia, is kidnapped. When the remains of a family elder are uncovered, the Skeleton Detective springs into action.

Italy, Lake Maggiore, Stresa • Kidnapping • Vacations

Where There's a Will. Berkley Prime Crime, 2004. 0425200264.

On the Hawaiian islands with his FBI pal John Lau, Oliver gets involved in a ten-year-old murder involving an old rancher named Torkel Torkelsson. The same night Torkel was killed, his brother Magnus disappeared in a small plane. When the plane's wreckage is finally discovered, Oliver must help discover who are the legitimate heirs to the cattle ranch kingdom.

Hawai'i, Big Island • Vacations

Unnatural Selection. Berkley Prime Crime, 2006. 9789780425210055.

The Isles of Scilly lie off the coast of Cornwall, and it is there that Oliver and his second wife, Julie, arrive when she is invited to a conference on biodiversity hosted by an eccentric Russian. Oliver has time to wander in a local museum, where he discovers one of their ancient exhibits contains the bones of a more recent vintage. To his surprise, the identification of the victim leads back to the conservation group that invited Julie to the islands, and to a new murder.

Biodiversity • England, Cornwall, Isles of Scilly

Little Tiny Teeth. Berkley Prime Crime, 2007. 9780425215302.

> Oliver goes up the Amazon with his friends, travel agent Phil Boyajian and John Lau of the FBI. But vacations are never easy for detectives, and soon it becomes obvious that their fellow passengers are up to no good. When one of the botanists is murdered, Oliver must decide if the threat is greater from within the jungle or onboard the boat.
>
> *Amazon River • Botany • Chayacuro • Drugs*

Uneasy Relations. Berkley Prime Crime, 2008. 9780425221761.

> When a find on the island of Gibraltar brings the world's scientists there to view the remains of Neanderthal man and *Homo sapiens*, anthropologist are questioning whether they coexisted peacefully. When two scientists close to the debate are murdered, it is up to the visiting Skeleton Detective, Gideon Oliver, to investigate.
>
> *Gibraltar • Neanderthal man*

Skull Duggery. Berkley, 2009. 9780425227978.

> Gideon and his wife Julie are vacationing at her relative's dude ranch when Village Police Chief Flaviano Sandoval asks him to examine a mummy found in the desert. The local coroner has made an incorrect examination, a fact that is echoed on a second case when Gideon works on a thirty-year-old case. But no case is as cold as the death of a Zapotec princess who for a thousand years has been actually a "he." How all this misdiagnosis will converge is part of the fun in this look at how Gideon spends his restful vacation time.
>
> *Coroners • Mexico, Oaxaca, Teotitlán del Valle • Vacations*

Kellerman, Jonathan ✍

Alex Delaware

Jonathan Kellerman is the husband of mystery writer Faye Kellerman. As a child psychologist, Alex Delaware is not afraid to consult with the Los Angeles Police Department on cases that involve children placed at risk. Often given access by his friend, Detective Milo Sturgis, Delaware finds himself drawn into cases that disturb and distress. These novels can be recommended to readers of the hard-boiled mystery. Readers may also enjoy Stephen White. See a Web site about the author at http://mysterynet.com/jkellerman/main. **HB** Series subjects: **California, Los Angeles • Children in jeopardy • Psychiatric evaluations • Psychologists**

> *When the Bough Breaks*. Atheneum, 1985. (UK: *Shrunken Heads*. Macdonald, 1985).
>
> *Blood Test*. Atheneum, 1986.
>
> *Over the Edge*. Atheneum, 1987.

Silent Partner. Bantam, 1989.

Time Bomb. Bantam, 1990.

Private Eyes. Bantam, 1992.

Devil's Waltz. Bantam, 1993.

Bad Love. Bantam, 1994.

Self-Defense. Bantam, 1995.

The Web. Bantam, 1996.

The Clinic. Bantam, 1997.

Survival of the Fittest. Bantam, 1997.

Monster. Random House, 1999.

Dr. Death. Random House, 2000.

Flesh and Blood. Random House, 2001.

The Murder Book. Ballantine, 2002.

A Cold Heart. Random House, 2003. 0345452550.

Damaged artists, trying to make it back from the brink, are being murdered, and cop pal Sturgis wants Delaware to help because the crimes are ritualistic and staged. The clues are coming fast and furious via an underground magazine and are signed by the "Faithful Scrivener," so Delaware finds himself working with Sturgis's fellow cop Petra Connor and her partner, Eric Stahl. When his investigation places someone he still cares for in danger, the resolution of this case becomes necessary to save her and find a murderer.

Serial killer

Therapy. Ballantine, 2004. 0345452593.

Two victims caught in a sexually compromising position present a homicide case for Lieutenant Milo Sturgis and an intriguing psychological dilemma for Delaware. The male victim is Gavin Quick, who was seeing the famous psychiatrist Dr. Mary Lou Koppel, perhaps because his mother is nuts and his father is a criminal. Equally intriguing is the fact that nothing is known of the woman victim. So why were they each shot once in the head executioner style, but she was impaled with a metal spike?

Rage. Ballantine, 2005. 9780345467065.

Troy Turner and Rand Duchay were children who murdered a child. While Troy died in prison, Duchay served his time and was released. Seeking Delaware's help as a psychologist, Duchay turns to him for treatment, but then Duchay is murdered. Delaware, with the help of Lieutenant Sturgis, decides they need to discover who is the killer of a killer. Could it be simple revenge, or does the first murder hold secrets about the second?

Gone. Ballantine, 2007. 9780345452610.

Initially the world is shocked by the story of Dylan Meserve and Michaela Brand, two acting students who were abducted, abused, and returned three days later. But then the investigation begins to pick apart their story, and the world believes they have perpetrated a hoax. Delaware is asked to evaluate Michaela for the court. When Michaela is murdered and Dylan disappears, Delaware turns to pal Milo Sturgis to begin a manhunt for the answers.

Abductions • Academia • Actors • Hoaxes

Obsession. Ballantine, 2007. 9780345452634.

Tanya Bigelow is worried that her aunt Patty, a nurse who helped Tanya through her obsessive-compulsive disorder, may have confessed to a murder prior to her death. When Sturgis asks once again for Delaware's help, the two discover more deaths on the way to an explanation of the mystery.

Deathbed confessions • Single mothers

Compulsion. Ballantine, 2008. 9780345465276.

Delaware and his friend LAPD Detective Sturgis are working on cases that all involve the use of luxury black automobiles. At the same time, a girl goes missing from the L.A. party scene. The question becomes, what will pull these cases all together and lead to a killer?

Serial killer

Bones. Ballantine, 2008. 9780345495136.

Los Angeles's Bird Marsh preserve becomes the burial ground for the victims of a new serial killer, who is being hunted by Lieutenant Milo Sturgis, LAPD's Special Case Investigator. When the killer turns from prostitutes as victims to burying the body of music tutor Selena Bass, Milo asks Delaware to help him find the connection. As the two begin to suspect the caretaker on the estate of the family who employed Bass, the young man disappears.

Birds • Nature preserves • Serial killer

True Detectives. Ballantine, 2009. 9780345495143.

Aaron Fox is an LAPD cop, and Moses Reed is a southern California P.I. They share one thing: a common mother. The case of the missing Caitlin Frostig has connections to both investigators and also brings Moses to his psychologist, Delaware. While the investigation focuses on Caitlin's father and her only boyfriend, Rory Stoltz, there are no easy answers for those seeking the truth, especially among Hollywood's movie community.

Brothers • Missing persons • Private investigator

Lanier, Virginia ✍

Jo Beth Sidden

Sidden owns a business called Bloodhounds, Inc. Her specialty is raising and training bloodhounds for search and rescue missions in the Okefenokee Swamp. Her challenges come both from her cases and from the men in her life, who do not trust her skills. This series can be recommended to traditional mystery readers. Readers may also enjoy Nevada Barr. **TR** Series subjects: **Dogs • Georgia, Okefenokee Swamp • Humor**

> *Death in Bloodhound Red.* Pineapple Press, 1995.
>
> *The House on Bloodhound Lane.* HarperCollins, 1996.
>
> *A Brace of Bloodhounds.* HarperCollins, 1997.
>
> *Blind Bloodhound Justice.* HarperCollins, 1998.
>
> *Ten Little Bloodhounds.* HarperCollins, 1999.

A Bloodhound to Die For. HarperCollins, 2003. 0060193883.

> Jimmy Joe Lane is a legend for turning a ninety-day sentence into a forty-year jail term, but when he escapes from prison, his fixation on Sidden means she is in danger of being stalked by this goofy jailbird. Relying on her ex-boyfriend, Sheriff Hank Cribbs, she manages to keep herself out of danger while she and her assistant Jasmine take the dogs out and try to find a woman with dementia who has wandered into the Okefenokee Swamp.
>
> *Georgia, Balsa City*

Maron, Margaret ✍

Deborah Knott

This is the second series started by this author, a change from her Sigrid Harald cop novels. Beginning her career as a lawyer in North Carolina, Knott is surrounded by all of her family members. Knowing her territory and her family, Knott's cases explore both as the character grows in stature and is elected judge of Colleton County. Readers may also enjoy Frances Fyfield, Lia Matera, and Julie Smith. See the author's Web site at http://www.margaretmaron.com. **SB TR** Series subjects: **Law • North Carolina, Colleton County**

> *Bootlegger's Daughter.* Mysterious Press, 1992.
>
> *Southern Discomfort.* Mysterious Press, 1993.

Shooting at Loons. Mysterious Press, 1994.

Up Jumps the Devil. Mysterious Press, 1996.

Killer Market. Mysterious Press, 1997.

Home Fires. Mysterious Press, 1998.

Storm Track. Mysterious Press, 2000.

Uncommon Clay. Mysterious Press, 2001.

Slow Dollar. Mysterious, 2002.

High Country Fall. Mysterious Press, 2004. 0892968087.

Balancing her feelings about getting engaged to Colleton County detective Dwight Bryant, Knott leaves for Blue Ridge country to fill in for a vacationing judge. Daniel Freeman, accused of the murder of a local doctor, is also a friend of some of Knott's extended family, who are living with her in the condo she is using. Then, with Dwight far away, Knott starts to have feelings for the local D.A.

North Carolina, Cedar Gap

Rituals of the Season. Mysterious Press, 2005. 9780892968091.

As her Christmas-time wedding beckons, Knott and her fiancé, Deputy Sheriff Dwight Bryant, find themselves investigating the death of Assistant District Attorney Tracy Johnson. What at first appeared to be an automobile accident turns out to be a murder when it is revealed Johnson was shot. Knott is distracted from the case when she believes a female death row prisoner might be innocent. Balancing both causes while renovating her farmhouse for her upcoming nuptials stresses out the judge, but it does lead to justice.

Automobile accidents • Christmas • Death row • Holidays • Weddings

Winter's Child. Mysterious Press, 2006. 9780892968107.

Newly married to Colleton County, N.C., chief deputy Dwight Bryant, Knott gets no rest when local troublemaker J. D. Rouse is found shot to death. While others are killed as the search for his killer progresses, Bryant is distracted when his ex-wife and eight-year-old son Cal go missing in Virginia.

Children in jeopardy • Missing persons • Virginia, Shaysville

Hard Row. Warner, 2007. 9780446582438.

Colleton County is the victim when parts of a human body are found throughout the countryside. New husband and deputy Dwight Bryant is assigned that case, while his wife's courtroom is filled with cases that reveal that the county also has a problem with hate. The victim was the husband missing from her courtroom's high-profile divorce case. The focus of all the anger is the undocumented migrant workers who now fill the fields. Knott also needs to deal with her new married life and an inherited stepson.

Divorce • Extended families • Migrant workers • Mutilation • Stepsons

Death's Half Acre. Grand Central, 2008. 9780446196109.

When husband and sheriff's deputy Dwight Bryant is caught up in a corruption case that exposes some local graft, Judge Knott finds herself dragged into a real estate case that leads to the murder of Candace Bradshaw. While Bradshaw's poor background is exposed by her death, Knott finds her own family relations, especially with her father, hold some surprises for her as well.

Fathers and daughters

Sand Sharks. Grand Central, 2009. 9780446196116.

While attending the North Carolina District Court Judges annual conference at the Sand Castle Hotel on the beach, Knott discovers the murdered body of a fellow judge named Pete Jeffreys. As she probes into the murder, she discovers that the dead judge was not everyone's favorite. Then a second judge is attacked. Is it possible that Knott will be the third victim?

North Carolina, Wrightsville Beach

McDermid, Val ✍

Tony Hill/Carol Jordan

Dr. Tony Hill is a psychological profiler teamed with police detective Carol Jordan. As the head of the National Profiling Task Force, Hill sets up a team of investigators who will help him put the pieces together on each case. Jordan will eventually rise to the rank of Detective Chief Inspector, but she will never be completely comfortable understanding Tony Hill. Readers may also enjoy Deborah Crombie and Kathy Reichs. See the author's Web site at http://www.valmcdermid.com. **TR** Series subjects: **England, Berkshire, Bradfield • Profilers • Serial killer**

The Mermaids Singing. HarperPrism, 1997. 0061011746. (UK: HarperCollins, 1995).

The Queer Killer, a murderer intent on torturing gay men, is loose in the town of Bradfield. The local police call in Tony Hill, a forensic psychologist for the Home Office, who is damaged himself. He is teamed for the time being with Detective Inspector Carol Jordan, who appears to be one of the few people who can understand him. The problem is that his profile does not work while the serial killer taunts the community.

Homosexuality

The Wire in the Blood. Penguin, 1997. 9780140275483. (UK: HarperCollins, 1997).

When a serial killer has made dozens of teenage girls disappear, it takes Dr. Hill and Jordan to figure out that one individual may be the reason why. Hill's

National Profiling Task Force plows forward with little success, until they lose one of their own to the killer.

Teenagers at risk

The Last Temptation. St. Martin's Minotaur, 2002. 0312290896.

Jordan goes undercover in Germany to bust an illegal immigration organization run by Tadeusz Radecki. While there, her police liaison, Petra Becker, asks for Tony's help in dealing with the torture and murder of psychologists doing experimental research. What they discover is that a serial killer's working methods echo the horrors of the Nazi era.

Drugs • Germany, Berlin • Nazis

The Torment of Others. HarperCollins, 2004. 9780007142903.

Two serial killers are plaguing Bradfield, and Hill is asked to help again. The first case is a possible copycat killer whose method matches incarcerated accused killer Derek Tyler. The second case involves a child molester who has the police looking for two missing victims. With a damaged Jordan trying to get back in the swing of things, the duo relies more on the help of Detective Inspector Don Merrick.

Children in jeopardy • Prostitutes

Beneath the Bleeding. Harper, 2009. 9780061688973. (UK: HarperCollins, 2007).

Forced into a hospital bed after being attacked by a patient, Hill is distracted by a new case brought to him by Jordan. Robbie Bishop, football star, has been poisoned with ricin. While Jordan's team investigates, an explosion occurs at the football stadium. Now the national security forces are on the case, and Hill must convince everyone that he knows why these incidents are occurring.

Poisons • Terrorism

Fever of the Bone. Harper, 2010. 9780061986482. (UK: Little, Brown, 2009).

When a teen named Jennifer Maidment is murdered in Worcester, Hill is asked to help. The killer is able to lure his victims to him through social networking, and soon more young people are dead, including one in Bradfield. As Jordan is drawn into the case, Hill realizes he will have to move fast to save lives.

Internet • Social networking • Teenagers at risk • World Wide Web

Reichs, Kathy ✍

Temperance Brennan

Tempe Brennan is the director of forensic anthropology in Quebec, Canada. She moved to Canada from North Carolina when her marriage failed, straining her relationship with her daughter Katy. The man who awaits her in Canada is homicide detective Andrew Ryan, with whom she will develop a relationship. Traveling from one location to another for each case, she is grounded by small things like her dog, Boyd. This series is the basis for the Fox TV series *Bones*. Readers may also enjoy Patricia Cornwell, Margaret Maron, and Val McDermid. **TR** Series subjects: **Canada, Québec, Montréal • Forensics • North Carolina**

Deja Dead. Scribner, 1997. 0684841177.

> As the newly minted province of Quebec forensic anthropologist, Brennan is called to the scene of a murder when a body is found stored in plastic garbage bags. Soon there are more victims, and Brennan is convinced she has a serial killer on her hands. Gaining the ear and admiration of the locals is another thing entirely, and she finds herself investigating as a lone wolf on this case.
>
> *Serial killer*

Death Du Jour. Scribner, 1999. 0684841185.

> When Brennan is asked to examine the exhumed remains of Sister Elisabeth Nicolet, a candidate for sainthood, she does not expect to be unable to locate the nun in her grave. Her second case involves deaths in a burning house, a case she jointly investigates with homicide detective Andrew Ryan. Ties to a strange cult eventually draw Brennan back to North Carolina and then to the ice storms of Montreal.
>
> *Arson • Children in jeopardy • Cults • Nuns • Sainthood • Winter*

Deadly Décisions. Scribner, 2000. 0684859718.

> When the Heathens motorcycle gang goes to war against the Vipers, it leavesa nine-year-old girl is left dead from a bullet wound. The investigation gets personal when Banks appears to be going over to the dark side along with her visiting nephew, Kit. To keep her own safe and to stop the gangs, Brennan digs deep into the gang life and a cold case from North Carolina.
>
> *Drugs • Gangs • Motorcycle gangs*

Fatal Voyage. Scribner, 2001. 0684859726.

> When an airplane goes down in the Smokey Mountains, Brennan is one of the disaster reaction team members who responds to the scene. She fears her own daughter may be among the wreckage. As she probes for a reason for the crash, she must sort out potential bombs, assassination attempts, and a prisoner transportation being done by Ryan's partner. Then she discovers a foot that does not belong to any of the passengers, and her dogged investigation leads to her being removed from the case at the request of the lieutenant governor. This only makes her more curious, and she launches a private investigation in the wilds of the mountains.
>
> *Aircraft accidents • Smokey Mountains*

Grave Secrets. Scribner, 2002. 0684859734.

> Asked to help identify the remains of people who disappeared during the long civil war in Guatemala, Brennan is diverted to examine the remains of a woman found in a septic tank. Is this the work of a serial killer? Could one of the bodies be the long-missing daughter of the Canadian ambassador? As she investigates, she finds herself attracted to Ryan's cop friend, Bartholome Galiano.
>
> *Guatemala, Guatemala City*

1

Bare Bones. Scribner, 2003. 0743233468.

> Brennan's dream vacation at the beach house in North Carolina with Ryan is disrupted when the remains of a baby are discovered in a wood-burning stove, Boyd digs up some remains at a resort, and a small plane crashes, killing two people. Brennan and Ryan toss aside any getaway plans and go to work together, leading to the discovery of the link among all three cases.
>
> *Drugs • Exotic animals • Smugglers • Vacations*

2

Monday Mourning. Scribner, 2004. 0743233476.

> When the bodies of three people are discovered in the basement of a pizza parlor, Brennan is given the job of examining the remains for clues. With her daughter Katy in North Carolina and her boyfriend Ryan distancing himself from her, she is struggling personally to stay positive. When the bodies prove to be teenagers, the police are led to a strong suspect, and Brennan gets back to work.
>
> *Pizza • Restaurants • Serial killer • Teenagers at risk*

3

Cross Bones. Scribner, 2005. 9780743233484.

> When an Orthodox Jew named Avram Ferris is murdered, Brennan is asked to examine the body to determine if it is suicide or murder. When a witness provides a photograph of a grave in Israel taken in 1963, Brennan and Ryan travel to that country to seek more information about this corpse, which may be connected to the battle at Massada. Led by the evidence provided by biblical scholar Jake Drum, they probe into the authenticity of a tomb that may contain the remains of the family of Jesus and find their own lives are threatened.
>
> *Israel • Massada • Religion*

Break No Bones. Scribner, 2006. 9780743233491.

> While instructing at an archaeology dig on South Carolina's Dewees Island, Brennan is stunned to discover a contemporary corpse among the ancient Native American bones she is lecturing on. Asked to stay on to conduct an investigation by her coroner friend Emma Rousseau, she is onsite when more deaths begin to occur. Meanwhile, nearby her ex-husband Pete is working a missing persons case, and the two are forced into proximity.
>
> *Missing persons • Native Americans • Religion • South Carolina, Dewees Island*

Bones to Ashes. Scribner, 2007. 9780743294379.

When Brennan accepts an assignment to help examine the remains of a young girl discovered in Acadia, she is back on her home turf and swamped with memories of her childhood friend Evangeline Landry. Haunted by her friend's disappearance when she was a child, Brennan must struggle with the emotions of dealing with discovering the long-sought-for truth about the disappearance. Meanwhile, Ryan has a series of corpses that may lead to the person responsible for the deaths of all these young people.

Canada, Nova Scotia, Acadia • Friendship • Serial killer

Devil Bones. Scribner, 2008. 9780743294386.

When the skull of a teenage girl is found encased in a voodoo shrine, Brennan is called in to examine the remains for clues. Then a headless boy's body turns up in a river, and the Charlotte community becomes aware that they may have a cult operating in their midst. When a local fundamentalist begins to lead a vigilante crusade to find the guilty parties, it puts Brennan on the hot seat.

Religion • Santeria • Vigilantism • Voodoo

206 Bones. Scribner, 2009. 9780743294393.

The prologue of this book tells us that Temperance is buried alive. The balance of the book is a flashback that explores how she is accused of mishandling the autopsy of Rose Jurmain, an heiress who has been missing from her Montréal home, while on a trip to Chicago with her ex-husband, Andrew Ryan. After she returns to her home, Temperance discovers that other deaths may be involved and that the killer wants her in the mix as well.

Illinois, Chicago

Spider Bones. Scribner, 2010. 9781439102398.

When a corpse found in Quebec is identified as John Lowery, U.S. citizen and Vietnam war casualty buried in North Carolina, it is up to Brennan to explain how a dead man's corpse was found in Canada. Brennan and Ryan journey to Hawaii to get answers from the military but eventually a third body appears. This one also seems to be John Lowery.

Hawai'i • Missing in action • Prisoners of war • Vietnam War, 1961–1975

Lawyer Detectives

Most courtroom thrillers will not qualify to be listed here, as they often have other intentions than to tell a straight mystery. However, sometimes those who work in the legal profession cannot resist the opportunity to leave the courtroom and get out in the streets to hunt for the perpetrators.

The Modern Practitioners

Connelly, Michael

Mickey Haller

Mickey Haller races around Los Angeles from one courtroom to another, balancing the lowball cases he has taken to keep his business going. He manages his time by working out of the backseat of a chauffeured Lincoln Town Car and has earned the nickname The Lincoln Lawyer. With two ex-wives, including D.A. Maggie McPherson, and guilt over his past behavior, he has as much to deal with as the clients he defends. He also happens to be the half-brother of Harry Bosch, Connelly's lone wolf police detective. Readers may also enjoy T. Jefferson Parker and John Sandford. See the author's Web site at http://www.michaelconnelly.com. **HB** Series subjects: **California, Los Angeles • Courtroom drama**

The Lincoln Lawyer. Little, Brown, 2005. 9780316734936.

Mickey Haller is one step above an ambulance chaser, but he thinks he has hit the big time when he lands the defense case for Louis Ross Roulet, a Beverly Hills real estate agent accused of beating a prostitute. Haunted by a previous case that resulted in his client being on death row, dealing with two ex-wives, and trying to make the big payoff keeps Haller on the move and deep in trouble. Then his investigator is killed, and Haller knows he is in over his head.

Assault

The Brass Verdict. Little, Brown, 2008. 9780316166294.

When fellow Hollywood defense attorney Jerry Vincent is murdered, it falls to Haller to defend his client, Walter Elliott, a studio executive, against murder charges. Accused of killing his wife and her lover, Elliott's case was built by Bosch. Haller is frightened when he discovers evidence that may indicate who killed Vincent and who might want to kill him. As Haller and Bosch see the weaknesses in each other's cases, the two must work together to discover the truth.

Brothers • California, Hollywood • Hollywood

The Reversal. Little, Brown, 2010. 9780316069489.

Reversing roles, Haller is hired to retry Jason Jessup, a man who has served twenty-four years in prison for a murder that new DNA evidence shows he did not do. Teamed with his ex-wife, D.A. Maggie McPherson, Haller insists that he will only take the case if Bosch will do the legwork. With the half-brothers feuding, his ex-wife sitting next to him at the prosecutor's table, most of the witnesses dead, and the whole world watching, Haller finds himself under enormous pressure to get this right.

Brothers • DNA • Retrials

Fyfield, Frances (pseud. of Frances Hegarty) ✍

Sarah Fortune

Working for a private firm in London, this lawyer is not your average solicitor. Her personal life is as complicated as her cases, and she is an intriguing character to read about. While trying to balance the important issues in her own personal life, she finds her professional career complicated by convoluted criminal cases that need her to act as a detective. Readers may also enjoy P. D. James (Cordelia Gray), Lia Matera, and Julie Smith. Visit the author's Web site at http://www.francesfyfield.co.uk. **TR** Series subjects: **Law**

> *Shadows on the Mirror.* UK: Heinemann, 1989. (US: Pocket, 1991).
>
> *Perfectly Pure and Good.* UK: Bantam, 1994. (US: Pantheon, 1994).
>
> *Staring at the Light.* UK: Bantam, 2000. (US: Viking, 2000).

Looking Down. UK: Little, Brown, 2004. 9780316861779.

> When Richard Beaumont witnesses a young woman falling to her death off the Cliffs of Dover, he withdraws from his wife and obsessively paints the scene over and over. Seeking a friendly ear for her sorrow, his wife Lilian turns to her downstairs neighbor, Sarah Fortune. When she gets involved with the local medical examiner, she decides to take up Richard's case despite their history as lovers.
>
> *Artists • Cliffs of Dover • Painters*

Safer Than Houses. UK: Little, Brown, 2005. 9780316727648.

> As a reward for her attentions from one of her lovers, Fortune is living in a flat that now is being claimed by the man's son. As he relentlessly pursues her, she meets the mild-mannered Henry, who has nearly the same issue with a different person. They cook up a scheme to switch flats, thinking that will solve everything, until someone turns to arson as the final solution.
>
> *Arson • Tenants*

Iles, Greg ✍

Penn Cage

Penn Cage returns to his hometown of Natchez, Mississippi, after a successful run as a prosecutor in Houston, with a second career as a thriller writer. After taking on the issues of his own family, he settles in to solve the problems of a Southern town, which brews its own crime. **TR HB** Series subjects: **Law • Mississippi, Natchez**

The Quiet Game. Dutton, 1999. 0525937935.

After abandoning his career in Houston, Penn Cage returns to his hometown of Natchez, Mississippi, only to discover that his physician father is being blackmailed. The intrigue revolves around the murder of a black man in 1967 and its infamy as a civil rights crime. Facing challenges from Judge Leo Marston, who had tried to ruin his father's practice with a malpractice suit, Penn receives help from the local publisher, Caitlin Masters. Penn finds himself balanced between seeking the truth and saving his own family from destruction.

    African American • Civil Rights • Trials

Turning Angel. Scribner, 2005. 9780743234719.

When high school senior, seventeen-year-old Kate Townsend, is drowned on a trip with Dr. Drew Elliot, the twenty-three year differences in their ages scandalizes the community when it is revealed they were having an affair. Penn, who is considering a run for the mayor's office, has to decide if defending his lifelong pal is worth throwing away his political ambitions.

    Affairs • Elections

The Devil's Punchbowl. Scribner, 2009. 9781416599265.

Penn Cage is a former prosecuting attorney who has moved home to Natchez, Mississippi, to become its mayor. When the town turns to gambling boats to raise revenue and attract tourists, it seems like a great idea. But there is something wrong with the *Magnolia Queen* and the crowd it attracts from Las Vegas. When Penn loses his old friend Tim Jessup to the new crime wave, he chooses to launch a campaign to free his town from the yoke of crime.

    Casinos • Gambling • Mayors

Martini, Steve ✍

Paul Madriani

Lawyer Madriani stars in a series of novels that may be more psychological thriller than detective fiction. They are included here to show the logical extension of the Perry Mason character into a modern setting. Unlike Mason, who remains static through the series and rarely deals with personal issues, Madriani is a volatile character with many complications in his personal life. His partner in crime is attorney Harry Hinds. Readers may also enjoy Michael Connelly, J. A. Jance (J. P. Beaumont), John Sandford, and William G. Tapply. See the author's Web site at http://www.stevemartini.com. **HB** Series subjects: **California, San Diego • Law**

    Compelling Evidence. Putnam, 1992.

    Prime Witness. Putnam, 1993.

Undue Influence. Putnam, 1994.

The Judge. Putnam, 1996.

The Attorney. Putnam, 2000.

The Jury. Putnam, 2001.

The Arraignment. Putnam, 2002. 0399148787.

When attorney Nick Rush is murdered, Madriani defends the man accused. This lowlife should have been Madriani's client, but Madriani had refused his case. Now the man holds the key to Nick's death. While chasing an insurance claim for Nick's widow, Madriani finds himself on the trail of a valuable ancient Mayan artifact and those who would kill to obtain it.

Antiquities • Mexico, Cancun

Double Tap. Putnam, 2003. 9780399150920.

A double tap is two shots to the head, and that is what kills computer software security programmer Madelyn Chapman. Her program, purchased by the government for an antiterrorism campaign, may have led to her execution by ex-army sniper Emiliano Ruiz. After his original lawyer quits, Madriani takes the case and discovers his client has deep hidden secrets that could affect his defense.

Computers • Military • Terrorism

Shadow of Power. Harper, 2009. 9780061230882.

Madriani and Hinds have taken on the tough job of defending the racist murderer Carl Arnsberg, who has been accused of murdering controversial author Terry Scarborough. Scarborough's book about Thomas Jefferson has proved so disturbing that there have been riots in the streets, but the letter that he threatened to reveal, which has now disappeared, may prove to be even more incendiary. When the elements of the case begin to threaten constitutional law, Madirani finds himself up against the Supreme Court.

Authors • Hate groups • Jefferson , Thomas • Racism • United States, Constitution • United States, Supreme Court

Guardian of Lies. Harper, 2010. 9780061230905.

Katia Solaz has had enough of living with her older husband, Emerson Pike, and she decides to return to her native country of Costa Rica. While journeying home, her husband is eliminated by the Mexicutioner. It falls to Madriani and Hinds to discover why the man was assassinated and to race to protect Katia, whom they believe may still be an intended target.

Assassins • Drugs • Nuclear threats

The Rule of Nine. Morrow, 2010.

As a hangover from the last case, Madriani's vow of silence is hard to keep when Joselyn Cole, a weapons expert, believes a new and equally devastating attack is planned on Washington, D. C. Meanwhile, the Mexicutioner has set Madriani up for a fall, so getting the confidence of anyone is going to be difficult, and the Mexicutioner is working with another mastermind named Thorn to bring about an attack on the United States.

Assassins • Nuclear threats

Tapply, William G. ✍

Brady Coyne

On a normal day, Boston-based lawyer Coyne works with wills and deeds. But his high-powered cases often force him to become a detective, so Coyne often needs to act more like a private investigator than an attorney. His cases can be recommended to any hard-boiled mystery reader. Tapply died in 2009 from leukemia. Readers may also enjoy Jeremiah Healy, Steve Martini, and Robert B. Parker. **HB** Series subjects: **Fishing • Law • Massachusetts, Boston**

> *Death at Charity's Point.* Scribner, 1984.
>
> *The Dutch Blue Error.* Scribner, 1985.
>
> *Follow the Sharks.* Scribner, 1985.
>
> *The Marine Corpse.* Scribner, 1986. (UK: *A Rodent of Doubt.* Collins, 1987).
>
> *Dead Meat.* Scribner, 1987.
>
> *The Vulgar Boatman.* Scribner, 1987.
>
> *A Void in Hearts.* Scribner, 1988.
>
> *Dead Winter.* Delacorte, 1989.
>
> *Client Privilege.* Delacorte, 1990.
>
> *The Spotted Cats.* Delacorte, 1991.
>
> *Tight Lines.* Delacorte, 1992.
>
> *The Snake Eater.* Otto Penzler, 1993.
>
> *The Seventh Enemy.* Otto Penzler, 1995.
>
> *Close to the Bone.* St. Martin's, 1996.

Cutter's Run. St. Martin's, 1998. 0312185618.

> In Maine to visit his girlfriend, Alexandria Shaw, Coyne offers a ride to an African American woman named Charlotte Gillespie. Shortly he hears that someone has poisoned her dog and painted red swastikas on her cabin home. When Charlotte disappears, Coyne must set down his fishing pole and seek the truth behind the hate crimes.
>
> *African American • Hate groups • Maine, Garrison • Racism*
>
> *Muscle Memory.* St. Martin's, 1999.
>
> *Scar Tissue.* St. Martin's Minotaur, 2000.

Past Tense. St. Martin's Minotaur, 2001.

First Light. Scribner, 2002.

A Fine Line. St. Martin's Minotaur, 2002. 0312303521,

When Walt Duffy, a famous nature photographer, is found dead in his garden, his friend and lawyer Coyne believes it may be murder. Duffy had asked Coyne to have authenticated some letters supposedly written by Meriwether Lewis. When Duffy's son Ethan goes missing, some clues point to an environmental group that is using arson as a weapon for their cause.

Arson • Eco-terrorism

Shadow of Death. St. Martin's Minotaur, 2003. 0312303777.

Ellen Stoddard is running for the U.S. Senate from Massachusetts, trying to be the first female elected from the state to this office. However, her husband Albert's odd behavior is threatening her campaign. When investigator Coyne hired is killed, he must seek the truth behind the politician's run for the Senate by hunting for the clues in New Hampshire.

Elections • New Hampshire, Southwick • Politicians

Nervous Water. St. Martin's Minotaur, 2005. 9780312337445.

Coyne hears from his estranged uncle Moze, who has terminal cancer and wishes to be reunited with his long-lost daughter, Cassie. Seeking clues to the disappearance of his cousin, Coyne begins to think that this is more than a missing persons case. How does all this tie to the long-unsolved murder of another of his uncles?

Families

Second Sight. Scribner, 2005. 0743260678.

Coyne is after Christa Doyle, a runaway on the island, while Jackson is chauffeur to Evangeline Fisherman, a musician who has come to the island to prepare for a humanitarian rock concert. When the rock star's bodyguard is murdered, both men find themselves hunting a killer. The clues lead to retreat run by a spiritualist that may be a cult.

Cults • Massachusetts, Martha's Vineyard • Musicians

Out Cold. St. Martin's Minotaur, 2006. 9780312337469.

One cold Boston morning, Coyne discovers the corpse of a teenager in his back yard with only his address in her pocket. Determined to discover her identity, he begins an investigation, with the help of his girlfriend, Evie Banyon. The girl's pregnancy leads the investigation to New Hampshire and a shady genetics lab. But as Coyne pushes forward, others push back, and he finds himself in danger as he seeks the truth.

Genetics • New Hampshire • Teenagers at risk

One-way Ticket. St. Martin's Minotaur, 2007. 9780312358297.

> Dalton Lancaster, a former client of Coyne's, is about to be released from the hospital after a terrible beating. While it is logical that his old gambling debts may be the reason, Lancaster convinces Coyne those days are long gone. When Lancaster's son is kidnapped, it becomes apparent that the sins of the father may be visited on the son.
>
> *Gambling • Kidnapping • Organized crime*

Third Strike. Scribner, 2007. 9781416532569.

> Coyne is on the island to help an old client who may have witnessed a crime. Jackson is asked by the widow to look into the death of a ferry boat worker who died in an explosion on a boat. The worker's death may be directly tied to the bitter strike that is hampering the island. The two friends decide to combine their skills to discover what bad things are going down in this vacation paradise.
>
> *Massachusetts, Martha's Vineyard • Strikes*

Hell Bent. St. Martin's Minotaur, 2008. 9780312358303.

> When his former lover Alexandria Shaw asks Coyne to represent her brother Gus Sinclair in a divorce case. Gus, a famous photojournalist who has had adjustment difficulties since losing his hand in Iraq, commits suicide before the case can be resolved. When Alexandria announces her suspicions about her brother's death, Coyne must resolve his personal issues and dive into a sticky case.
>
> *Iraq War, 2003 • Photojournalism • Post-traumatic stress disorder*

Chapter 3

Private Detectives

Private Investigators

The origins of private detectives as characters can be traced to the development of the Pinkerton Agency and its famous motto, "We never sleep." From the emblem of the omnipresent and constantly alert human eye comes the logical abbreviation of private investigator (P.I.) to private eye.

Ignoring some early forerunners, including Sherlock Holmes, it could be said that the fictional private detective as we know it developed within the pages of the very popular and proletarian pulp magazines of the 1920s. A story by John Carroll Daly in the December 1922 issue of *Black Mask* magazine, "The False Burton Combs," is considered the first private eye short story. In the June 1, 1923, issue of *Black Mask* magazine, a story by Daly, the "Knights of the Open Palm," introduced the private detective Race Williams. Following in the footsteps of Daly, and under the leadership of the magazine's editor, Joseph T. "Cap" Shaw, many authors began to develop similar characters. Other authors offered stories to such pulps as *Dime Detective, Thrilling Detective Stories, Detective Fiction Weekly,* and *Action Detective.*

Although Daly's short stories were the most popular features in *Black Mask,* as a novelist he was less successful than another *Black Mask* contributor, Dashiell Hammett, who used his own experiences as a Pinkerton agent to create a series of novels from his *Black Mask* works. These novels featured a nameless detective, remembered as The Continental Op. But Hammett's crowning achievement was *The Maltese Falcon,* in which he created the archetypical private detective, Sam Spade.

Following the same pattern and cobbling together his own short stories as well, Raymond Chandler moved from the pages of *Black Mask* into novel format with his private detective, Phillip Marlowe. Hammett and Chandler popularized the private detective in novel format, legitimized it as a literary form, and raised the playing field for other practitioners.

After the Second World War, the popularity of the paperback format proved to be a springboard for the career of Mickey Spillane. His Mike Hammer novels galvanized the field with their surprising popularity, but proved to be less of a literary achievement than those of his predecessors. Almost a throwback to the days of the pulps, his character's excessive violence, mistreatment of women, and promotion of political points of view that are now unpopular make his works challenging to read today.

When Ross Macdonald's Lew Archer novels appeared on the best-seller lists in the late 1960s and early 1970s, they pushed Spillane's pulpy style of writing out of the way to make room for a more soft-boiled private detective and plots based on the psychology of the crime rather than the physiology of the detective. Macdonald's painfully developed family tragedies proved that there was more to private eye writing than just plot-driven violence. When Macdonald passed the torch, it was to writers like Robert B. Parker, who studied Hammett and Chandler and used the lessons learned to develop a contemporary private detective with modern sensibilities accompanied by the ability to stand tall in a fight.

In 1972, P. D. James wrote *An Unsuitable Job for a Woman*, featuring one of the first modern female private detectives. Although female detectives had been around as long as male ones, they often were cast in the mold of the effervescent Honey West, an oversexed woman whose sole purpose seemed to be taking off her clothes at some point during her case. James's detective was a capable woman challenged to run an inquiry agency when it fell into her lap. In 1974 Maxine O'Callaghan's Deliah West appeared in a short story in *Alfred Hitchcock's Mystery Magazine*. In 1977 Marcia Muller created Sharon McCone, an American woman P.I. with a social conscience, but her work received little recognition upon publication. These two groundbreaking efforts bore full fruit in 1982, when Muller's second McCone adventure was published, as well as Sue Grafton's *A Is for Alibi* and Sara Paretsky's *Indemnity Only*. Whether in response to the increased awareness of women's roles in the mystery field or serving as a catalyst for the advent of the woman character and writer, these female private detectives led a revolution that transformed the private detective novel and the rest of the mystery field.

Another development that transformed the private detective novel took place at roughly the same time. When Michael Z. Lewin was able to have his private detective set up shop in Indianapolis, it helped break the New York–Southern California regional grip on the fictional private detective.

In today's market, we have male and female private detectives in equal numbers, private detectives setting up shop in every region of the world, and novels whose first release is in paperback format. Riding the most popular mystery fiction trend of the 1990s, the historical, we even have private detectives like Nate Heller, by Max Allan Collins, or Roman detectives, created by Lindsay Davis and Stephen Saylor.

Repeatedly declared a dead art form, the private detective novel has proved to be quite resilient. Its continuing popularity may be traced to its most basic component, the required feisty independence of the investigator. The vast majority of private detectives are "lone wolf" detectives, working without the support that backs up a police detective. Fiercely loyal to their clients, private detectives risk all even if the client proves unfaithful. Private detectives usually find themselves fighting corruption in society as well as trying to solve murders. Similar to the amateur, the private detective does what many readers wish they could do: confront authority, triumph over impossible odds, and right the wrongs of society. Since the mid-1970s the private detective has afforded the modern reader all the same advantages that most of mystery fiction enjoys: diversity of characters, regionalism, and contemporary themes.

The Modern Practitioners

Barnes, Linda ✍

Carlotta Carlyle

Tall, red-haired, and driving a cab, this Boston P.I. works in a contemporary American society that allows her to stretch her wings as an investigator. Her ward, Paoline, adds complications to her life, as does the occasional man who wanders into her world. Readers may also enjoy Sue Grafton, Jeremiah Healy, Sara Paretsky, and Robert B. Parker. See the author's Web site at http://www. lindabarnes.com. **TR** Series subjects: **Massachusetts, Boston**

> *A Trouble of Fools.* St. Martin's, 1987.
>
> *The Snake Tattoo.* St. Martin's, 1989.
>
> *Coyote.* Delacorte, 1990.
>
> *Steel Guitar.* Delacorte, 1991.
>
> *Snapshot.* Delacorte, 1993.
>
> *Hardware.* Delacorte, 1995.
>
> *Cold Case.* Delacorte, 1997.
>
> *Flashpoint.* Hyperion, 1999.

The Big Dig. St. Martin's Minotaur, 2001. 0312282702.
> All of Boston is disrupted by The Big Dig, an enormous underground highway project, and Carlyle has signed on as an operative for Foundation Security to work undercover searching for on-site corruption at the Horgan Construction site. By night she is working a missing persons case brought to her private eye firm by the very rich Dana Endicott, who has lost her friend, Veronica James.
>
> *Construction*

Deep Pockets. St. Martin's Minotaur, 2004. 0312282710.

When an African American Harvard professor named Wilson Chaney is blackmailed over his affair with a student, Denali Brinkman, he hires Carlyle to stop the threat. Denali was a lonely Native American student, finding solace as a single sculler and eventually illegally moving into the boathouse to avoid her dorm mates. What shocks Carlyle is that Denali committed suicide by immolation, taking the boathouse with her. So the big question is, who knew about the affair and how did they get Chaney's incriminating letters?

Academia • Affairs • African American • Extortion • Rowing • Suicide

Heart of the World. St. Martin's Minotaur, 2006. 9780312333877.

Paolina Fuentes is now fifteen, and she longs to fit in, be cool, and find love. When she is contacted by someone representing her Colombian drug-lord father Roldan, she jumps at the chance to finally gain his love and attention. When Paolina disappears, big sister Carlyle begins a desperate hunt that takes her from Cambridge to Miami to Colombia.

Children in jeopardy • Fathers and daughters

Lie Down with the Devil. St. Martin's Minotaur, 2008. 9780312333891.

When her mobbed-up boyfriend Sam Gianelli has to go on the lam to avoid a murder charge, Carlyle is at loose ends. A woman named Jessica Franklin approaches Carlyle with evidence questioning Sam's loyalty to her, then is killed in a hit-and-run. Distracted on Cape Cod by a fidelity case that teams her with her old boss, Joseph Mooney, Carlyle is juggling many things when the evidence begins to indicate that Sam may be guilty as charged.

Massachusetts, Cape Cod

Barre, Richard ✍

Wil Hardesty

If Raymond Chandler defined California as one of the premier regions for the private eye, contemporary authors like Barre extend that definition into a new generation. Hardesty is a Vietnam vet who has turned to private investigating. Hardesty's joy in surfing has been spoiled by the death of his young son in a surfing accident, an accident that may have been his fault. Readers may also enjoy Robert Crais and Michael Connelly. **TR HB**

The Innocents. Walker, 1995.

Bearing Secrets. Walker, 1996.

The Ghosts of Morning. Berkley, 1998.

Blackheart Highway. Berkley, 1999.

The Burning Moon. Capra Press, 2003. 1592660118.

> Vinh Tien is on the *Bui Doi*, or *Dust of Life*, having escaped from Vietnam with his family to establish a new life in America. But his children remain aloof from his strict ways, and older son Jimmy has been on the streets for three years, following the lead of Vinh's gangster brother, Luc Tuan Tien. When Jimmy steals one of Vinh's fishing boats and disappears with his pregnant wife Wen, Vinh hires Hardesty to find out how their boat ended up sunk in the waters off San Miguel Island. Hardesty discovers the Treasury Department's ATF agents are also interested in this case, because Jimmy was an informant in a plan to bring down Luc.

> *Fathers and sons • Organized crime • Vietnamese War, 1961–1975*

Beaton, M. C. (pseud. of Marion Chesney) ✍

Agatha Raisin

British novelist Beaton retires her businesswoman detective Raisin to the Cotswolds, where dead bodies are never in short supply. Being a Londoner initially sets Agatha outside the society she wishes to enter, but her acumen as a detective earns her grudging respect. Written in a cozy style, these novels use humor as well as the traditional plots and have a touch of romance between Agatha and her neighbor, James Lacey. By book 14, Agatha Raisin has opened a private detective agency, with the expected success, and has a young protégée named Toni Gilmour. Readers who enjoy Beaton's work may also enjoy Donna Andrews, Agatha Christie (Jane Marple), Diane Mott Davidson, Carolyn G. Hart (Annie Darling), Joan Hess (Claire Malloy), Katherine Hall Page, or Valerie Wolzien. See a Web site about this author at http://www.booksnbytes.com/authors/beaton_mc.html. **SB**
Series subjects: **England, Cotswold, Carsely • Humor**

> *Agatha Raisin and the Quiche of Death.* St. Martin's, 1992.

> *Agatha Raisin and the Vicious Vet.* St. Martin's, 1993.

> *Agatha Raisin and the Potted Gardener.* St. Martin's, 1994.

> *Agatha Raisin and the Walkers of Dembley.* St. Martin's, 1995.

> *Agatha Raisin and the Murderous Marriage.* St. Martin's Press, 1996.

> *Agatha Raisin and the Terrible Tourist.* St. Martin's Press, 1997.

> *Agatha Raisin and the Wellspring of Death.* St. Martin's Press, 1998.

> *Agatha Raisin and the Witch of Wyckhadden.* St. Martin's Minotaur, 1999.

> *Agatha Raisin and the Wizard of Evesham.* St. Martin's Press, 1999.

> *Agatha Raisin and the Fairies of Fryfam.* St. Martins Minotaur, 2000.

> *Agatha Raisin and the Love from Hell.* St. Martin's Minotaur, 2001.

Agatha Raisin and the Day the Floods Came. St. Martin's Minotaur, 2002. 0312207670.

Without her former love James Lacey, now in a monastery in France, Raisin heads off to the South Pacific for some rest and relaxation. When a bride drowns on her honeymoon and another woman appears to have committed suicide in a Costwold river while wearing a wedding dress, the detective in Agatha is awakened, especially if it allows her to be teamed up with her handsome, mystery-writing neighbor, John Armitage.

Brides • South Pacific • Suicide

Agatha Raisin and the Case of the Curious Curate. St. Martin's Minotaur, 2003. 0312207689.

Tristan Delon has come to Carsely as the new curate. The women of the village find themselves drawn to the handsome man, and the local vicar is jealous of his new competition. When Delon is stabbed to death in the vicar's study, Raisin, suffering from problems in her own love life, who decides to find the murderer.

Religion

Agatha Raisin and the Haunted House. St. Martin's Minotaur, 2003. 0312207697.

Mrs. Witherspoon is a crabby old woman living in a haunted house called Ivy Cottage. Raisin's handsome new neighbor, Paul Chatterton, is eager for the detective to discover the truth, and both of them are challenged when Mrs. Witherspoon is murdered.

England, Cotswold, Hebberdon • Ghosts

The Deadly Dance. St. Martin's Minotaur, 2004. 0312304366.

Raisin Investigations is opened by the forceful and former amateur detective Agatha Raisin, who is thinking that the Cotswolds will provide a bevy of clients. Indeed it does, but missing cats are a priority. It is not until the wealthy divorcee Catherine Laggat-Brown arrives bearing a death threat aimed at her twenty-one-year-old daughter Cassandra that Raisin finds a case worthy of her talents.

The Perfect Paragon. St. Martin's Minotaur, 2005. 9780312304485.

Robert Smedley hires Raisin to determine if his wife is cheating on him. Desperate for a client, she accepts the case, but she is soon distracted by the corpse of a teenage girl. Then Smedley is murdered with weed killer, and Raisin finds herself hired by the grieving widow, whom she had been following. With Sir Charles Fraith's help, Raisin boldly moves forward in the search for both victims' killer.

Love, Lies and Liquor. St. Martin's Minotaur, 2006. 9780892960255.

Raisin cannot keep away from her ex-husband James Lacey, so when she receives his invitation to go on holiday to the seaside town of Snoth-on-Sea, she goes. Imagine her discomfort when a guest in the hotel, Geraldine Jankers, with whom she has argued, is found strangled with Raisin's scarf. But shortly two more victims are discovered, and Raisin must use all of her new P.I. skills to rise to her own defense.

England, Sussex, Snoth-on-Sea • Resorts

Kissing Christmas Goodbye. St. Martin's Minotaur, 2007. 9780312349110.

A wealthy widow, Phyllis Tamworthy, hires Raisin to prevent her from being poisoned during the holidays. Too late. And speaking of the holidays, Raisin decides to invite her old boyfriend, James Lacey, to the Cotwolds. Distracted by her plans, Raisin puts her new teenage trainee Toni Gilmour to work on the missing pet cases in which her agency still specializes.

Christmas • Holidays • Poisons • Teens • Widows

A Spoonful of Poison. St. Martin's Minotaur, 2008. 9780312349127.

Returning to the public relations business, Raisin is asked to help promote a church charity event. When an elderly woman takes a dive off the St. Odo the Severe tower and plunges to her death, Raisin returns to the role of detective. LSD is the root cause, and it becomes the job of Raisin and her attractive employee Toni Gilmour to pick from the six jam providers to find which one has been spicing her recipe. Meanwhile, someone has made off with the profits from the celebration, and a suicide decreases the number of suspects.

England, Cotswold, Comfrey Magna • LSD • Poisons • Suicide

There Goes the Bride. Minotaur, 2009. 9780312387006.

When James Lacey's bride-to-be Felicity is shot to death just before her wedding, the suspicion falls on none other than Agatha Raisin. Believing her innocent, the bride's mother hires Agatha's firm, so she and sidekick Toni Gilmour launch an investigation.

England, Cotswold, Hewes • Weddings

Busy Body. Minotaur, 2010. 9780312387013.

When John Sunday, of the Health and Safety Board, decides this year's village Christmas tree is unsafe to install on is church tower pedestal, he earns the scorn of the town and is murdered. When the prime suspect hires Raisin and Toni to clear her name, the two leap into a festival holiday stew of suspects.

Christmas • Holidays

Black, Cara ✍

Aimée Leduc

Aimée Leduc is the daughter of a private investigator who tracked the lost souls of the World War II European theater until he was killed by a terrorist bomb. His death left his agency to his daughter, who chose to move into the arena of corporate computer security. Her mother disappeared when Aimée was eight years old, and she is still haunted by that loss. Her agency specializes in computer security, and she partners with computer expert René Friant. These novels can be recommended to any traditional mystery reader. Readers may

also enjoy Sue Grafton, Sara Paretsky, and any other of the many international writers published by Soho. See a Web site about this author at http://www.carablack.com. **TR**
Series subjects: **Computer security** • **France, Paris** • **Mothers and daughters**

Murder in the Marais. Soho, 1998. 1569471592.

> When Nazi hunter Soli Hecht reminds Leduc of her father's legacy, Leduc agrees to do a computer job that leads to her placing one-half of an old photograph in the hands of an old woman who is dead with a swastika carved into her forehead. Leduc's third-person narration is mixed with the story of Hartmuth Griffe, an old Gestapo officer now disguised as a trade minister for the new united Germany, who in reality is the puppet of the neo-Nazi group The Werewolves.
>
> *Holocaust* • *Nazis*

Murder in Belleville. Soho, 2000. 1569472114.

> Leduc is asked to meet with her friend Anais's sister, whose husband Philippe, a defense minister, may be having an affair. When Leduc arrives for the meeting, she sees a car bomb kill the alleged mistress, a woman who was leading a double life. As she probes into this mystery, she uncovers some international intrigue in the Belleville district that may involve Islamic fundamentalists.
>
> *Affairs* • *Islamic fundamentalism* • *Terrorism*

Murder in the Sentier. Soho, 2002. 1569472785.

> Having yearned for years for information about her mother, Leduc is ready to believe a recently released radical named Jutta Hald, who claims to have known her mother in prison. The story reveals that a gang of radicals ripped off some art in the 1960s, and now someone is killing the gang members in search of the hidden loot. While Leduc is scrambling to help these former radicals, she is also desperate to find out how her mother fits into this story.
>
> *Art* • *Gangs* • *Radicals*

Murder in the Bastille. Soho, 2003. 1569473641.

> Being a good Samaritan by trying to return a cell phone to a woman dining in the same restaurant wearing the same outfit, Leduc is attacked and left blinded by her injuries. When the other woman is found murdered, Leduc decides to probe into the case after the police dismiss it as the work of a serial killer. Dependent on her partner René to act as her eyes, she discovers that her other senses are up to the task.
>
> *Blindness*

Murder in Clichy. Soho, 2005. 1569473838.

> Having taken up meditation at the Cao Dai temple in Paris, Leduc agrees to exchange an envelope for a package for her trainer, the Vietnamese nun Linh. When the exchange leads to the death of Thadee Baret, Leduc is left holding the money and the ancient jade that was part of the exchange. When Linh and Ren

disappear, Leduc is on her own to find out who was involved and extricate herself from the middle of these violent forces.

Indochinese War, 1946–1954 • *Jade* • *Jewels*

Murder in Montmartre. Soho, 2006. 9781569474105.

When Leduc's childhood cop friend Laure Rousseau is accused of the murder of her partner Jacques, Leduc jumps to her defense. Her investigation takes her into a wornout working class neighborhood for witnesses and up against all the police forces who are working to convict a cop killer.

False accusations • *Separatists*

Murder on the Ile Saint-Louis. Soho, 2007. 9781569474440.

When a mysterious phone call leads Leduc to an abandoned baby, she finds herself a caregiver while trying to solve the mystery. Could the caller have been the body found floating in the Seine that night? Her investigation leads her to some environmentalists, whose protests are disrupted by violence.

Babies • *Environment*

Murder in the Rue de Paradis. Soho, 2008. 9781569474747.

A marriage proposal from Yves Robert surprises Leduc, but not more than the call a short time after that, which takes her to the morgue to identify. The only clue she has is that the murderer was wearing a chador. As she probes into his last assignment as a journalist, she uncovers a war being waged around the world that leads back to an ancient conflict.

Journalists • *Kurds* • *Turkish militants*

Murder in the Latin Quarter. Soho, 2009. 9781569475416.

Leduc is shocked when an illegal Haitian immigrant named Mireille tells her that they are sisters. Could her long-dead father have had an affair that produced an offspring? When Mireille disappears, Leduc sets out to discover the truth about her family. What she discovers is that the current state of Haitian affairs in France is a violent world of intrigue.

Affairs • *Fathers and daughters* • *Haiti* • *Sisters* • *Water rights*

Murder in the Palais Royal. Soho, 2010. 9781569476208.

First René is shot, and Leduc is devastated. Then mysterious money shows up in their accounts, and the government is taking an interest in their business affairs. Finally Leduc realizes she is being set up as the fall guy for René's shooting.

False accusations • *Neo-Nazis*

Bruen, Ken

Jack Taylor

Ex-Garda Jack Taylor, an unofficial investigator, or finder of things, is one of the most damaged characters in all of mystery and crime fiction. While his cases occasionally make him rise to a standard nearing normality for most, it is almost a guarantee that the pressures of his investigations will make him abandon any pledges of sobriety that he makes. The real power of this series is Bruen's writing style, which combines a poetic and musical-flavored, dialogue-driven narrative with some of the most hard-boiled writing that readers can find. These novels can be recommended to any hard-boiled mystery reader. Readers may also enjoy James Lee Burke, James M. Cain, James Crumley, or Patricia Highsmith. See a Web site about this author at http://www.kenbruen.com. **HB** Series subjects: **Alcoholism • Drugs • Ireland, Galway**

 The Guards. St. Martin's Minotaur, 2003. 0312303556. (Ireland: Brandon, 2001).

Ann Henderson thought her sixteen-year-old daughter Sarah had committed suicide, until a man called and said, "She was drowned." So Ann hires Taylor, and a melancholy singer named Catherine B. gives Taylor the clue he needs to look at Bartholomew Planter, a rich man with an interest in young women. When Taylor invites Sutton along for part of the investigation, it leads to the accidental death of a pedophile connected to Planter, which leaves Sutton happy and Taylor on a bender.

SH

Children in jeopardy • Pedophilia

The Killing of the Tinkers. St. Martin's Minotaur, 2004. 0312304110. (Ireland: Brandon, 2002).

A Tinker named Sweeper asks Taylor to investigate the death of four of his brother tinkers. With the help of a cop pal from London named Keegan, Taylor decides to take pity on someone he sees as a reflection of himself and hunt for the killer. The problem is that Taylor cannot be released from his own demons long enough to concentrate on the case.

Gypsies • Tinkers

The Magdalen Martyrs. St. Martin's Minotaur, 2005. 9780312353513. (Ireland: Brandon, 2003).

Bill Cassell, Galway's chief mobster, has called in the favor owed to him by Taylor. Bill's request is that Taylor find Rita Monroe, a now elderly woman who years ago saved Bill's mum from the tortures of the Catholic nuns at Magdalen. The narrative swings between the violence imposed on the young women by the nuns and the abuse that Taylor puts his own body through every day in his personal struggles.

Catholicism • Nuns • Organized crime

🏅 **The Dramatist.** St. Martin's Minotaur, 2006. 9780312316471. (Ireland: Brandon, 2004).

Taylor is clean for once, but that may be only because his dealer is in jail. When called to the Mountjoy Prison for an interview with him, Taylor accepts the job of looking into the death of the dealer's sister. As he launches a reluctant investigation, he crosses paths with Ann Henderson and the man who abuses her. If he can focus long enough, he might be able to tie his case to another where a playwright's works may be a clue to the killer's identity.

🔘

Ireland, Dublin • Prisoners

Priest. St. Martin's Minotaur, 2007. 9780312341404. (UK: Bantam, 2006).

Father Joyce has been decapitated in the confessional of his church as a consequence of his pedophilia. Other priests are nervous, and for whatever reason, they turn to Taylor, recently released from the psychiatric ward. While Taylor still suffers painful guilt over the death of a child, he agrees to pursue the priest killer and stop more killings from happening.

Children in jeopardy • Decapitations • Guilt • Pedophilia • Priests • Religion

Cross. St. Martin's Minotaur, 2007. 9780312341428. (UK: Bantam, 2007).

With his surrogate son Cody lying in a hospital, the victim of a gunshot meant for Taylor, our hero is left out on the street with a big case of the guilts. Ridge, his old partner on the Garda, needs his help when a young boy is crucified. Taylor stumbles through the case, and soon the boy's sister is also murdered. Now Taylor must pull himself together in order to stop the carnage.

Crucifixions • Teenagers at risk

Sanctuary. St. Martin's Minotaur, 2009. 9780312384418. (Ireland: Transworld Ireland, 2008).

Jack Taylor returns to Galway when his old police partner Ridge is dying of cancer. When the serial killer Benedictus sends him a list of victims, he is stirred out of his post-alcohol haze to take action. When no one else seems convinced that a serial killer is in action, it falls to Taylor to confront the ultimate evil.

Serial killer

The Devil. St. Martin's Minotaur, 2010. 9780312646967. (Ireland: Transworld Ireland, 2010).

Taylor makes it all the way to the airport in an attempt to leave Ireland, only to be denied entry to the United States. When he turns back to Galway and the airport bar, he meets the mysterious Kurt, who seems to know a great deal about Taylor's life. Days later, when he is asked to investigate a student's murder, the name "Mr. K" arises. How does this all connect, and will Taylor be able to stay sober enough to deal with it all? Has Taylor finally met the Devil himself?

Confessions • Devil

Crais, Robert ✍

Elvis Cole/Joe Pike

Beginning his life as a spirited wisecracker, Cole matures into a modern knight who is not shy about using force to right wrongs. Pairing Cole with a tough sidekick named Joe Pike, Crais continues to explore the American landscape, using Southern California in a similar fashion to Raymond Chandler. Cole's life is complicated by his relationship with Lucy Chenier, whose son Ben adds something missing to Elvis's outlook. Joe Pike becomes the lead character in some of the later novels. These novels can be recommended to any hard-boiled mystery reader. Readers may also enjoy Richard Barre, Dennis Lehane, and Harlan Coben. See the author's Web site at http://www.robertcrais.com. **HB** Series subjects: **California, Los Angeles**

> *The Monkey's Raincoat*. Bantam, 1987.
>
> *Stalking the Angel*. Bantam, 1989.
>
> *Lullaby Town*. Bantam, 1992.
>
> *Free Fall*. Bantam, 1993.
>
> *Voodoo River*. Hyperion, 1995.
>
> *Sunset Express*. Hyperion, 1996.
>
> *Indigo Slam*. Hyperion, 1997.
>
> *L.A. Requiem*. Doubleday, 1999.

The Last Detective. Doubleday, 2003. 0385504268.

> Lucy suffers the ultimate parental nightmare when she leaves her ten-year-old son Ben in Elvis's care and the boy disappears. Cole and Pike search desperately for the boy with the help of LAPD Detective Carol Starkey, while fending off interference from Lucy's ex-husband, Richard Chenier. As the search gets more and more frenetic, it appears that a secret from Cole's past may be the key to finding the boy.
>
> *Children in jeopardy • Missing persons*

Forgotten Man. Doubleday, 2005. 0385504284.

> Cole is woken up in the middle of the night by a phone call from the police telling him his father has been found dying in an alley. With Pike and Starkey's help, Cole decides to backtrack his father's life and discovers that there was a good

reason he stayed away all these years. Now Cole may be in the sights of a vengeful killer looking to close the books on his family.

Fathers and sons

The Watchman. Simon & Schuster, 2007. 9780743281638.

Larkin Conner Barkley is living the out of control L.A. life of the rich and famous when one night her car plows into another one. That coincidence marks her as the only witness in a secret federal investigation, and now she is a target. When the Feds cannot protect her, her family hires Joe Pike and his former training officer, Bud Flynn, to protect the unwilling Barkley. It is up to Pike to use all of his senses to take out the bad guys before they take out Larkin.

Automobile accidents • Bodyguards • Witnesses

Chasing Darkness. Simon & Schuster, 2008. 9780743281645.

Three years prior to the opening of this case, Cole had provided the evidence to free Lionel Byrd from a charge of murder. Now he has been found dead, apparently a suicide, with photos of seven women at the time of their deaths. As the community turns on Cole for freeing a killer, he and Pike go back to work to try to prove that the original evidence was correct.

Evidence • Guilt • Serial killer • Suicide

The First Rule. Putnam, 2010. 9780399156137.

Pike's acquaintance Frank Meyer and Frank's entire family are slaughtered one day in what looks like a well-planned military operation. While all point to Frank's background as the cause, Pike is not so sure and begins to explore the murders from a different angle: the Meyer's Serbian maid and her missing nephew.

Organized crime • Revenge • Serbia

Crumley, James ✐

Milo Milodragovitch/C. W. Sughrue

Lost in the worst sensibilities of the 1970s, both of Crumley's P.I.s struggle with a world full of alcohol, drugs, and violence. Crumley follows in the literary tradition of Hammett, Chandler, and Macdonald, but adds a sense of weariness and hopelessness to the private eye legends. Crumley passed away in 2008. Readers may also enjoy Lawrence Block (Matthew Scudder), Ken Bruen, and James Lee Burke. **HB** Series subjects: **The West**

The Wrong Case. Random House, 1975.

The Last Good Kiss. Random House, 1978.

Dancing Bear. Random House, 1983.

The Mexican Tree Duck. Mysterious Press, 1993.

Bordersnakes. Mysterious Press, 1996.

The Final Country. Mysterious Press, 2001.

The Right Madness. Viking Penguin, 2005. 9780670034062.

> First Sughrue's psychiatrist friend Dr. William MacKinderick comes to him with a story about someone stealing his files, which contain private information about MacKinderick's clients. Then MacKinderick's clients start to die. Now Sughrue has to hit the road to try to figure out who has a reason to attack a random group of people who needed care.
>
> *Montana, Missoula* • *Psychiatrists*

Davis, Lindsey ✍

Marcus Didius Falco

The closest thing ancient Rome has to a P.I. is private informer Marcus Didius Falco. Using the voice of a contemporary P.I. and humor, Falco takes the reader into the back streets of Rome and on grand adventures in the Empire. Eventually the detective matures into a husband and father, but these duties do not deter him from being a seeker of truth. Readers should be aware that this series mixes humor with the historical. Readers may also enjoy Steven Saylor. See the author's Web site at http://www.lindseydavis.co.uk. **SB TR Historical.** Series subjects: **Historical (0000–1000)** • **Humor** • **Italy, Rome (Ancient)**

> *The Silver Pigs.* UK: Sidgwick, 1989. (US: Crown, 1989).
>
> *Shadows in Bronze.* UK: Sidgwick, 1990. (US: Crown, 1991).
>
> *Venus in Copper.* UK: Hutchinson, 1991. (US: Crown, 1991).
>
> *The Iron Hand of Mars.* UK: Hutchinson, 1992. (US: Crown, 1992).
>
> *Poseidon's Gold.* UK: Hutchinson, 1993. (US: Crown, 1994).
>
> *Last Act in Palmyra.* UK: Century, 1994. (US: Mysterious, 1996).
>
> *Time to Depart.* UK: Century, 1995. (US: Mysterious, 1997).
>
> *A Dying Light in Corduba.* UK: Century, 1996. (US: Mysterious, 1998).
>
> *Three Hands in the Fountain.* UK: Century, 1997. (US: Mysterious, 1999).
>
> *Two For the Lions.* UK: Century, 1998. (US: Mysterious, 1999).
>
> *One Virgin Too Many.* UK: Century, 1999. (US: Mysterious, 2000).
>
> *Ode to a Banker.* UK: Century, 2000. (US: Mysterious, 2001).
>
> *The Body in the Bath House.* UK: Century, 2001. (US: Mysterious, 2002).

The Jupiter Myth. Mysterious, 2002. 0892967773. (UK: Century, 2002).

> Falco is visiting Londinium when he is called by Helena's uncle to investigate a body found stuffed head first into the well of a bar. When the victim turns out to be Verovolcus, a disgraced member of the court of King Togidubnus, it becomes

imperative that the detective figure out who killed him before things turn politically ugly.

England (Ancient), Britannia, Londinium • *Families*

1

The Accusers. Mysterious, 2004. 0892968117. (UK: Century, 2003).

Falco agrees to investigate the life of Roman senator Rubirius Metellus, who supposedly committed suicide when publicly exposed as being corrupt, partially based on evidence Falco gathered. He finds himself caught between two warring lawyers. At stake is the fortune of the Metellus family, and Falco finds plenty of intrigue among the relatives eager to first save and then divide the spoils.

Families • *Inheritance* • *Lawyers* • *Suicide*

2

Scandal Takes a Holiday. Mysterious, 2004. 0892968125. (UK: Century, 2004).

When the famous *Roman Daily Gazette* gossip columnist Infamia disappears, the case falls to Falco. Off to the port city of Ostia, he finds himself up against pirates who are holding members of families for ransom.

Gossip columnists • *Italy, Rome (Ancient), Ostia* • *Pirates*

See Delphi and Die. St. Martin's Minotaur, 2006. 9780312357658. (UK: Century, 2005).

Falco and Helena go undercover with a travel group to try to discover who is responsible for deaths amongst tourists traveling with Seven Sights Tours. Their destination is Olympia in Greece. With hisFalco's own brother-in-law on the hot seat as an employee of the business, he and Helena find themselves acting more like detectives and less like tourists among athletes preparing for the competition.

Greece, Olympia • *Olympics*

3

Saturnalia. St. Martin's Minotaur, 2007. 9780312361297. (UK: Century, 2007).

When his old nemesis Veleda, the German revolutionary, has escaped house arrest, and Sextus Gratianus Scaeva is murdered, Falco is set on her trail. To add to his woes, his own brother-in-law is missing, and he finds himself working again with the empire's chief spy, Anacrites. Meanwhile, the city is preparing for the annual bacchanal, called Saturnalia, which will not help Falco investigate matters at all.

Holidays • *Saturnalia*

Alexandria. St. Martin's Minotaur, 2009. 9780312379018. (UK: Century, 2009).

While on vacation in Alexandria in AD 77, Marcus Didius Falco has dinner with the director, Theon, the director of the famous Alexandrian library. When the librarian is found dead in a locked-room situation, Falco is asked to help solve the mystery. When other deaths occur, Falco realizes that the succession to the directorship of the library may be a greater issue then he first thought.

Egypt, Alexandria • *Libraries*

Nemesis. US: Minotaur, 2010. 9780312595425. (UK: Century, 2010).

> Falco is mourning two deaths. As he settles the estate of his father, he is forced to investigate the disappearance of two business acquaintances of the freedman Claudii. The art dealer Modestus and his wife are missing, and Falco and Pertonius must try to outsmart Anacrite's troops and get to the facts first.
>
> *Death • Fathers and sons • Missing persons*

Estleman, Loren D. ✍

Amos Walker

An anachronism, Amos Walker is the best modern representative of the great P.I.s who have come before. Estleman's skill as a writer and his respect for the genre allow him to use all the conventions of the private eye to his advantage. Walker's stomping grounds are Detroit, a city that goes through many changes during the run of this series. A reader with a sense of the history of the private investigator will love this series. Readers may also enjoy Robert B. Parker and Bill Pronzini. See the author's Web site at http://www.lorenestleman.com. **TR HB** Series subjects: **Michigan, Detroit**

> *Motor City Blue*. Houghton Mifflin, 1980.
>
> *Angel Eyes*. Houghton Mifflin, 1981.
>
> *The Midnight Man*. Houghton Mifflin, 1982.
>
> *The Glass Highway*. Houghton Mifflin, 1983.
>
> *Sugartown*. Houghton Mifflin, 1985.
>
> *Every Brilliant Eye*. Houghton Mifflin, 1986.
>
> *Lady Yesterday*. Houghton Mifflin, 1987.
>
> *Downriver*. Houghton Mifflin, 1988.
>
> *General Murders*. Houghton Mifflin, 1988.
>
> *Silent Thunder*. Houghton Mifflin, 1989.
>
> *Sweet Women Lie*. Houghton Mifflin, 1990.
>
> *Never Street*. Mysterious Press, 1997.
>
> *The Witchfinder*. Mysterious Press, 1998.
>
> *The Hours of the Virgin*. Mysterious Press, 1999.
>
> *A Smile on the Face of the Tiger*. Mysterious, 2000.
>
> *Sinister Heights*. Mysterious Press, 2002.

Poison Blonde. Forge, 2003. 0765304473.

> Pop star Gilia Cristobal is being blackmailed because she is in this country illegally, hiding from a murder charge in her native land, of which she is innocent.

She hires Walker to find out why her blackmailer has missed picking up the last three payments. What Walker discovers indicates that the threat of blackmail may go away, only to be replaced by something more dangerous: murder.

Blackmail • Illegal immigrants • Music

Retro. Forge, 2004. 0765304481.

When a madam named Beryl Garnet asks Walker to deliver her ashes to her son Delwayne after she dies, he does not realize the trouble he will be in. Finding the son, who has been living in Canada since he avoided the Vietnam War draft, Walker ends up suspect number one when Delwayne is killed. As he scrambles to save his own skin, he uncovers the murder of the son's father, a boxer named Curtis Smallwood, who was killed in the 1940s. The odd thing is that both murders were committed with the same gun.

Boxers • Canada, Toronto • Draft dodgers

Nicotine Kiss. Forge, 2006. 9780765312235.

Walker can credit Jeff Starzek with saving his life just one month before this case begins, so when he gets a call from the man's sister Rose asking for help, he responds. It seems Jeff has disappeared, and the Feds want him on a counterfeiting charge tied to terrorism. Still recovering from the last bullet wound, Walker finds bad people shooting at him again, and he needs to move quickly to solve this one.

Counterfeiting • Homeland Security • Religion • Terrorism

American Detective. Forge, 2007. 9780765312242.

Walker is hired by former Detroit Tigers pitcher Darius Fuller, who wants Walker to investigate his daughter Deidre's fiancé, Hilary Bairn, a man Fuller believes to be a fortune hunter. When Fuller's daughter is murdered, Walker needs to shift gears and try to beat the loan shark to Bairn before he disappears permanently.

Finances • Loan sharks • Weddings

Amos Walker: The Complete Story Collection. Tyrus, 2010. 9781935562245.

A collection of the following stories: "Greektown," "Robbers' Roost," "Fast Burn," "Dead Soldier," "Eight Mile & Dequindre," "I'm in the Book," "Bodyguards Shoot Second," "The Prettiest Dead Girl in Detroit," "Blond and Blue," "Bloody July," "The Anniversary Waltz," "Needle," "Cigarette Stop," "Deadly Force," "People Who Kill," "Pickups and Shotguns," "The Crooked Way," "Redneck," "Dogs." "Safe House," "Kill the Cat," "Slipstream," "Lady on Ice," "Snow Angels," "Major Crimes," "Square One," "Man Who Love Noir," "Sunday," "Necessary Evil," "Trust Me," "The Woodward Plan," "Rumble Strip," and "Sometimes a Hyena."

Short stories

The Left-Handed Dollar. Forge, 2010. 9780765319548.

>Mob lawyer Lucille "Lefty Lucy" Lettermore hires Walker to gather evidence to prove that mobster Joseph "Joey Ballistic" Ballista's old conviction for attempted murder can be thrown out in order to clear his record. The problem is that the car bombing victim was Walker's close friend, investigative reporter Barry Stackpole. Putting money ahead of friendship, Walker takes the case and finds himself alone in a battle to set history right.

>>*Friendship • Organized crime*

Grafton, Sue ✍

Kinsey Millhone

The most popular of the female private detectives, Kinsey Millhone works out of her office in Santa Teresa, California. Her ability to work the mean streets while maintaining a perky personality appeals to a great number of readers and has made her the best-selling character of the 1990s. The good news for her fans is that she ages one year for every two books, so she should have a long and healthy career. Readers may also enjoy Linda Barnes, Marcia Muller, and Sara Paretsky. See the author's Web site at http://www.suegrafton.com. **TR** Series subjects: **California, Santa Teresa**

>*"A" Is for Alibi.* Holt, 1982.

>*"B" Is for Burglar.* Holt, 1985.

>*"C" Is for Corpse.* Holt, 1986.

>*"D" Is for Deadbeat.* Holt, 1987.

>*"E" Is for Evidence.* Holt, 1988.

>*"F" Is for Fugitive.* Holt, 1989.

>*"G" Is for Gumshoe.* Holt, 1990.

>*"H" Is for Homicide.* Holt, 1991.

>*"I" Is for Innocent.* Holt, 1992.

>*"J" Is for Judgment.* Holt, 1993.

>*"K" Is for Killer.* Holt, 1994.

>*"L" Is for Lawless.* Holt, 1995.

>*"M" Is for Malice.* Holt, 1996.

>*"N" Is for Noose.* Holt, 1998.

>*"O" Is for Outlaw.* Holt, 1999.

>*"P" Is for Peril.* Putnam, 2001.

>*"Q" Is for Quarry.* Putnam, 2002.

"R" Is for Ricochet. Putnam, 2004. 0399152288.

Nord Lafferty is an old, tired tycoon whose daughter Reba is getting out of prison after embezzling money from her boss, Alan Beckwith's, real estate company. Hired to shepherd Reba home from prison, Millhone finds herself the go-between when cop acquaintance Cheney Phillips reveals an IRS investigation into Beckwith that he wants Reba to help with. The problem is that Reba has a mind of her own, and it does not have the same moral code as Millhone.

   Ex-convicts • Fathers and daughters

"S" Is for Silence. Putnam, 2005. 9780399152979.

Daisy's mom Violet Sullivan disappeared on the Fourth of July weekend in 1953when she was a girl, and now she wants Kinsey to find out what happened. With a cold case over thirty years old, Millhone plunges into all the rumors that swirled around the woman after she left, giving herself five days to solve the mystery.

   California, Serena Station • Missing persons • Mothers and daughters

"T" Is for Trespass. Putnam, 2007. 9780399154485.

Enter Solana Rojas, a sociopath using an assumed identity to take jobs in the care-giving industry in order to steal even more identities. She is hired to care for Gus Vronsky, Millhone's neighbor. When Millhone is set on her trail, it becomes a challenge to the private eye like no other she has ever had. As Solana and Milhone share the narrative, the reader sees the case from both points of view.

   Care giving • Elder abuse • Identity theft • Sociopaths

"U" Is for Undertow. Putnam, 2009. 9780399155970.

Michael Sutton is troubled by a memory of something being buried around the same time that four-year-old Mary Claire Fitzhugh went missing years ago. It falls to Millhone to deal with real memory, false memory, and the passage of time in order to discover the truth about Sutton's confession.

   False memory • Kidnapping • Memory

Hall, Tarquin ✍

Vish Puri

Vish Puri is a Punjabi who advertises himself as India's most private investigator. Happily married to Rumpi and challenged by his extended family, he is essentially a happy man. Of large enough girth to be nicknamed "Chubby" and in his fifties, his main source of income is doing background checks for arranged marriages. But when called upon, he brings a determination to his work that means he will persistently pursue his investigation to the bitter end, using master disguises and a team of helpful sidekick investigators. Told with a sensibility that echoes the great thinking detectives of the Golden Age, these books will be enjoyed by readers of the traditional mystery. Readers may also enjoy Earl Derr Biggers, Arthur Conan Doyle, H. R. F. Keating, and Alexander McCall Smith. Visit the author's Web site at http://tarquinhall.com. **TR** Series subjects: **Humor • India, Delhi**

The Case of the Missing Servant. Simon & Schuster, 2009. 978-1-4165-8368-4. (UK: Hutchinson, 2009).

> Puri is given a big case when a prominent lawyer named Ajay Kasliwal is accused of murdering his maidservant, Mary, who is missing. Assembling his own team of Bow Street Runners for help, he travels through greater India searching for clues about the mysterious servant girl. While this is happening, he is unexpectedly sidetracked by the visit of his Mummy-ji and her meddling in his detective business.
>
> *India, Jaipur • India, Jharkhand • Lawyers • Mothers and sons • Servants*

The Case of the Man Who Died Laughing. Simon & Schuster, 2010. 9781416583691.

> When Dr. Suresh Jha is murdered in front of the members of the Rajpath Laughing Club by the goddess Kali, it falls to Puri to find out why, when asked for help by Inspector Singh. Jha was a proponent of rationalism and an opponent of the many gurus, so Puri, despite believing in mysticism himself, finds himself testing the truths spoken by Jha's chief adversary, Mararaj Swami.
>
> *Gurus • Mysticism • Swamis*

Hughes, Declan ✍

Ed Loy

Ed Loy fled from his homeland of Ireland to work as a private investigator in Los Angeles. His ties to Dublin are strong, including the influence of his family. He returns to his homeland to deal with his self-inflicted demons. Readers may also enjoy Benjamin Black, Ken Bruen, and John Connolly. Visit the author's Web site at http://www.declanhughesbooks.com. **TR** Series subjects: **Families • Ireland, Dublin**

The Wrong Kind of Blood. US: Morrow, 2006. 9780060825461. (UK: John Murray, 2006).

> After twenty years in Los Angeles as a P.I., Ed Loy has returned to Ireland to bury his Mom. He finds no peace when Linda Dawson, a former school chum, asks him to find her missing husband, a financial controller for a construction company. Then another old acquaintance, Tommy Owens, shows up on the run from a drug gang, with a pistol that may or may not have been used to commit a murder. Old Irish shadows plague Ed when the ghost of his father appears, and the gang members start making his life miserable.
>
> *Drugs • Fathers and sons • Missing persons • Mothers and sons*

The Color of Blood. Morrow, 2007. 9780060825492. (*The Colour of Blood*. UK: John Murray, 2007).

> When dentist Shane Howard receives pornographic pictures of his missing daughter Emily, he hires Loy to find her and bring her home. When people start dying, Loy realizes that he is up against major forces who will stop at nothing to keep their secrets safe, and that the answers may lie within the Howard family itself.
>
> *Dentists • Pornography*

The Price of Blood. Morrow, 2008. 9780060825515. (*The Dying Breed*. UK: John Murray, 2008).

> Before he dies, Father Vincent Tyrrell wants Loy to locate missing jockey Patrick Hutton. Gone for ten years, the missing man's disappearance still stirs concerns in the present that lead to a few murders before Loy can start to see the light at the end of the tunnel. As he tackles the Halligan family and the corruption that surrounds the horse-racing industry, he finds himself in personal jeopardy.
>
> *Horse racing • Jockeys*

All the Dead Voices. US: Morrow, 2009. 9780061689888. (UK: John Murray, 2008).

> Loy is balancing two cases. The first involves investigating the death of Paul Delaney, an up-and-coming soccer star who may had a drug problem. He was hired for his second case by Ann Fogarty, who is not convinced the police charged the right man for the murder of her father decades ago. As he investigates, Loy finds that Ann's father and Paul may have had a connection that drags organized crime into the picture.
>
> *Fathers and daughters • Irish Republican Army (IRA) • Organized crime • Soccer*

City of Lost Girls. US: Morrow, 2010. 9780061689901. (UK: John Murray, 2010).

> When filmmaker Jack Donovan receives threats and some of his female extras disappear from his set, he turns to Loy for help. This has happened re, to Donovan befso Loy begins an investigation to find a serial killer who is preying on this film director.
>
> *California, Los Angeles • Hollywood • Motion pictures • Serial killer*

Kerr, Philip ✍

Bernard Gunther

Kerr wrote a trilogy that covers the prewar, war, and postwar years of Nazi Germany. His lead character is a world-weary P.I. named Gunther, who becomes his eye on the times. This series captures European history with a master's touch and could appeal to any reader who enjoys historical fiction. As a mystery, this series should be recommended to any hard-boiled mystery reader. Readers may also enjoy Max Allan Collins, Ken Kuhlken and Charles Todd. See the author's Web site at http://www.philipkerr.co.uk. **HB Historical.** Series subjects: **Historical (1900–1999)** • **Nazi Germany** • **Nazis** • **World War II**

> *March Violets.* Viking, 1989.
>
> *The Pale Criminal.* Viking, 1990.
>
> *A German Requiem.* Viking, 1991

The One from the Other. Putnam, 2006. 9780399152993.

> Gunther is managing a hotel near Dachau in 1949 when his wife Kirsten dies in a mental hospital. Out of despair, he returns to detective work when a woman wants confirmation that her Nazi husband is dead, so she can remarry. This sets Gunther on a search for some missing Nazis. As he probes into these post–World War II issues, he finds he is in conflict with the American occupation forces and the newly formed spy organization, the CIA. Gunther must decide if proving his point is worth his own life.
>
> *Germany, Munich*

A Quiet Flame. Putnam, 2009. 9780399155307.

> Fleeing to Argentina to dodge his Nazi past, Gunther is blackmailed by Colonel Montalbán into investigating the murder of Grete Wohlauf. Grete's murder is reminiscent of a case Gunther worked in the 1930s in Germany, and a serial killer from the Nazi era may have immigrated with the rest of the asylum-seeking Germans.
>
> *Argentina, Buenos Aires* • *Cancer* • *Serial killer*

 If the Dead Rise Not. Putnam, 2010. 9780399156151.

> Moving back in time to 1934, Berlin is making preparations for the 1936 Olympics, and Gunther is the house detective at Berlin's Adlon Hotel. When he discovers the theft of a Chinese box, it ties him into the behind-the-scenes maneuvering to prevent an American boycott of the games and to an American mobster. Leaping forward to the mid-1950s, when he has left Argentina for Batista's Cuba, he finds himself involved in the death of a killer from his past that will bring back into his life the same American mobster who plagued him so long ago.
>
> **BA**
>
> *Cuba* • *Germany, Berlin* • *Olympics* • *Organized crime*

King, Laurie R.

Mary Russell/Sherlock Holmes

It is dangerous to play with a legend, but King has proven herself worthy of tackling the best. Her creation, Mary Russell, is a protégée of and accomplice to the legendary private detective, Sherlock Holmes. Beginning as a teenage waif and maturing into a full partner, the relationship that develops between the two characters is almost as important as the mystery cases that attract their detective skills. Less pastiche and more history, these novels can be recommended to readers who are not particularly Holmesian by nature. They can also be recommended to traditional mystery readers. Readers may also enjoy Arthur Conan Doyle, Sharyn Newman, and Anne Perry. See the author's Web site at http://www.laurierking.com. **TR** **Historical.** Series subjects: **Historical (1900–1999)** • **Holmes, Sherlock** • **Teams** • **Victorian England**

> *The Beekeeper's Apprentice; or on the Segregation of the Queen.* St. Martin's, 1994.
>
> *A Monstrous Regiment of Women.* St. Martin's, 1995.
>
> *A Letter of Mary.* St. Martin's, 1997.
>
> *The Moor.* St. Martin's, 1998.
>
> *O Jerusalem.* Bantam, 1999.

Justice Hall. Bantam, 2002. 0553111132.

> A desperate visitor comes to the home of Holmes and Russell one night to lay out the tragedy of Marsh Hughenfort, recently returned to England after the death of his brother, the Duke of Beauville. A family history leading back to a First World War scandal still plagues Justice Hall, the ancestral home. The question for the detective duo is, what does this have to do with today's heirs?
>
> *England, Arley Holt* • *England, London* • *World War I*

The Game. Bantam, 2004. 0553801945.

> Rudyard Kipling once wrote about Kim, and in this adventure Russell and her husband Sherlock find themselves off to India in pursuit of the English spy, Kimball O'Hara. As they pursue the boy-hero grown up to a life of intrigue, their lives are threatened on the steamer they take passage on. Once in India, traveling incognito, they find themselves threatened from all sides until the danger leads them to a deadly end.
>
> *Espionage* • *India* • *Shipboard*

Locked Rooms. Bantam, 2005. 9780553801972.

> When Russell and her husband Holmes travel back to her hometown of San Francisco, she is on a journey of recovery and reconciliation regarding her father's estate. When she is shot at, the great thinking detective networks with Dashiell Hammett, a Pinkerton agent. The facts about the death of her family and her status as an orphan make Russell face demons from the past.
>
> *California, San Francisco* • *Earthquakes* • *Hammett, Dashiell* • *Wills*

The Art of Detection. Bantam, 2006. 9780553804539.

> When San Francisco Detective Kate Martinelli is investigating the death of Sherlockian Philip Gilbert in contemporary times, the author also reveals how this death relates to an unpublished Holmes story that brings in the characters from this series.
>
> *Bibliomystery* • *California, San Francisco*

The Language of Bees. Bantam, 2009. 9780553804546.

> Estranged son Damian Adler has returned to the lives of Mary and Sherlock while searching for his missing wife Yolanda and their child. With a troubled past and a link to a cult for whose text he is the resident illustrator, Damian is a challenge to the loving relationship between the two detectives.
>
> *Art* • *England, London* • *England, Sussex* • *Fathers and sons* • *Missing persons*

The God of the Hive. Bantam, 2010. 9780553805543.

> It is the summer of 1924, and this book picks up where the last case left off, when Damian Adler was incapacitated by a bullet wound. He has been shot by Reverend Thomas Brothers, whose fervent religious beliefs include a psychic energy released by death. Mary is on the run from the police with Damian's daughter Estelle, while Holmes makes a desperate attempt to save his son's life by fleeing to Holland.
>
> *England, London* • *Fathers and sons* • *Granddaughters* • *Holland* • *Psychics* • *Religious fanatics*

Kuhlken, Ken ✍

Thomas Hickey/Alvaro Hickey/Clifford Hickey

Thomas Hickey suffers the restlessness that was common as the Great Depression was winding down and America was preparing to fight a world war. His noir lifestyle makes him a perfect candidate to lead an investigation in the dark cases that come his way. Kuhlken is able to capture the 1940s in a way that should appeal to any historical fiction reader. Late in the series the focus shifts to Tom's extended family. Readers may also enjoy Harold Adams, Max Allan Collins, and Philip Kerr. See the author's Web site at http://www.kenkuhlken.net. **HB** **Historical.** Series subjects: **California, San Diego** • **Historical (1900–1999)**

> *The Loud Adios.* St. Martin's, 1991.
>
> *The Venus Deal.* St. Martin's, 1993.
>
> *The Angel Gang.* St. Martin's, 1994.

The Do-Re-Mi. Poisoned Pen, 2006. 9781590583371.

> Among the hippie communes, marijuana fields, and redwoods of Evergreen, California, a gathering of free-thinkers has flocked together for a music jamboree

in 1972. When Clifford Hickey arrives, intent on meeting his brother and showcasing his talent on the festival's stage, he is caught in a nightmare. When shots are fired in the night, Clifford discovers the local corrupt cops and a vicious motorcycle gang are all out to pin the murder of local Jimmy Marris on Clifford's adopted Mexican brother, Alvaro. Clifford makes a call home to Lake Tahoe and rouses the patriarch of the family, the retired and ill Tom Hickey.

Adoption • Fathers and sons • Motorcycle gangs • Music • Police corruption

The Vagabond Virgins. Poisoned Pen, 2008. 9781590584613.

In 1979, Alvaro Hickey is studying the law and working for an immigration lawyer when he is approached by Lourdes Shuler. Her twin sister Lupe is missing in the Baja, where a local election is being disrupted by visits from the Virgin Mary urging residents to vote against the Partido Revolucionario Institucional party. He turns to his brother Clifford for help, and the two venture across the border to try to decide if the missing sister is the visiting virgin.

Elections • Mexico, Baja • Missing persons • Nazis

The Biggest Liar in Los Angeles. Poisoned Pen, 2010. 9781590586976.

The year is 1926, and Tom Hickey is delivering meat for a friend of his father and keeping one eye on his wayward underage sister Florence. He has also taken over leadership of a swing band, and when one of his African American band mates brings in a broadside that maintains a lynching has taken place in a park in Los Angeles, it stops Tom cold. The dead man is an old friend who rescued him as a child, and now Tom decides finding out what happened to his friend Franklin Gaines is his new mission.

African American • California, Los Angeles • Lynching

Lippman, Laura ✎

Tess Monaghan

Beginning her professional career as a newspaper reporter, Monaghan migrates to private eye status when she decides to start her own business after being laid off from her newspaper. Her cases show off the city of Baltimore, making the city's neighborhoods a character in the novels. Monaghan's extended family and complicated love life with her boyfriend Crow add flavor to the adventures. Readers may also enjoy Linda Barnes, Jan Burke, Sue Grafton, and Nancy Pickard. ⊞ Series subjects: **Maryland, Baltimore**

Baltimore Blues. Avon, 1997.

Charm City. Avon, 1997.

Butchers Hill. Avon, 1998.

In Big Trouble. Avon, 1999.

The Sugar House. Morrow, 2000.

In a Strange City. Morrow, 2001.

The Last Place. Morrow, 2002. 0380978199.

While seeing a psychiatrist in court-ordered anger management sessions, Monaghan is hooked into looking at some dead end homicide cases by her friend Whitney. Whitney belongs to a foundation interested in lowering the number of domestic-abuse homicides, and they are funding Monaghan's research. What troubles Tess is that the open cases she is given all seem bogus, while the foundation's chair is her old nemesis, Luisa O'Neal. As she probes into the death of Lucy Fancher, who was decapitated, she meets the man who found Lucy's head, Toll Facilities cop Carl Dewitt. The two detectives form an unlikely partnership and weasel their way into a statewide hunt for a serial killer that is being conducted by various law enforcement agencies.

Cold case • Serial killer

By a Spider's Thread. Morrow, 2004. 0060506695.

Mark Rubin, an Orthodox Jew and furrier, comes home from work on a Friday before Labor Day to discover his wife and three children have disappeared. With no evidence of a crime and no police help, he turns to Monaghan for help. She manages to do her job, perhaps better than she has on any other case. However, what she discovers is not comfortable for her or her client. While her client does everything possible to irritate her, Tess slowly develops a feeling for him that makes her teach him about life while he teaches her about being Jewish.

Jewish families • Missing persons

 ### No Good Deeds. Morrow, 2006. 9780060570729.

Why would Crow bring a homeless boy home to Monaghan? While Monaghan worries about her stuff, Lloyd Jupiter steals their car and crashes it, disappearing into the night. This is unfortunate, because he may hold the key to the murder of Assistant U.S. District Attorney Gregory Youssef. Tess inadvertently gives the boy's identity away to the killer when she does a newspaper interview, and Crow leaves her in order to hunt down and then protect the young boy from street vengeance.

Homeless

Another Thing to Fall. Morrow, 2008. 9780061128875.

When the Mann of Steel television production company arrives in Baltimore, they hire Monaghan to protect one of the stars. But while her eyes are on Selene Waites, another company member is beaten to death. When some questionable photographs of Waites surface, it leads to a previous death that may have consequences for the current cast.

Stalking • Television

McCall Smith, Alexander ✍

Precious Ramotswe

The first thing that readers need to know is that the stories in these books are much more about Precious and the landscape of Botswana then they are about the crimes brought to her business. Each novel reads like an interrelated series of short stories. As a detective, Precious is much more likely to rely on her intuition than on clues, but she is always able to use her Solomon-like decisions to resolve her cases. Meanwhile, her personal life is displayed with gusto, and readers are fascinated. Along with great secondary characters like Mr. J. L. B. Matekoni, Mma Makutsi, and the orphans, she reigns as one of the most interesting female characters in the genre. Readers may also enjoy M. C. Beaton, Agatha Christie, and James McClure. Visit the author's Web site at http://www.mccallsmith.com. **TR** Series subjects: **Adoption • Botswana, Gabarone • Orphans • Romance**

The No. 1 Ladies' Detective Agency. Anchor, 2002. 1400034779. (UK: Polygon, 1998).

> Precious Ramotswe must solve various puzzles, including a wandering daughter, a fake insurance claim, medical malpractice, and other simple, ordinary concerns. But within the quiet revelations are also the truths of this African nation: its language, culture, and religions. Broadcast over the arid surfaces of this fascinating country, Mma's detective skills allow her to display her concerns about the role of women in Botswana society as well as her passionate love for an Africa not changed by Western ways.
>
> *Insurance • Medical malpractice • Missing persons*

Tears of the Giraffe. Anchor, 2002. 1400031354. (UK: Polygon, 2000).

> Picking up right where the first novel left off, the main case in this novel involves Mma Ramotswe's search for the reason behind the ten-year-old disappearance of Michael Curtin. Michael's mother Andrea was to know the reason why her son is dead, and Mma Ramotswe will eventually find out, but not really by using great detective skills. Instead, the discovery of the truth follows the same method used to reveal the truth about the other characters and other stories in this novel: intuition.
>
> *Mothers and sons*

Morality for Beautiful Girls. Anchor, 2002. 1400031362. (UK: Abacus, 2001).

> When an important government official's brother is poisoned, the case falls to Mma Ramotswe. At the same time, she is looking into the backgrounds of the finalists in the Miss Beauty and Integrity Contest. While all this detective activity is going on, she must also deal with issues with Mr. J. L. B. Matekoni and relies on Mma Makutsi more and more.
>
> *Beauty contest • Contests • Poisons*

The Kalahari Typing School for Men. Pantheon, 2002. 037542217X. (UK: Polygon, 2003).

> Mma Ramostwe is pressured by outside forces when Mma Makutsi opens a typing school for men and an American-trained detective opens a competitive agency called Satisfaction Guaranteed Detective Agency. When an engineer who feels badly about his past asks for help to right some wrongs, Mma Ramostwe has a case she can sink her teeth into.
>
> *Abortion*

The Full Cupboard of Life. Pantheon, 2003. 0375422188. (UK: Abacus, 2003).

> With Mma Holonga considering marriage, it falls to Mma Ramostwe to decide which of the four eligible men is a suitable candidate for a husband. With her own marriage plans still up in the air, it is a challenge to Mma Ramostwe to focus on the affairs of the heart. This is especially true with Mr. J. L. B. Matekoni having agreed to jump out of an airplane as a stunt for a fund-raiser.
>
> *Weddings*

In the Company of Cheerful Ladies. Pantheon, 2004. 0375422714. (UK: Abacus, 2004).

> When her own house has been burglarized and the culprit left his pants behind as a clue, Ramotswe has to apply her detective skills to her own case. With her husband Mr. J. L. B. Matekoni left a man short at work and Mma Makutsi trying to fall in love during dance lessons, Mma Ramotswe is beginning to feel like the world is aligning against her. Then, out of her past steps a man who will challenge her resolve as well: ex-husband Note Mokoti.
>
> *Burglary*

Blue Shoes and Happiness. Pantheon, 2006. 9780375422720. (UK: Abacus, 2006).

> Mma Ramotswe, traditionally built, has decided to go on a diet. With food on her mind, she finds herself investigating a cook suspected of stealing food from the kitchen where she works. Meanwhile, her agency is dealing with witchcraft, a pair of blue shoes, a dream about feminism, and a cobra in the office.
>
> *Cooking • Diets*

The Good Husband of Zebra Drive. Pantheon, 2007. 9780375422737. (UK: Polygon, 2007).

> Why would some patients in a hospital, in the same bed, die at the same time each week? That conundrum falls in Mma Ramotswe's lap, while her husband, Mr. J. L. B. Matekoni, has launched his own investigation into a case of infidelity. Will the newly engaged Mma Makutsi leave the agency?
>
> *Affairs • Doctors • Hospitals*

The Miracle at Speedy Motors. Pantheon, 2008. 9780375424489. (UK: Little Brown, 2008).

> When some threatening letters arrive at the agency, it disturbs Mma Ramotswe and Makutsi to the point of distraction. Miracles are questioned at the agency

when a woman believes her mother is not her birth parent, a heart-shaped headboard throws a romance into question, and a doctor believes he can make a wheelchair-bound girl walk again. The question becomes which of these threads will mean the most to Mma Ramostwe and the cast of characters who surround her agency.

Doctors • Mothers and daughters

Tea Time for the Traditionally Built. Pantheon, 2009. 9780375424496. (UK: Little Brown, 2009).

With abundant energy and little knowledge of the game, Mma Ramotswe and Makutsi integrated themselves into the Kalahari Swoopers in order to determine who is sabotaging the soccer games of this local team. Meanwhile, both women wrestle with love and deal with the men in their lives.

Soccer

The Double Comfort Safari Club. Pantheon, 2010. 9780375424502. (UK: Little Brown, 2010).

Ramotswe balances three cases in her latest adventure. The most complicated one takes her and Mma Grace Makutsi north to the Okavango River Delta region when the executor of an American will needs to find a safari tour guide who was helpful to a dead woman. Meanwhile, Mma Makutsi's fiancé has been hurt in an accident, and that causes a conflict with the man's family. Finally, a priest and his wife raise an issue of infidelity that Mma Ramotswe must resolve.

Botswana, Okavango River Delta

Muller, Marcia ✍

Sharon McCone

One of the pioneer contemporary female private eyes, McCone begins her career at All Souls Collective in San Francisco. Eventually situations force her to branch out as an independent investigator and to open McCone Investigations. Her cases are always complex puzzles and often concern a social issue. Her relationships with her coworkers, family, and lovers also make the series interesting. Readers may also enjoy Linda Barnes, Sue Grafton, and Sara Paretsky. See a fan's Web site at http://interbridge.com/marciamuller. **TR** Series subjects: **California, San Francisco**

Edwin of the Iron Shoes. McKay, 1977.

Ask the Cards a Question. St. Martin's, 1982.

The Cheshire Cat's Eye. St. Martin's, 1983.

Games to Keep the Dark Away. St. Martin's, 1984.

Leave a Message for Willie. St. Martin's, 1984.

Double (with Bill Pronzini). St. Martin's, 1984.

There's Nothing to Be Afraid Of. St. Martin's, 1985.

Eye of the Storm. Mysterious Press, 1988.

There's Something in a Sunday. Mysterious Press, 1989.

The Shape of Dread. Mysterious Press, 1989.

Trophies and Dead Things. Mysterious Press, 1990.

Where Echoes Live. Mysterious Press, 1991.

Pennies in a Dead Woman's Eyes. Mysterious Press, 1992.

Wolf in the Shadows. Mysterious Press, 1993.

Till the Butchers Cut Him Down. Mysterious Press, 1994.

The McCone Files. Crippen and Landru, 1995.

A Wild and Lonely Place. Mysterious Press, 1995.

The Broken Promise Land. Mysterious Press, 1996.

Both Ends of the Night. Mysterious Press, 1997.

While Other People Sleep. Mysterious Press, 1998.

A Walk Through Fire. Mysterious Press, 1999.

McCone and Friends. Crippen and Landru, 2000.

Listen to the Silence. Mysterious, 2000.

Dead Midnight. Mysterious, 2002.

The Dangerous Hour. Mysterious, 2004. 0892968044.

McCone Investigations is now open for business. Julia Rafael is arrested, and the agency is thrown into turmoil when Supervisor Alex Aguilar accuses the McCone operation of stealing his credit cards. As McCone and her detectives work a case to save themselves, it becomes apparent to McCone that neither Rafael or Aguilar is the target. She is.

Hispanic Americans • Politicians

Vanishing Point. Mysterious Press, 2006. 9780892968053.

There is no down time after a honeymoon for a private eye, so when she returns to work, McCone takes on a twenty-two-year-old cold case. Laurel Greenwood, a San Luis Obispo artist and mother, disappeared without explanation. As McCone's team begin their exploration of the past, they discover disturbing evidence about the woman they want to believe in.

California, San Luis Obispo • Missing persons

The Ever-Running Man. Warner, 2007. 9780446582421.

> Renshaw & Kesell International, a security firm in which McCone's husband Hy Ripinsky is a partner, is suffering a series of bombings. Does this have something to do with the kidnappings the firm tries to prevent, or is there something rotten within the corporation? Then the bomber turns to murder. As the McCone agency works the case, it begins to drive a stake between husband and wife.
>
> *Bombs • Security services*

Burn Out. Grand Central, 2008. 9780446581073.

> On a break at her ranch in order to recover from the last case and to consider closing up her agency, McCone witnesses an abuse victim's trauma and hears about a murder. Soon her detective instincts are too strong for her to stick to her resolve to rest, and she is investigating on her own. The mystery swirls around a Native American family, a ranch manager named Ramon Perez, and the missing members of his extended family.
>
> *California, High Sierra • Dysfunctional families • Native Americans • Ranches*

Locked In. Grand Central, 2009. 9780446581059.

> McCone is shot in the face when sh interrupts a burglary at her agency and is left paralyzed and able to communicate only by blinking her eyes. Each member of her agency and her husband Hy gets a shot at helping solve the crime.
>
> **SH**
>
> *Locked-in syndrome*

3

Coming Back. Grand Central, 2010. 9780446581066.

> In rehabilitation for her wound from the previous case, McCone is concerned when a fellow patient, Pipe Quinn, stops coming to her treatments. A visit to Quinn's home proves she is in danger, then both Quinn and Adah Joslyn from McCone Investigations disappear. Everyone at the office is now on full alert to solve the mystery and save one of their own.
>
> *Missing persons • Rehabilitation*

Paretsky, Sara ✍

V. I. Warshawski

Dramatic action and a hard-boiled edge highlight the cases of Chicago female P.I. Warshawski. She is not the easiest person to like, and her prickly nature often sets her against her own support network. But that same personality quirk is the quality that makes her the determined detective that most of her clients need. An eye on social concerns highlights the series, and readers will find that Warshawski's cases are darker than those of Marcia Muller's Sharon McCone or Sue Grafton's Kinsey Millhone. Readers may also enjoy Lawrence

Block (Matthew Scudder) and Jeremiah Healy. See the author's Web site at http://www. saraparetsky.com. **HB** Series subjects: **Illinois, Chicago**

> *Indemnity Only.* Dial, 1982.
>
> *Deadlock.* Dial, 1984.
>
> *Killing Orders.* Morrow, 1985.
>
> *Bitter Medicine.* Morrow, 1987.
>
> *Blood Shot.* Delacorte, 1988. (UK: *Toxic Shock.* Gollancz, 1988).
>
> *Burn Marks.* Delacorte, 1990.
>
> *Guardian Angel.* Delacorte, 1992.
>
> *Tunnel Vision.* Delacorte, 1994.
>
> *Windy City Blues.* Delacorte, 1995.
>
> *Hard Time.* Delacorte, 1999.
>
> *Total Recall.* Delacorte, 2001.

 Blacklist. Putnam, 2003. 0399150854.

Someone has been breaking into Larchmont Hall mansion, and Warshawski is hired to find out who the culprit is. Larchmont had been the property of the Drummond family, but it was abandoned for three years. Geraldine Graham, the matriarch of the family that previously owned it and sold it to the Drummonds, can see a light in the attic from her retirement community. But it is Paretsky who finds the dead body of a black reporter floating in the weed-filled swimming pool and who will see how the past affects the present.

African Americans • Journalists

Fire Sale. Putnam, 2005. 9780399152795.

Warshawski has returned to the south side of Chicago as a fill-in for her ailing high school basketball coach. Confronted by contemporary issues at her old school, such as poverty, gangs, and drugs, she decides to mobilize the team by seeking corporate sponsorship from a fellow alumnus of the school, By Smart founder Buffalo Bill Bysen. As she deals with an explosion at a local factory, she also deals with the disappearance of nineteen-year-old Billy Bysen.

Academia • Arson • Basketball • Missing persons • Romance • Sabotage

Hardball. Putnam, 2009. 9780399155932.

Warshawski's latest case is a cold one: find Lamont Gadsden, an African American who disappeared in 1967. As she probes, she discovers her own father might have had a connection to the man, so she tries to finds his old partners to ask questions. What does all this have to do with a visit by Martin Luther King Jr. to Chicago and the murder of a black woman named Harmony Newsome? When her cousin Petra, in town to work on a political campaign, takes an interest in the case and is then kidnapped, she knows she is raising the ghosts of something that will only get uglier as it goes along.

African Americans • Kidnapping • Politicians

Body Work. Penguin, 2010. 9780399156748.

Petra, Warshawski's young cousin, has taken a job at the avant-garde Club Gouge, where a body painting exhibition is troubled when a young woman named Nadia Guaman's art enrages a veteran named Chad Vishnesk. When Nadia is murdered outside the club and the police arrest Chad, Warshawski is hired by his family to prove him innocent. Warshawski discovers there is more behind the scenes of the club than she first realized, and that even The Body Artist may have secrets that need to be revealed.

Art • Organized crime • Performance art • Veterans

Parker, Robert B. ✍

Spenser

Working out of Boston, this P.I. managed to become the most popular of the male P.I.s in the 1990s, when the women private eye characters were dominant. Spenser and his tough African American enforcer Hawk combine interesting and tough methods to help their clients. Their appearances as TV characters did not hurt the popularity of this series. Robert B. Parker died of a heart attack in 2010. Readers may also enjoy Linda Barnes, Loren D. Estleman, Jeremiah Healy, and William Tappley. See the fan Web site for this author at http://www.linkingpage.com/spenser. **HB** Series subjects: **Massachusetts, Boston • Teams**

The Godwulf Manuscript. Houghton Mifflin, 1974.

God Save the Child. Houghton Mifflin, 1974.

Mortal Stakes. Houghton Mifflin, 1975.

Promised Land. Houghton Mifflin, 1976.

The Judas Goat. Houghton Mifflin, 1978.

Looking for Rachel Wallace. Delacorte, 1980.

Early Autumn. Delacorte, 1981.

A Savage Place. Delacorte, 1981.

Ceremony. Delacorte, 1982.

The Widening Gyre. Delacorte, 1983.

Valediction. Delacorte, 1984.

A Catskill Eagle. Delacorte, 1985.

Taming a Sea-Horse. Delacorte, 1986.

Pale Kings and Princes. Delacorte, 1987.

Crimson Joy. Delacorte, 1988.

Playmates. Putnam, 1989.

Stardust. Putnam, 1990.

Pastime. Putnam, 1991.

Double Deuce. Putnam, 1992.

Paper Doll. Putnam, 1993.

Walking Shadow. Putnam, 1994.

Thin Air. Putnam, 1995.

Chance. Putnam, 1996.

Small Vices. Putnam, 1997.

Sudden Mischief. Putnam, 1998.

Hush Money. Putnam, 1999.

Hugger Mugger. Putnam, 2000.

Potshot. Putnam, 2001.

Widows Walk. Putnam, 2002.

Back Story. Putnam, 2003. 0399149775.

Paul Giacomon asks Spenser to look into a cold case: the death of his friend's mother during a bank robbery in the 1970s by The Dread Scott Brigade. Expecting at least some cooperation from the FBI, Spenser discovers that not only the bad guys want this investigation to go away, so do the good guys. When his work draws the attention of Sonny Karnofsky, it puts Susan and Spenser in the target zone of a mob hit man.

Bank robberies • Cold case • Organized crime • Underground movements

Bad Business. Putnam, 2004. 0399151451.

When Spenser is hired to tail a wayward husband by his wife, Marlene Rowley, he is amused to discover that she is being tailed, and so is he. However, things get complicated when the husband, Trent, is shot. Digging into the murdered man's company, Kinergy, to solve the murder, he discovers that there was more in this man's life than an itch to wander from his wife.

Corruption • Husbands and wives • Sex

Cold Service. Putnam, 2005. 0399152407.

Hawk has been shot in the back by some Ukrainian mobsters and is determined to seek revenge. The first order of business is to get himself back in condition, so while he is recuperating Spenser does some digging for his friend. It looks like

Boots Podolak and his whole organization are going to feel the wrath of these two best friends.

Massachusetts, Marshport • Organized crime • Revenge • Ukrainian mobsters

School Days. Putnam, 2005. 9780399153235.

When a young man named Jared Clark confesses to a school shooting, his grandmother, Lily Ellsworth, believing him innocent, hires Spenser to find out the truth. Every door is closed to Spenser, as everyone is convinced the right shooter is behind bars.

Academia • Private schools • Teenagers at risk

Hundred-Dollar Baby. Putnam, 2006. 9780399153761. (Dream Girl. UK: Harpenden).

April Kyle (*Ceremony; Taming a Sea-Horse*) needs Spenser's help again when her exclusive escort service is threatened by the mob. When taking care of the threat proves easy, Spenser is not surprised to discover his friend and client has not been honest with him about the real problem. It will take his best effort, and his muscle Hawk, to straighten out April's life again.

Organized crime • Prostitutes

Now and Then. Putnam, 2007. 9780399154416.

When a man comes to Spenser with a tale of his wife's odd behavior, Spenser is able to record evidence of the infidelity. The down side is that the recording also reveals that the lover, Perry Alderson, is involved in an underground group called Last Hope, which helps terrorists find the weapons they need. Soon people are dying everywhere and Spenser needs to leap into action to stop more killings and shut down Last Hope.

Affairs • Terrorism

Rough Weather. Putnam, 2008. 9780399155192.

When an invasion interrupts a wedding on an island and the bride is kidnapped by the Gray Man, Spenser finds he is no longer a guest, he is a detective. Heidi Bradshaw had asked Spenser to be nearby during the wedding, so the first place Spenser looks is into the background of the now-missing bride.

Islands • Kidnapping • Massachusetts, Buzzard's Bay • Weddings

Chasing the Bear: A Young Spenser Novel. Philomel, 2009. 9780399247767.

When Spenser was a teen, he was raised by his father and two uncles. Between lessons on life and boxing instructions from his uncles, the young boy takes on the case of a friend who is kidnapped by her alcoholic father and stands up to some racists out to get a Hispanic friend.

Coming-of-age • Fathers and sons

The Professional. Berkley, 2009. 9780399155949.

> When each of four women who have had an affair with Gary Eisenhower approaches Spenser looking for relief from his blackmail, he discovers that he is not the only one on the man's trail. One of the husbands is not pleased with any investigation and sends some muscle to Spenser to make sure he understands. As Spenser tries to rein in a blackmailer, people start to die, and the case begins to spin out of control.
>
> *Affairs • Blackmail*

Painted Ladies. Berkley, 2010. 9780399156854.

> The famous painting *Lady with a Finch* by Dutch artist Franz Hermenszoon is being held for ransom, so art consultant Dr. Ashton Prince hires Spenser for protection. A bomb kills Prince at the payoff, and Spenser is left holding the bag. When his investigation turns from the theft to the life of Prince, things begin to get ugly.
>
> *Art • Extortion • Holocaust*

Pronzini, Bill ✐

Nameless

This long-running series features the San Francisco P.I. without a name (eventually revealed to be "Bill"). Pronzini has long been considered one of the better writers in the field, and one of the series' strengths is the inclusion of a play-fair puzzle in each. Nameless is given a host of personal demons to fight as well as interesting cases to solve over the course of the series. Eventually, as he ages, he takes on some employees, like African American Tamara Corbin and ex-Seattle cop Jake Runyon. One of Nameless's cases is a joint venture with Colin Wilcox, while another is a joint venture with Marcia Muller, Pronzini's wife. Readers may also enjoy Lawrence Block (Matthew Scudder), Loren D. Estleman, and Jeremiah Healy. **TR** **HB** Series subjects: **California, San Francisco**

> *The Snatch.* Random House, 1971.
>
> *The Vanished.* Random House, 1973.
>
> *Undercurrent.* Random House, 1973.
>
> *Blowback.* Random House, 1977.
>
> *Twospot* (with Collin Wilcox). Putnam, 1978.
>
> *Labyrinth.* St. Martin's, 1980.
>
> *Hoodwink.* St. Martin's, 1981.
>
> *Scattershot.* St. Martin's, 1982.
>
> *Dragonfire.* St. Martin's, 1982.

Casefile. St. Martin's, 1983.

Bindlestiff. St. Martin's. 1983.

Quicksilver. St. Martin's, 1984.

Nightshades. St. Martin's, 1984.

Double (with Marcia Muller). St. Martin's, 1984.

Bones. St. Martin's, 1985.

Deadfall. St. Martin's, 1986.

Shackles. St. Martin's, 1988.

Jackpot. Delacorte, 1990.

Breakdown. Delacorte, 1991.

Quarry. Delacorte, 1992.

Epitaphs. Delacorte, 1992.

Demons. Delacorte, 1993.

Hardcase. Delacorte, 1995.

Spadework. Crippen and Landru, 1996.

Sentinels. Carroll & Graf, 1996.

Illusions. Carroll & Graf, 1997.

Boobytrap. Carroll & Graf, 1998.

Crazybone. Carroll & Graf, 2000.

Bleeders. Carroll & Graf, 2002.

Spook. Carroll & Graf, 2003. 0786710861.

When a motion picture company befriends a damaged street person named Spook and he is murdered, they hire Nameless's agency to discover who would do something like this. The case falls to Jake Runyon and Tamara Corbin. As the ops probe into the case, they discover that there was most likely a specific reason to target this mysterious man of the streets.

Homeless

Scenarios. Five Star, 2003. 0786243260.

A collection of the following short stories: "It's a Lousy World," "The Pulp Connection," "Dead Man's Slough," "The Ghosts of Ragged-Ass Gulch," "Cat's-Paw," "Skeleton Rattle Your Mouldy Leg," "Incident in a Neighborhood Tavern," "Stakeout," "La Bellezza delle Bellezze", "Souls Burning," "Bomb Scare," "The Big Bite," "Season of Sharing" (with Marcia Muller), and "Wrong Place, Wrong Time."

Short stories

Nightcrawlers. Forge, 2005. 9780765309310.

Nameless and Runyon take on a personal case when Runyon's gay son's lover is one of the victims of a hate crime in the Castro District. Meanwhile, Tamara needs help when she stumbles on what she believes to be a pedophile in the midst of one of his adventures and disappears from sight.

> *Hate crimes • Homosexuality • Pedophilia*

Mourners. Forge, 2006. 9780765309327.

Hired to follow financial advisor James Troxell, the crew discovers he is prone to odd behavior like attending the funerals of complete strangers who have one thing in common: they were all women who died violently. While on the case, each op is touched by his or her own personal relationship crisis, which ties his or her emotional state to that of Troxell.

> *Funerals • Mourning*

Savages. Forge, 2007. 9780765309334.

Nameless is the op who did the background check that cleared Nancy Ogden to marry Brandon Mathias. Now Nancy is dead, and her sister Celeste wants the agency to determine if Brandon was the murderer. As this case is developing, Jake steps into the middle of an arson case that nearly takes his life.

> *Arson • Background checks • Husbands and wives*

Fever. Forge, 2008. 9780765318183.

Mitchell Krochek hires the agency to find his wife, Janice. She is addicted to Internet gambling and has left and does not want to go home. But when she disappears and it looks like foul play, the ops regret their decision to honor her request. Meanwhile Jake is dealing with a young man whose behavior has his family worried.

> *Families • Gambling • Husbands and wives • Internet*

Schemers. Forge, 2009. 9780765318190.

The agency is first approached by Gregory Pollexfen, a rare book collector who is missing eight volumes from his secured collection. While the investigation gets underway, the collector's brother-in-law is found shot to death inside the sealed collection room, and the crew has a locked-room puzzle to solve. Meanwhile, Jake is trying to solve a case of a stalker terrorizing a married couple, and Tamara is dealing with a con man in her life.

> *Bibliomystery • Book collecting • Con men • Stalking*

Betrayers. Forge, 2010. 9780765318206.

Crime strikes at home when Kerry finds some cocaine in the couple's adopted daughter's room and Emily goes into complete denial. It distracts Kerry from his own case dealing with harassment. Meanwhile Tamara is hunting the con man who hurt her and trying to save people from his latest scheme. While all this is going on, Jake is dealing with a skip case that is going to turn ugly.

> *Con men • Drugs • Skip trace*

Rozan, S. J. ✍

Lydia Chin/Bill Smith

Stories in this unique series are told by two narrators: half the books are narrated by Chinese American Lydia Chin (the odd-numbered books), and the other half are from Bill Smith's perspective (the even-numbered books). One of the intriguing questions in the series is, just what is the relationship between these two investigators? This becomes especially true in the later titles in the series. Using the greater New York landscape as a map, Rozan creates interesting puzzles from interesting perspectives and has become one of the leading voices of the genre in the new millennium. Readers may enjoy Sue Grafton, Dennis Lehane, Sujata Massey, and Sara Paretsky. **TR** Series subjects: **Asian Americans • New York, New York • Teams**

> *China Trade.* St. Martin's, 1994.
>
> *Concourse.* St. Martin's, 1995.
>
> *Mandarin Plain.* St. Martin's, 1996.
>
> *No Colder Place.* St, Martin's, 1997.
>
> *A Bitter Feast.* St. Martin's, 1998.
>
> *Stone Quarry.* St. Martin's Minotaur, 1999.
>
> *Reflecting the Sky.* St. Martin's Minotaur, 2001.
>
> *Winter and Night.* St. Martin's Minotaur, 2002.

The Shanghai Moon. Minotaur, 2009. 9780312245566.

The Shanghai Moon is a brooch combining the diamonds of Rosalie Gilder's mother and the jade of ancient China, which was made in Shanghai in pre–World War II times. It disappeared during the war and reappears in the hands of a Chinese official named Wong Pan, who is in New York to sell the jewels. On his trail is Joel Pilarksy, who asks Lydia for her help and then is promptly murdered. Reluctantly, Lydia reaches out for help to her estranged investigative partner, Bill Smith.

> *Jade • Jewels • World War II*

On the Line. Minotaur, 2010. 9780312544492.

When Bill gets a call on Lydia's cell from her kidnapper, he is given twelve hours to rescue her. Her tormenter is a serial killer who wants Bill to play a game that includes no cops but plenty of clues to a puzzle, which if he does not solve, could lead to Lydia's death.

> *Kidnapping*

Saylor, Steven ✍

Gordianus the Finder

This is the second of two Roman private detectives (see Lindsey Davis's Marcus Didius Falco). Saylor has a much more serious approach to writing about the Roman period than Davis. Using the palette of ancient times to paint a solid mystery, Saylor's novels could easily be read by any historical fiction reader. Readers may also enjoy Sharan Newman. See the author's Web site at http://www.stevensaylor.com. **TR** **Historical.** Series subjects: **Historical (BC)** • **Italy, Rome (Ancient)**

> *Roman Blood.* St. Martin's, 1991.
>
> *Arms of Nemesis.* St. Martin's, 1992.
>
> *Catilina's Riddle.* St. Martin's, 1993.
>
> *The Venus Throw.* St. Martin's, 1995.
>
> *A Murder on the Appian Way.* St. Martin's, 1996.
>
> *The House of the Vestals.* St. Martin's, 1997.
>
> *Rubincon.* St. Martin's, 1999.
>
> *Last Seen in Massilia.* St. Martin's Minotaur, 2000.
>
> *A Mist of Prophecies.* St. Martin's Minotaur, 2002.

The Judgment of Caesar. St. Martin's Minotaur, 2004. 0312271190.
> While Caesar is battling with the two claimants to the Egyptian throne, Cleopatra and Ptolemy, Gordianus has sailed there with his sick wife, hoping to cure her in the waters of the Nile. Captured by his bitter enemy Pompey, he manages to escape a death threat, only to find himself investigating the death of a wine taster. The intended victim appears to be Caesar himself, and the apparent poisoner is none other than Gordianus's estranged adopted son, Meto.
>
> *Egypt, Alexandria* • *Poisons*

A Gladiator Dies Only Once. St. Martin's, 2005. 9780312271206.
> A collection of short stories including "The Consul's Wife," "If a Cyclops Could Vanish in the Blink of an Eye," "The White Fawn," "Something Fishy in Pompeii," "Archimedes's Tomb," "Death by Eros," "A Gladiator Dies Only Once," "Poppy and the Poisoned Cake," and "The Cherries of Lucullus."
>
> *Short stories*

The Triumph of Caesar. St. Martin's Minotaur, 2008. 9780312359836.
> With the Roman Civil War over and Gordianus in retirement, things should be calmer in the old man's life. But when Julius Caesar's wife, Calpurnia, wants Gordianus to prevent his generals from assassinating him, it is hard for the man to say no. Using the journals of his dead friend Hieronymus, the first person

Calpurnia hired to get the job done, he ventures forward to name the person his friend could not.

Assassinations • Journals

Spillane, Mickey ✍

Mike Hammer

Spillane is the most popular mystery author of his period in terms of sales. His P.I., Mike Hammer, is a throwback to the pulp days and an unacceptable investigator to some contemporary readers because of changes in sensibilities. However, *I, The Jury* remains one of the most surprising mystery novels of all time. **HB** Series subjects: **New York, New York**

I, the Jury. Dutton, 1947.

My Gun Is Quick. Dutton, 1950.

Vengeance Is Mine! Dutton, 1950.

One Lonely Night. Dutton, 1951.

The Big Kill. Dutton, 1951.

Kiss Me, Deadly. Dutton, 1952.

The Girl Hunters. Dutton, 1962.

The Snake. Dutton, 1964.

The Twisted Thing. Dutton, 1966.

The Body Lovers. Dutton, 1967.

Survival . . . Zero! Dutton, 1970.

The Killing Man. Dutton, 1989.

Black Alley. Dutton, 1996.

The Goliath Bone (with Max Allan Collins). Harcourt, 2008. 9780151014545.

When Hammer keeps two graduate students from being killed, he discovers they have a rare artifact: the thigh bone of Goliath. This bone represents a key to the religions of the factions in conflict in the Middle East, and the various entities are all in search of the relic. Now it is up to the aging Hammer to be their best defense, even against all the forces of good who want to get their hands on it.

Goliath • Relics • Terrorism

The Big Bang (with Max Allan Collins). Houghton Mifflin Harcourt, 2010. 9780151014484.

In this novel set in the 1960s, Hammer is on the spot when a bike messenger is attacked, and that leads him into the world of drugs. The clues point to a character named The Snowbird, and Hammer decides it is time to take him down.

Drugs

Stabenow, Dana ✍

Kate Shugak

Kate Shugak is a former investigator for the Anchorage district attorney, who now works private investigations on cases that involve all the wildness that defines Alaska. Shugak left active service after killing a child molester and being injured in the line of duty. She is an Aleut who now lives on a 160-acre homestead near a national park and the community of Niniltna. She has a romantic interest in cop Jack Morgan, and her best friend is Alaska State Trooper Jim Chopin. The novels are dependent on the location, as Stabenow takes full advantage of her own homeland to display the reasons behind the crimes that are committed. Readers may also enjoy Sue Henry, Karin Slaughter, and John Straley. **TR** Series subjects: **Alaska** • **Aleuts**

A Cold Day for Murder. Berkley, 1992. 042513301X.

When a national park ranger who is also the son of a congressman disappears, the investigator sent to figure out what happened also disappears. Feeling they need a topnotch investigator, the forces turn to their former colleague Kate Shugak, who now lives in the wilderness and knows the territory better than anyone. As she investigates, she must travel into the villages of the remote Alaskan countryside to find the answers.

Park rangers • *Parks*

A Fatal Thaw. Berkley, 1993. 0425135772.

When Roger McAniff begins to kill one spring, investigative forces feel that once the manhunt is over, they will have solved the crimes. When forensics show that Lisa Getty was shot with a different rifle from all the others, the investigation is turned over to Shugak. As she explores the countryside for a killer, she finds herself in the crosshairs of his rifle.

Serial killer

Dead in the Water. Berkley, 1993. 042513749X.

Signed on to the *Avilda* as a crabber, Shugak has gone undercover to try to find out why two crew members never returned from the last voyage into the Bering Sea. She finds that by turning to the Aleuts on the remote islands in the sea, she will find the guidance she needs to solve this case.

Bering Sea • *Commercial fishing* • *Fishing* • *Undercover operations*

A Cold-blooded Business. Berkley Prime Crime, 1994. 042514173X.

Kate gets hired as a roustabout in Prudhoe Bay so that she can discover who is bringing cocaine into RPetCo's territory. The big oil company is nervous enough, having just suffered a big spill, and does not need or want a scandal. Kate learns that the oil company is made up of people whom she can really care for and surprisingly, she can even admit that environmentally the company is doing all they can. Her anger rises when she discovers someone may be smuggling ancient native artifacts off the Slope, and her investigation of this leads accidentally to the solution of the drug problem.

Alaska, Prudhoe Bay • *Antiquities* • *Oil*

Play with Fire. Berkley Prime Crime, 1995. 0425147177.

Alaskans are taking advantage of a forest fire to harvest a crop of mushrooms growing on the wasteland. Then Kate finds a body. She is mushrooming with Bobby Clark, a wheelchair-bound friend, and Bobby's pickup, a video journalist named Dinah Cookman. Days after her discovery, the body is identified as Daniel Seabolt, a teacher who had been driven from the small town of Chistona when he dared to introduce evolution into the school curriculum. Oddly, Kate had been investigating his disappearance at the request of Daniel's young son, but once the body is properly identified, the son fires Kate at the request of his fundamentalist preacher grandfather.

Evolution • *Fundamentalism*

Blood Will Tell. Berkley Prime Crime, 1996. 0399141243.

Ekaterina Shugak, Shugak's grandmother, is concerned when two of her tribal council are killed under suspicious circumstances. She believes their deaths tie into a battle to retain control over some Aleut land that developers are interested in. She turns to Shugak for help, and the investigator decides to winter in Anchorage and help her people.

Alaska, Anchorage • *Developers*

Breakup. Putnam, 1997. 0399142509.

When a plane crash leaves rubble in her remote location, Shugak is left with the mess and a body. As investigators probe the wreckage, she is dealing with the spring breakup and an increase in bear attacks, including tourists in the line of fire. But perhaps even more dangerous, she is dealing with the death of her grandmother and the appeal for her to take over as her people's leader.

Aircraft accidents • *Bears*

Killing Grounds. Putnam, 1998. 0399143564.

When the evil Cal Meany is murdered, Shugak finds herself rising to the defense of her own family, which has fallen under suspicion. The problem is that there are too many suspects who would want this man dead. With the help of Jack Morgan, she tries to find a real perpetrator before the police do. When Meany's own daughter is murdered, it puts a different twist on the investigation.

Alaska, Prince William Sound • *Fishing* • *Salmon fishing*

Hunter's Moon. Putnam, 1999. 0399144684.

> Shugak and Morgan are working as big game hunter guides and take a group of obnoxious German hunters out into the wilderness. When one man shoots another, it is passed off as an accident, until another shooting occurs. Then weather isolates the whole hunting party. Now the two detectives realize they are in a kill zone and need to figure out what is going on before they are left for dead in the wild.
>
> *Hunting*

Midnight Come Again. St. Martin's Minotaur, 2000. 0312205961.

> When the Russian mafia's activities force Chopper Jim Chopin to go undercover in Russia to bring down the bad guys, the last thing he expects to find is Shugak, who has been missing for months from her home, undercover there as well. With each stepping on the other's toes, the case is burst wide open, and people start to get hurt.
>
> *Alaska, Bering* • *Russian mafia* • *Undercover operations*

The Singing of the Dead. St. Martin's Minotaur, 2001. 0312209576.

> When Shugak is hired to handle security for the state senate campaign of Anne Gordaoff, she finds herself on the spot when two people are murdered. While people are dying in the present, the clue to the reason lies in Alaskan history and the notorious madam Angel Beecham, murdered in 1915. Meanwhile, Jack's son Johnny has shown up on Kate's doorstep, and she is providing some security for him as well.
>
> *Politicians* • *Prostitutes*

A Fine and Bitter Snow. St. Martin's Minotaur, 2002. 0312205481.

> When park ranger Dan O'Brian loses his job because of his stance against oil drilling in the preserve where she lives, Shugak jumps to his defense. When her childhood mentors are attacked for the same reason and Dan is blamed, Shugak goes on the offensive to stop this environmental range war.
>
> *Environment* • *Oil*

A Grave Denied. St. Martin's Minotaur, 2003. 0312306814.

> Johnny Morgan discovers the corpse of Len Dreyer frozen in a glacier, and Jim Chopin would like to have Shugak's help on this one. As she investigates Dreyer's background, she loses her cabin to an arsonist, so Jim asks her not to investigate anymore. Shugak needs revenge and proceeds down a dark path to find the killer.
>
> *Arson* • *Glaciers*

A Taint in the Blood. St. Martin's Minotaur, 2004. 0312306830.

> Charlotte Muravieff's mother is behind bars for murder and is dying of cancer, so Charlotte turns to Shugak to launch a post-conviction defense. Thirty years ago Victoria went to jail for setting fire to her house and murdering her young son William. Now Shugak is in Anchorage and working on a new angle to the

incident, and it draws the interest of the surviving members of the family. Unfortunately, it also draws a killer.

Alaska, Anchorage • Arson • Families • Mothers and daughters

1

A Deeper Sleep. St. Martin's Minotaur, 2007. 9780312343224.

Louis Deem is a ne'er-do-well from Niniltna whom the justice system cannot ever compile enough evidence to convict. Unafraid, Shugak takes on an investigation of the man and soon finds she has placed her extended family in danger. With Chopin's help, she hopes to finally bring Deem down.

Revenge

2

Whisper to the Blood. Minotaur, 2009. 9780312369743.

Shugak has finally accepted the one job she never wanted: chairperson of the Ninilta's Native Association. Her first crisis arises when a mining company wants to dig in the Iqaluk Wildlife Refuge and the town is split on the issue. When people are murdered, Shugak knows she must seek justice no matter which side of the issue she is on.

Mining • Wildlife refuges

3

A Night Too Dark. Minotaur, 2010. 9780312559090.

With the gold mine now an inevitability, Global Harvest company men are all over the park. When Dewayne Gammons appears to have been eaten by a bear after leaving a suicide note in his company truck, Shugak and Chopin are a little confused. But not as confused as when a week later Gammons walks out of the woods, unable to tell anyone what happened. Now, whose body was eaten by the bear?

Bears • Mining

Winspear, Jacqueline ✍

Maisie Dobbs

Maisie Dobbs has risen above the challenges thrown at her. Traded into a life a servitude to Lady Rowan Compton by her father, Franki Dobbs, Maisie was lucky enough to impress her employer so that she was educated above her station. After her experiences as a nurse on the battle fronts of World War I, and after the disappearance of the doctor who was her love, she returns to England to open her own investigative agency, which practices psychology as much as it does detection. With veteran Billy Beale as her assistant and Inspector Stratton as her police contact and love interest, Dobbs has all she can handle in between the two world wars. Readers who enjoy this series will also like Kerry Greenwood and Anne Perry. See the author's Web site at http://www.jacquelinewinspear. com. **TR** Series subjects: **Historical (1900–1999) • World War I**

Maisie Dobbs. Soho, 2003. 1569473307.

Maisie Dobbs is hired to follow Celia Davenham by her husband when Christopher believes his wife is having an affair. As Maisie follows Celia to the grave of a World War I casualty, it brings home the state of affairs in London ten years after the war to end all wars. It also reminds Dobbs of her own past and the lost love left behind on the battlefields of World War I.

Romance

Birds of a Feather. Soho, 2004. 1569473684.

The murder of a young woman attracts the attention of Dobbs and Inspector Stratton. When her agency is hired to locate Charlotte Waite, the missing daughter of businessman Joseph Waite, it ties into the first murder and the murder of a third woman. What is the meaning of the white feathers left at the crime scenes? When her own employee Beale is suspected of being involved in the killings, Dobbs must draw on all her skills to pick the right clues to find the real murderer.

Drugs • Serial killer

Pardonable Lies. Holt, 2005. 9780805078978.

Dobbs and Billy have three cases to balance. First, a thirteen-year-old farm girl named Aril Jarvis has been charged with murder, and Dobbs is asked to take up her defense. Second, Queen's Counsel Sir Cecil Lawton's wife has died, and to honor her request he is seeking information about his son Richard, a pilot during the war, who never returned. Finally, Dobbs's friend Priscilla asks her to investigate the death of her brother on the battlefields of France, a country Dobbs would rather avoid because of her own war experiences.

Memory

Messenger of Truth. Holt, 2006. 9780805078985.

Georgina Bassington Hope was a classmate of Dobbs at Girton College, and she calls upon the detective when her twin brother, artist Nick Bassington Hope, falls from a scaffold while installing his exhibition and she suspects murder. With Inspector Stratton convinced it was an accident, it is up to Dobbs to prove that the sister's intuition is correct.

Art • Artists • Brothers and sisters

An Incomplete Revenge. Holt, 2008. 9780805082159.

James Compton's company wants to buy a brickworks and some land in the village of Heronsdene, but before they do they want Dobbs to investigate a series of fires set in the village. The harvest of hops brings workers to the village, including some gypsies never trusted by anyone. Are they to blame? Is the landowner, Alfred Sandermere, hated so much? Can this all be tied to a Zeppelin crash during the Great War that no one wants to talk about?

England, Kent, Heronsdene • Gypsies • Hops • Zeppelins

Among the Mad. Holt, 2009. 9780805082166.

> Dobbs is nearly a victim when a bomber blows himself up near her on Christmas Eve in London. In the economic depression, everyone is suffering, but no one more than the veterans of Wotld War I. Because the prime minister has received threatening letters, Dobbs is asked to joined a team with Scotland Yard and Special Branch personnel to hunt down the band of terrorists. The group has only forty-eight hours to stop another attack from happening.
>
> *Bombs • Christmas • Terrorism • Veterans*

1

The Mapping of Love and Death. Harper, 2010. 9780061727665.

> When a World War I trench is uncovered long after the war, it sets off bad memories for too many people. The American parents of cartographer Michael Clifton, found in the pit, hire Dobbs to investigate when his wounds indicate he was murdered. The search begins for a nurse thought to have been his lover and now thought to have been his murderer.
>
> *Cartographers • Nurses*

2

Crime Specialist Detectives

3

Certain occupations lend themselves to aiding in criminal investigations while maintaining status as private individuals. Occasionally these individuals will find their relationships with professionals are cordial, and cooperation will be mutual in the investigation. On other occasions, they will find themselves at odds with the investigation and sometimes championing the causes of the weak and unrepresented.

The Modern Practitioners

Barr, Nevada ✍

Anna Pigeon

Today, writers always look for a hook, and for Barr it was to use her experience as a park ranger to create a unique setting for each of her novels about park ranger Anna Pigeon. Pigeon is a federal law enforcement officer. As she travels about the country, transferred from one national park to another, she finds a death to investigate at each stop. Her family is important to her, and eventually she marries, but the distances she travels will always create stress in her life. Readers may also enjoy Jean Hager and Tony Hillerman. See the author's Web site at http://www.nevadabarr.com. **TR** Series subjects: **National parks** • **Park rangers**

> *Track of the Cat.* Putnam, 1993.
>
> *A Superior Death.* Putnam, 1994.
>
> *Ill Wind* (UK: *Mountain of Bones*). Putnam, 1995.
>
> *Firestorm.* Putnam, 1996.
>
> *Endangered Species.* Putnam, 1997.
>
> *Blind Descent.* Putnam, 1998.
>
> *Liberty Falling.* Putnam, 1999.
>
> *Deep South.* Putnam, 2000.
>
> *Blood Lure.* Putnam, 2001.
>
> *Hunting Season.* Putnam, 2002.

Flashback. Putnam, 2003. 0399149759.

Assigned to the islands of the Dry Tortugas National Park off Key West, Florida, Pigeon is involved in the investigation of a small craft that blows up in the waters one day. Living on Garden Key island in isolation, she rummages through a box of letters written by her great-great-aunt when she was on the same island during the Civil War. While haunted by the past, history empowers Pigeon's current investigation and leads her to an unexpected conclusion.

> *Boats • Bombs • Civil War, 1861–1865 • Dry Tortugas National Park • Families • Florida, Dry Tortugas National Park • Florida, Florida Keys • Mudd, Samuel*

High Country. Putnam, 2004. 0399151443.

Four Yosemite Park employees are missing in a winter storm, and Ranger Pigeon is sent undercover to the park to discover why. Taking the cover of a waitressing job in the Ahwahnee Hotel, she learns about a downed plane that contained illegal drugs. When her own life is on the line, she pushes herself to find the solution in the ice and snow of the Sierra Nevada mountains.

> *California, Yosemite National Park • Drugs • Yosemite National Park*

Hard Truth. Putnam, 2005. 0399152415.

Rocky Mountain National Park is Pigeon's new assignment, and she is called when two traumatized children come out of the woods into Heath Jarrod's "handicamp." Jarrod has been confined to a wheelchair since a mountain-climbing accident, and she bonds with the children, persuading Pigeon to investigate the cause of their distress: one other girl is still out there. Pigeon discovers a cult set-up just outside the borders of the park and needs to decide if Robert Proffit is a spiritual leader or a pedophile.

> *Children in jeopardy • Cults • Colorado, Rocky Mountain National Park • Rocky Mountain National Park*

Winter Study. Putnam, 2008. 9780399154584.

Pigeon returns to the Isle Royale National Park, this time to be a team member of Winter Study, a wolf and moose group. When the team finds itself tracking a large and formidable wolf through the bitter cold, they begin to wonder if they are searching for a new species. Then Homeland Security decides the project may need to be shut down to use the park as a buffer against penetration from Canada.

> *Homeland Security • Isle Royale National Park • Michigan, Isle Royale National Park • Wolves*

Borderline. Putnam, 2009. 9780399155697.

Needing to recover from her last assignment, Pigeon and husband Paul decide to raft downriver in the Big Bend National Park in Texas. When they paddle up to a drowning pregnant woman giving birth, Pigeon is able to save the child. When a sniper gets interested in the rafting party and their guide is taken out, everyone's lives are in danger. At the same time, Mayor Judith Pierson has announced her candidacy for governor of Texas and will drag Pigeon and Paul into her campaign.

> *Big Bend National Park • Births • Immigration • Rafting • Texas, Big Bend National Park*

Burn. Minotaur, 2010. 9780312614560.

On administrative leave, Pigeon heads for New Orleans to stay with her friend Geneva Akers, a jazz singer. One of Geneva's fellow tenants is a scary guy named Jordan, who may have something to do with pedophilia. Seattle actress Clare Sullivan's house has burned to the ground, and her confused discussion with the police leads to her being suspect number one. Now on the run, she crosses into Pigeon's world as she hunts for the truth about her family. When someone tries to put a voodoo curse on Pigeon, she decides to work some of her own voodoo and get to the root cause of what is spoiling her vacation.

> *Children in jeopardy • Louisiana, New Orleans • Pedophilia • Voodoo*

Benn, James R. ✍

Billy Boyle

What makes Billy Boyle unique is that he is a Boston police detective who was supposed to sit out the Second World War in Washington with a cushy desk job. Unfortunately for Boyle but fortunately for the reader, he was assigned to the office of his uncle, General Dwight D. Eisenhower. Following the Supreme Commander to the European front means Boyle and the reader will witness all the major events of that challenging period as American soldiers contribute to the liberation of Europe. Readers may also enjoy Alan Furst. View the author's Web site at http://www.jamesrbenn.com. 📺 Series subjects: **Soldiers • World War II**

The First Wave. Soho, 2007. 9781569474716.

> When the Allies invade North Africa in 1942, Billy finds himself in the first wave of boats to hit the beach. While his unit's job is to arrange the surrender of the Vichy French defending the shores, he finds the task is complicated by the numerous forces all fighting each other and any semblance of the law. Then some American soldiers are murdered. When he discovers his girlfriend Diana, a British spy, has been captured by the enemy, to rescue her, he must sort out a black market underworld conspiracy interested in a new drug called penicillin.
>
> *Algeria • Penicillin • Spies*

Blood Alone. Soho, 2008. 9781569475164.

> When Billy is sent in advance of the landing to contact the local mafia on the island of Sicily, he is carrying a message from Lucky Luciano as protection. Waking in a field hospital with limited memory, he tries to piece together his mission. His biggest problem is that he is up against a mobster named Vito Genovese, who wants to continue his counterfeiting ways.
>
> *Amnesia • Counterfeiting • Organized crime • Italy, Sicily*

Evil for Evil. Soho, 2009. 9781569475935.

> Sent to his ancestral homeland of Ireland, Boyle is supposed to recover all the rifles and ammunition that the IRA stole from a U.S. Army depot. What he discovers is that everyone is willing to assume certain things about him because of his heritage. What he has to discover is whether the IRA, the Germans, or even some of his own men might have been behind the raid.
>
> *Irish Republican Army (IRA) • Ireland*

Rag and Bone. Soho, 2010. 9781569478493.

> With major distrust existing between the Polish representatives living in London and their Russian counterparts over the blame for the Katyn Massacre, it comes as no surprise that blood is shed. When a Russian secret policeman is found murdered in the style of the massacre, suspicion falls on Boyle's friend, Lieutenant Kazimierz. Boyle's assignment is to find the truth, no matter who gets hurt in the process.
>
> *England, London • Katyn Massacre*

Box, C. J. ✍

Joe Pickett

Joe Pickett is an honest and hard-working family man who covers the wide open spaces of Wyoming as a game warden for the Wyoming Game and Fish Department. A bad shot himself, he learns how to be a detective over the course of the series, often while in opposition to local sheriff Bud Barnum. Pickett matures into a world-weary man who is often disappointed by what he sees, but he maintains his steadfast dedication to protecting his family and the environment even after being fired. Readers may also enjoy Tony Hillerman, William Kent Krueger, and Dana Stabenow. View the author's Web site at http://www.cjbox.net. **TR** Series subjects: **Environment • Game wardens • Husbands and wives • Wyoming, Twelve Sleep County, Saddlestring**

Open Season. Putnam, 2001. 0399147489.

> Joe Pickett is the only game warden in Twelve Sleep County, Wyoming, a job he got despite having ticketed the governor for illegal fishing and being the worst shot on the testing range. He was placed in this position by his longtime mentor, Vern Dunnegan, whom the community still respects. When Vern brings a major corporation's interest in building a pipeline to the county and it may involve an endangered species, things get tense. Three men are found dead in a remote part of the wilderness, but not before one dies on Joe's woodpile, involving his family in a desperate plot against Joe and the environment.
>
> *Endangered animals*

Savage Run. Putnam, 2002. 0399148876.

> When underground environmental terrorist Stewie Woods and his new wife Annabel Bellotti are blown up in a cow pasture while spiking trees, it falls to warden Pickett to discover why. Partially motivated by his own wife Marybeth's former relationship with Woods, Pickett is working the case as he gathers evidence of other deaths of people sympathetic to the environment. When he begins to get an inkling of a conspiracy, he finds himself in danger as well.
>
> *Assassins • Conspiracies*

Winterkill. Putnam, 2003. 0399150455.

> Pickett stumbles into this case when Lamar Gardiner, the locally hated district supervisor of the Twelve Sleep National Forest, is killed in a remote area while doing some illegal elk hunting. In the forest is a group of people called The Sovereign Citizens, all survivors of either Ruby Ridge or Waco. When the federal agents arrive, they are as eager to wipe out the renegades as they are to find a murderer. This disturbs Pickett, because also in the woods is Jeannie Keeley, birth mother to his adopted daughter, April.
>
> *Adoption • Federal Bureau of Investigation • Survivalists*

Trophy Hunt. Putnam, 2004. 0399152008.

> When mutilated animals, and later a few humans, show up in Pickett's territory, it leads to the creation of the Northern Wyoming Murder and Mutilations Task Force. Not really a team player, Pickett finds himself following clues the others would dismiss, including testimony from the paranormal expert Cleve Garrett. While the residents talk about aliens from space, Pickett knows he will find the reason here on the land he protects.
>
> *Mutilation • Task forces*

Out of Range. Putnam, 2005. 9780399152917.

When Will Jensen, a game warden in Jackson, kills himself, Picket is temporarily assigned to the big city. Picket is a fish out of water and is ill-equipped to handle the pressure of the various groups who vie for his attention. And in the back of his mind, he still has some doubts about Will's suicide.

Suicide • Wyoming, Jackson

In Plain Sight. Putnam, 2006. 9780399153600.

Pixkett returns to the peace and quiet of Saddlestrings from Jackson, only to get embroiled in a family feud. Opal Scarlett is missing, and her two sons, Hank and Arlen, are less interested in where their mother is than in dividing up the estate. His daughter Sheridan is best friends with Hank's daughter, so Pickett is drawn even deeper into this case. Meanwhile, John Wayne Keeley has been released from prison and is coming to Saddlesprings to take revenge on Pickett, who is Keeley's daughter's guardian.

Ex-convicts • Families • Revenge

Free Fire. Putnam, 2007. 9780399154270.

Having been fired as a game warden, Pickett is sent by Wyoming's new governor, Spencer Rulon, to Yellowstone to investigate a strange circumstance. Lawyer Clay McCann has just walked away from a charge of murder in the deaths of four campers, who may have had some secrets of their own. With his pal, falconer Nate Romanowski, as a sidekick, he delves into a remote part of the national park to try to find the answers to the governor's questions.

Corruption • Lawyers

Blood Trail. Putnam, 2008. 9780399154881.

As special agent for the governor, Pickett is called when an elk hunter is butchered like the animal he was hoping to hunt and kill. The bad news is that his nemesis, Randy Pope, the man who fired him, is heading the investigation. When an antihunting activist named Klamath Moore arrives in town, some of the officials think he is the murderer. Pickett does not and springs his pal Romanowski from jail in order to stop a serial killer who is loose in the woods.

Hunting • Serial killer

Below Zero. Putnam, 2009. 9780399155758.

When Pickett's daughter Sheridan receives a text message from the family's long-dead foster daughter April Keeley, Pickett is stunned. He feels responsible for her death, and if it is true that she is alive, Pickett will do anything to make sure he is not the reason she does not survive again. Could April really be traveling with ecoterrorists on a cross-country reign of destruction?

Adoption • Eco-terrorism • Fathers and daughters • Serial killer • South Dakota, Black Hills • Text messages

Nowhere to Run. Putnam, 2010. 9780399156458.

Joe is winding down his service in Baggs, Wyoming, when some strange occurrences on the local level make him want to hang around town. For years the residents have wondered about the ultimate fate of an Olympic runner who disappeared in the woods. Unwittingly, Joe walks into an ambush. This attack will open the doors needed for him to set on the trail of two mountain men who have crossed over to the dark side, while the world descends onto a community that just wants to be left alone.

Kidnapping • Mountain men • Wyoming, Baggs

Burke, Jan ✍

Irene Kelly

As a news reporter, Irene Kelly crosses paths with all the wrong people while covering the crime beat in Southern California. Allied with homicide detective and sometime lover Frank Harriman, she finds herself walking a deadly beat that causes her personal suffering. Readers may also enjoy Barbara D'Amato, Laura Lippman, and Mary Willis Walker. See the author's Web site at http://www.janburke.com. **TR HB** Series subjects: **California, Las Piernas •** **Journalist**

Goodnight, Irene. Simon & Schuster, 1993.

Sweet Dreams, Irene. Simon & Schuster, 1994.

Dear Irene. Simon & Schuster, 1995.

Remember Me, Irene. Simon & Schuster, 1996.

Hocus. Simon & Schuster, 1996.

Liar. Simon & Schuster, 1998.

Bones. Simon & Schuster, 1999.

Flight. Simon & Schuster, 2001.

Bloodlines. Simon & Schuster, 2005. 074322390X.

This novel tells three reporters' stories, each separated by twenty years, which deal with the death of a wealthy family and a missing heir to a fortune. In 1958, novice reporter Conn O'Connor gets involved when his mentor Jack Corrigan is nearly killed after finding a blood-spattered car buried on a farm. Twenty years later, Kelly finds herself mentored by O'Connor. Finally, in 1998 Kelly takes two reporters under her wing to bring closure to this forty-year-old crime when the car is finally unburied to reveal its secrets.

Children in jeopardy • Kidnapping

Kidnapped. Simon & Schuster, 2006. 9780743273855.

> The reader is shown who killed graphic artist Richard Fletcher in the first chapter of this book, before the narrative jumps five years to the present, in which Kelly has written a series of articles focusing on missing children. It renews interest in the case of Jenny Fletcher, a toddler who went missing when her father was murdered. It also develops new leads, which make some begin to doubt the conviction of Mason Fletcher, including Kelly, her husband Frank, and Caleb Fletcher. Caleb has always been convinced her brother was innocent and now intends to use her forensic skills to prove it. All of this new attention focuses a light on the strange family of adopted children maintained by its patriarch, multimillionaire Graydon Fletcher.
>
> *Adoption* • *Children in jeopardy* • *Dysfunctional families* • *Forensics* • *Kidnapping*

Evanovich, Janet ✍

Stephanie Plum

Not everyone who loses a job would want to be a bounty hunter, but Plum does. And when she does, the wild humor that is the specialty of this series becomes evident. Allied with her pal Ranger and sometime friend Morelli, she grows into a fairly good detective, even willing to use her own grandmother in her schemes. These comic novels can be recommended to any traditional mystery reader. Readers may also enjoy Sparkle Hayter and Joan Hess. See the author's Web site at http://www. evanovich.com. **TR** Series subjects: **Bounty hunters** • **Humor** • **New Jersey, Trenton**

> *One for the Money*. Scribner, 1994.
>
> *Two for the Dough*. Scribner, 1996.
>
> *Three to Get Deadly*. Scribner, 1997.
>
> *Four to Score*. St. Martin's Press, 1998.
>
> *High Five*. St. Martin's Press, 1999.
>
> *Hot Six*. St. Martin's Press, 2000.
>
> *Seven Up*. St. Martins Press, 2001.
>
> *Hard Eight*. St. Martin's Press, 2002.

Visions of Sugar Plums. St. Martin's Press, 2002. 0312306326.

> How appropriate that Plum is chasing a bail-jumper named Sandy Claws just four days before Christmas. But who is the mysterious young man named Diesel who appears in her house, and what do the elves have to do with this case?
>
> *Christmas* • *Holidays*

To the Nines. St. Martin's Press, 2003. 0312265867.

> When his work visa expires, Samuel Singh goes on the lam and leaves Vinnie holding the bag. He sends Ranger and Plum after the man, but Plum's source is

murdered right in front of her. With Plum having finally settled on Morelli, it compromises her good intentions to be thrown together with her other man, especially when they all end up in Sin City.

Nevada, Las Vegas

Ten Big Ones. St. Martin's Press, 2004. 0312289723.

Plum is in the deli when the street gang the Red Devils rob the joint. When it becomes known that Plum could put their leader Anton Ward, aka The Junkman, in jail, her life is threatened. What better place for her to hide than Ranger's apartment, but she still thinks it would be better not to let her cop boyfriend Morelli know where she is.

Gangs

Eleven on Top. St. Martin's Press, 2005. 9780312306267.

Plum has decided to leave the bounty hunting business to someone else and pursue a career in nickel-and-dimed-to-death jobs. However, an old acquaintance has different plans for her, and his scary attentions mean Plum needs to ally herself with Morelli and Ranger for protection. Her former coworker Lula is making a hash of Plum's former job, and reluctantly Plum is drawn back into the world of chasing really bad people. This time around she is going to work for Ranger.

Twelve Sharp. St. Martin's Press, 2006. 0312349483.

When Ranger is accused of kidnapping his own daughter, things get really confusing, because Stephanie ends up living with both of the men she loves. Their goal becomes retrieving a ten-year-old girl who needs to be saved from a very bad man.

Children in jeopardy

Lean Mean Thirteen. St. Martin's Press, 2007. 9780312349493.

Dickie Orr, Plum's ex-husband, has mysteriously disappeared under suspicious circumstances, and Plum is suspect number one. That might be because she was seen with Dickie just before his death while doing a favor for Ranger. As she tries to clear her name, Dickie's shady business partners become more and more convinced that Plum is the key to a $40 million payoff.

Ex-husbands

Fearless Fourteen. St. Martin's Press, 2008. 9780312349516.

When Loretta Rizzi cannot make her bail and skips town, Plum ends up babysitting her teenage Goth son Zook. When the bad guys who are behind the gambling interests in this case think that Morelli is holding the stash, it falls to Plum and a gang of teens to defend him. Meanwhile, Plum and Ranger are bodyguarding a musician whose brother may be sitting on the take from a big-time bank robbery.

Bank robberies • Goths • Musicians • Teenagers at risk

Finger Lickin' Fifteen. St. Martin's Press, 2009. 9780312383282.

> When their office clerk Lula witnesses the beheading of celebrity chef Stanley Chipotle, she appears to be next on the killer's list. Plum takes on her case while balancing a special request from Ranger. He needs her to look into some strange activities at Rangeman Security that are putting that agency at risk. When Grandma Mazur and Lula enter the cooking contest as bait for the killer, that creates chaos for Plum.
>
> *Chefs • Security*

Sizzling Sixteen. St. Martin's Press, 2010. 9780312383305.

> When Vinnie is kidnapped by Bobby Sunflower because he owes his bookie six figures, it is up to the remaining staff of his bail bond business to find and free him. The group develops a wide range of schemes, including trying to rob Sunflower to pay him with his own money. Will Plum be able to pull this off and save her job?
>
> *Kidnapping • Ransom*

Larsson, Stieg ✍

Mikael Blomkvist/Lisbeth Salander

This surprisingly popular series of novels is an interesting study of Swedish social struggles buried in a crime novel format. Featuring the crusading journalist Mikael Blomkvist, the books' real strength is the strange yet fascinating character Lisbeth Salander. Unfortunately, although ten books were planned for this series, Larsson died after completing only three. Readers may also enjoy Denise Mina, Henning Mankell, and Jo Nesbø. View a Web site about the author at http://www.stieglarsson.com. **HB** Series subjects: **Computer hackers • Journalist • Magazine publishing • Sweden, Stockholm**

The Girl with the Dragon Tattoo. Knopf, 2009. 9780307269751. (Sweden: Män Som Hatar Kvinnor. Norstedt, 2005).

> Mikael Blomkvist is a financial journalist who has just mishandled his work on his own magazine and faces a term in jail for libel. With a bit of free time on his hands before he is sentenced, he finds himself called to the home of one of Sweden's riches industrialists. Henrik Vanger wants Mikael to write his life story as a cover for investigating the forty-year-old disappearance of his niece, Harriet Vanger. While Mikael finds himself surrounded by a family tree's worth of suspects who were around on the day that Harriet disappeared, his own life is being investigated by a renegade investigator and computer hacker named Lisbeth Salander. When the two cross paths, it leads to a battle of wits that calls into question issues of loyalty and justice.
>
> *Industrialists • Islands • Missing persons • Rape • Sweden, Hedeby Island*

The Girl Who Played with Fire. Knopf, 2009. 9780307269980. (Sweden: Flickan Som Lekte Med Elden. Nordstedt, 2006).

> *Millennium* magazine, now in the hands of others while Mikael is on leave, is about to release an issue with a story about sex trafficking when the two authors are murdered. The fingerprints on the gun belong to Lisbeth, and Mikael feels compelled to try to rescue her. Perhaps he has forgotten that Lisbeth rarely needs anyone to help her with anything.
>
> *Human trafficking • Sex*

The Girl Who Kicked the Hornet's Nest. Knopf, 2010. 9780307269997. (Sweden: Luftslottet Som Sprängdes. Norstedt, 2007).

> Lisbeth barely managed to survive the last adventure, and now she is recovering from a head wound in a hospital while awaiting trial for murder. Her father, and her hated nemesis, is just down the hall recovering from injuries she gave him. Trying to gather evidence to prove her innocent, Mikael finds himself up against Sweden's spy organization. Meanwhile, Erica has her hands full trying to manage the magazine without any help from Mikael.
>
> *Spies • Trials*

3

Ex-Cop Detectives

The number of professional investigators who have retired from active duty but are willing to be dragged back into an investigation seems endless. Being stripped of their badges, their support organizations, and the funds to investigate are minor inconveniences to determined ex-professionals, now perhaps more properly labeled amateurs. It is their previous experiences that make these ex-detectives such proficient investigators, despite giving up their guns.

Block, Lawrence ✍

Matt Scudder

Retired from the police force and troubled by alcoholism, Block's Scudder is one of the most dramatic of the "recovering" cops. Acting as a private detective, Scudder works the underbelly of New York, and the city comes alive in the hands of this author. Readers may also enjoy James Crumley, Loren D. Estleman, and Robert B. Parker. See the author's Web site at http://www.lawrenceblock.com. **HB**
Series subjects: **Alcoholism • New York, New York**

> *The Sins of the Fathers.* Dell, 1976.
>
> *In the Midst of Death.* Dell, 1976.

Time to Murder and Create. Dell, 1977.

A Stab in the Dark. Arbor House, 1981.

Eight Million Ways to Die. Arbor House, 1982.

When the Sacred Ginmill Closes. Arbor House, 1986.

Out on the Cutting Edge. Morrow, 1989.

A Ticket to the Boneyard. Morrow, 1990.

A Dance at the Slaughterhouse. Morrow, 1991.

A Walk Among the Tombstones. Morrow, 1992.

The Devil Knows You're Dead. Morrow, 1993.

A Long Line of Dead Men. Morrow, 1994.

Even the Wicked. Morrow, 1997.

Everybody Dies. Morrow, 1998.

Hope to Die. Morrow, 2001.

All the Flowers Are Dying. Morrow, 2005. 0060198311.

And the rematch is on. Scudder, having let a killer walk in his last adventure, now is trying to retire and enjoy life. When he and Elaine are personally threatened by the serial killer, he must call upon all of his remaining resources to save his extended family.

Retirement • Serial killer

Connolly, John ✍

Charlie Parker

Charlie "Bird" Parker is a former New York detective who turns to alcohol and loses everything when his family is murdered by a serial killer. Eventually he returns to do what he does best: hunt down the bad people. Connolly can be a very dark writer, and some of the scenes in Parker's adventures are gruesome to read. He also is not shy about applying magical realism and spectrals from the past to enhance the tension in his stories. Readers may also enjoy Lawrence Block, Ken Bruen, and James Lee Burke. See the author's Web site at http://www.johnconnollybooks.com. **HB** Series subjects: **Alcoholism • Maine, Scarborough • Supernatural**

Every Dead Thing. Simon & Schuster, 1999. 0684857146. (UK: Hodder & Stoughton, 1999).

When Parker's wife and daughter are killed by a ritual dissection performed by a serial killer, he quits the force. Eventually he pulls back from the alcoholism that has enveloped his life to look for a missing woman named Catherine Demeter. He allies himself with two gay hit men, a Creole psychic and his old FBI pal

Woolrich, to help put the clues together to stay on the trail of a killer known as the Traveling Man.

Children in jeopardy • Louisiana, New Orleans • Virginia

Dark Hollow. Pocket, 2009. 0743203321. (UK: Hodder & Stoughton, 1999).

Parker has moved back home to Maine, where he is going to operate as a private investigator. Rita Ferris approaches him and asks for help getting her husband Billy to pay his child support, a decision that costs her her life. Now Parker finds himself in opposition to mobster Tony Celli, who believes that Parker's pal Purdue has his $2 million swag. When it appears that Purdue is searching for his birth parents, it is going to leave a trail of bodies, and Caleb Kyle, a serial killer from Parker's youth whom his cop grandfather investigated, reappears.

Organized crime • Parents • Private investigator • Serial killer

The Killing Kind. Atria, 2002. 0743453344. (UK: Hodder & Stoughton, 2001).

When Grace Peltier is found dead in the backseat of her car, it falls to Parker to prove that she did not commit suicide. When an investigation uncovers a mass grave of Aroostook Baptists who died forty years ago, Parker realizes that the two investigations are tied together. Now he is forced to confront The Fellowship, a new threat to the community that includes the evil Elias Pudd.

Mass murderer • Religion

The White Road. Atria, 2003. 0743456386. (UK: Hodder & Stoughton, 2002).

When Parker's girlfriend, psychologist Rachel Wolfe, becomes pregnant with his child, it does not keep the private investigator from running off to South Carolina. Earl Larousse's daughter Marianne has been raped, and her African American boyfriend Atys Jones is accused. When only Parker stands against the belief that Jones is innocent, he is led down a dark path that he is reluctant to follow.

African American • Rape • South Carolina, Charleston

The Black Angel. Atria, 2005. 9780743487863. (UK: Hodder & Stoughton, 2005).

Parker is living with Rachel and their daughter Sam when he accepts a job for his partner, Louis. Louis's cousin Alice, a prostitute, is missing. Trips to New York City, Mexico, and the Czech Republic are necessary as Parker finds himself in pursuit of a statue called the Black Angel.

Czech Republic • Mexico • New York, New York • Prostitutes

The Unquiet. Atria, 2007. 9780743298933. (UK: Hodder & Stoughton, 2007).

Rebecca Clay needs protection from an ex-con stalker named Frank Merrick, so she turns to Parker. Merrick believes Rebecca can reveal where her father Daniel, a child psychiatrist, is so that Merrick can learn the fate of his own daughter.

Child psychiatrists • Fathers and daughters • Psychiatrists

The Reapers. Atria, 2008. 9780743298933. (UK: Hodder & Stoughton, 2008).

This case is turned over to Parker's partner Louis. Louis was once a member of an assassination team called The Reapers, and now their top killer is coming for him. Now Louis and Angel must work to save their own lives.

Assassins • Hit men • Homosexuality

The Lovers. Atria, 2009. 9781416569541. (UK: Hodder & Stoughton, 2009).

With his license suspended, Parker is tending bar in Portland. He has lots of time on his hands, so he decides to look into the suicide of his father. When William Parker was a New York cop, he shot an unarmed couple and then turned his gun on himself. When Parker's probing uncovers stories from the past including his own birth, he is frightened by what he discovers.

Bartenders • Maine, Portland • New York, Pearl River

The Whisperers. Atria, 2009. (UK: Hodder & Stoughton, 2009). 9781439165195.

When a recently returned veteran takes his own life, his father wants an explanation. He turns to Parker, who discovers that many soldiers in the Stryker C unit have killed themselves. When it appears the men may have been smuggling things home, Parker finds himself up against powerful forces that may put his own life in danger.

Antiquities • Iraq War, 2003 • Soldiers • Suicide

Krueger, William Kent ✍

Corcoran O'Connor

Cork O'Connor is part Irish, part Ojibwe Indian. He drifts from law enforcement jobs to special cases investigated as a private citizen and runs a small restaurant in his hometown. Once a Chicago cop, he now is settled in the more remote areas of Minnesota, where he tries to carve out some normality for his family and himself. He is not afraid to ally himself with his roots, including his mentor, Ojibwe elder Henry Meloux. Readers may also enjoy Steve Hamilton and Dana Stabenow. The author's Web site can be viewed at http://www.williamkentkrueger.com. **TR** Series subjects: **Minnesota, Aurora • Minnesota, Tamarack County • Native Americans • Ojibwe**

Iron Lake. Atria, 1998. 0671016962.

When a judge commits suicide the same night an Indian boy goes missing, the former sheriff of Aurora is inclined to investigate anyway. Fighting his guilt over losing his job and messing up his family relationships, Connor is desperate to get this one right. What he finds is that when the new gambling money is mixed with the old legions, it is not always clear which path to take.

Blizzards • Judges • Suicide • Windigo

Boundary Waters. Atria, 1999. 0671016989.

When a musician named Shiloh disappears into the Boundary Waters, her father William Raye hires Connor to find her. Joining a search party made up of the FBI, an ex-con, and two Native Americans, Connor finds he does not work well with others. Nor will he like the two killers who are also searching for Shiloh to make sure she never comes back to tell a tale from the past.

Fathers and daughters • Minnesota, Boundary Waters • Mothers and daughters • Winter

Purgatory Ridge. Atria, 2001. 0671047531.

When an explosion claimed by the Eco-Warrior blows up a lumber mill and kills the chief of the Iron Lake Ojibwe, Charlie Warren, Connor is called in by the sheriff who replaced him. As he probes into the case, he discovers that the Ojibwe who opposed the logging of their sacred land may have had a hand in the event, which sets him at odds with his wife Jo, who is their attorney. While mill owner Karl Lindstrom makes it hard for Connor, things really get messy when Jo and his son are held for ransom.

Bombs • Environment • Hostages • Lumber • Mills

 Blood Hollow. Atria, 2004. 0743445864.

Charlotte Kane disappears on New Year's Eve, but her body is not discovered until three months late when the snow melts. Sheriff Arne Soderberg is inclined to lock up her Ojibwe boyfriend, Solemn Winter Moon. When Solemn skips town to avoid arrest, it is up to Connor to determine why the community has a second corpse. No one expects Solemn to return from the wilderness claiming to have had a vision of Jesus.

Religion

 Mercy Falls. Atria, 2005. 9780743445887.

Returned to the force in Aurora, Sheriff Connor is on a domestic dispute call on the Ojibwe reservation when someone tries to shoot him in a carefully planned ambush, but wounds his deputy. Meanwhile, the body of a Chicago businessman named Eddie Jacoby is found at the foot of Mercy Falls. With a private investigator in town to help and the victim's brother having ties to Jo, Connor feels like he has been thrown under the wagon. Who wants him dead?

Businessmen • Hit men

Copper River. Atria, 2006. 9780743278409.

Wounded by a hitman while on the run from the incidents that occurred in the previous case, Connor seeks sanctuary in a small Upper Peninsula town, where his cousin, Jewell DuBois, lives. Jewell is not happy to see him, but her fourteen-year-old son Ren takes to Connor like a father. When a young girl is found floating in the Copper River and then his cousin falls under suspicion of murder, Connor is on the spot to investigate with the help of Dina Willnert, a Chicago private eye.

Hit men • Michigan, Bodine • Teenagers at risk

 Thunder Bay. Atria, 2007. 9780743278416.

Giving up public service, Connor is now a private investigator willing to take cases like the one offered by Henry Meloux. Henry believes he sired an heir whom he has never seen, and he hopes Connor can track him down. When Connor is able to find Henry Wellington, a wealthy miner living in Thunder Bay, it leads to an attack on Henry. Connor dives into the past, seeking the answers to a contemporary crime.

Canada, Ontario, Thunder Bay • Gold

Red Knife. Atria, 2008. 9781416556749.

When Ojibwe Red Boyz gang member Lonnie Thunder is accused of murdering the daughter of a white gang leader named Buck Reinhardt, it falls to Connor to arrange a peace conference. Before the olive branch can be passed, someone murders both the Red Boyz leader Alex Kingbird and his wife. Now Tamarack County is going to go to war, unless Connor can find a murderer.

Gangs • Race relations

Heaven's Keep. Atria, 2009. 9781416556763.

When a plane carrying Jo and some Native American dignitaries crashes in the wilds of the Rocky Mountains, Connor is devastated. Months afterward, he is approached by two women with evidence that the pilot was not who was listed as a victim of the accident. Now Conner travels west to uncover a conspiracy that may have caused the death of his Jo.

Aircraft accidents • Husbands and wives • Wyoming

Vermilion Drift. Atria, 2010. 9781439153840.

Connor is looking for Lauren Cavanagh, the missing sister of Vermilion One mine owner Max Cavanagh. Cavanagh is not the most popular man in Tamarack County, because he has been negotiating with the government to use his mine as a nuclear waste depot.. Then Connor has to explain the six dead people in the mine and how the most recent victim was killed with his gun.

Brothers and sisters • Mining • Nuclear waste

Langton, Jane

Homer Kelly

Retired from his police career as a lieutenant detective, Kelly is a New England resident and Emersonian scholar. He exhibits the sensibilities of the New England area through his personality and his actions. He finds himself using his detective skills to solve many crimes, and his wife Mary is a great sidekick. **TR**

> *The Transcendental Murder.* Harper & Row, 1964. (Also published as *The Minuteman Murder.* Dell, 1976).
>
> *Dark Nantucket Noon.* Harper & Row, 1975.
>
> *The Memorial Hall Murder.* Harper, 1978.
>
> *Natural Enemy.* Ticknor and Fields, 1982.
>
> *Emily Dickinson Is Dead.* St. Martin's, 1984.
>
> *Good and Dead.* St. Martin's, 1986.
>
> *Murder at the Gardner.* St. Martin's, 1988.
>
> *The Dante Game.* Viking, 1991.
>
> *God in Concord.* Viking, 1992.
>
> *Divine Inspiration.* Viking, 1993.
>
> *The Shortest Day.* Viking, 1995.
>
> *Dead as a Dodo.* Viking, 1996.
>
> *The Face on the Wall.* Viking, 1998.
>
> *The Thief of Venice.* Viking, 1999.
>
> *Murder at Monticello.* Penguin, 2001.
>
> *The Escher Twist.* Viking, 2002.

The Deserter: Murder at Gettysburg. St. Martin's Minotaur, 2003. 0312301863.

Shifting between the past and the present, Kelly investigates the reasons behind the desertion accusation against his wife Mary's great-great-grandfather Seth Morgan. Centering on the battle at Gettysburg during the Civil War, the modern sleuths try to find a compelling reason for a historical tragedy.

Civil War, 1861–1865 • Gettysburg • Massachusetts, Concord

Steeplechase. St. Martin's Minotaur, 2005. 9780312301958.

Kelly, now a best-selling author, is writing a book about Massachusetts called *Steeplechase* and has uncovered a strange story from nineteenth-century Nashoba. A revered chestnut tree brings two clergymen into conflict, and their tale is told in alternating chapters with Kelly's tale. While Reverend Josiah Gideon's son-in-law lies physically shattered by the Civil War, the good reverend finds himself in conflict with the more conservative Reverend Horatio Biddle. The events of 1868, including the photographs and drawings included in the text, add a special air to this tragic tale of a church that gets lost to history.

Churches • Massachusetts, Nashoba • Trees

Lescroart, John T. ✍

Dismas Hardy

Once a cop and once a lawyer, Dismas Hardy is in conflict with himself as much as he is in conflict with the bad guys. Set in San Francisco, Lescroat's stories use his character's Irish background to the maximum. Hardy bounces among various legal jobs, trying to find himself and protect the innocent. Readers may also enjoy Terence Faherty and Don Winslow. See the author's Web site at http://www.johnlescroart. com. **HB** Series subjects: **California, San Francisco**

Dead Irish. Fine, 1989.

The Vig. Fine, 1990.

Hard Evidence. Fine, 1993.

The Thirteenth Juror. Fine, 1994.

The Mercy Rule. Delacorte Press, 1998.

Nothing But the Truth. Delacorte Press, 1999.

The Hearing. Dutton, 2001.

The Oath. Dutton, 2002.

The First Law. Dutton, 2003. 0525947051.

Hardy's cop pal Abe Glitsky takes center stage here when he is promoted away from the homicide desk, but he cannot stop investigating when his best friend's father is murdered. Hardy's client, John Holiday, is the chief suspect, and when Glitsky and Hardy begin to go down a path to prove his innocence, they find themselves wrapped up in a police conspiracy to prevent the truth from being revealed.

Police corruption

The Second Chair. Dutton, 2004. 0525947752.

Both Dismas and cop pal Glitsky have been kicked upstairs, and that makes them wish for the good old days when they were "first chair." Now relegated to being second chair in associate Amy Wu's case, Dismas finds himself energized when a series of mistakes puts their high-school-aged client Andrew North's freedom on the line. Meanwhile Glitsky's search for a serial killer puts him back in the saddle as an investigator.

Serial killer

The Motive. Dutton, 2005. 0525948449.

Sergeant Dan Cuneo is handling a case of arson in an old Victorian house in San Francisco in which mogul Paul Hanover and his lover, Missy D'Amiens, were killed. Is this arson, or murder-suicide? When Mayor Kathy West comes under pressure for results and asks administrator Abe Glitsky to oversee Cuneo, sparks fly. Meanwhile, Hardy has been hired by his old college girlfriend, who is Hanover's daughter-in-law, who is accused of murder.

Arson • Politicians

1

Betrayal. Dutton, 2008. 9780525950394.

Attorney Charlie Bowen has disappeared, and Hardy agrees to take on the job of shutting down his business by cleaning up his outstanding cases. The one case that proves problematic deals with an attempt to overturn the murder conviction of National Guard reservist Second Lieutenant Evan Scholler. Scholler is accused of the murder of his former friend, an ex-SEAL and Iraq conflict contractor named Ron Nolan. While Nolan had a relationship with Scholler's girlfriend Tara on the home front, the two men got involved in an incident in Iraq that killed men in Scholler's platoon plus innocent Iraqi civilians. As Hardy probes the government's business with private contractors, he finds a conspiracy that might lead to treason.

Contractors • Iraq War, 2003

2

A Plague of Secrets. Dutton, 2009. 9780451228321.

A politically charged case opens with the murder of Dylan Volger, a marijuana dealer working out of the coffee shop owned by Maya Townshend, the mayor's niece. When the prosecution decides to make her an example, Hardy gets to work. His partner Glitsky is distracted when his son is in a car accident and left in a coma.

Coma • Drugs • Marijuana

3

Rogue Detectives

Mystery fiction authors have had a little fun twisting the natural order of things by creating rogues who must function as detectives. Sometimes they do it for their own roguishness, sometimes for pure profit, and at other times they are defending their own names. But whatever their motivations, it is always interesting when someone sets a thief to catch a thief.

Block, Lawrence ✍

Bernie Rhodenbarr

At times a detective out of desperation, Bernie is an extension of the Raffles tradition in a modern American setting. He finds himself allied with a pet groomer named Carolyn Kaiser and occasionally at odds with a slightly crooked cop named Kirschmann. Eventually trying to settle down to life as a used bookseller does not keep Rhodenbarr from being tempted by the dark side of burglary. Readers may also enjoy Simon Brett (Melita Pargeter) and Jonathan

Gash. See the author's Web site at http://www.lawrenceblock.com. **TR** Series subjects:
New York, New York

> *Burglars Can't Be Choosers.* Random House, 1977.
>
> *The Burglar in the Closet.* Random House, 1978.
>
> *The Burglar Who Liked to Quote Kipling.* Random House, 1979.
>
> *The Burglar Who Studied Spinoza.* Random House, 1980.
>
> *The Burglar Who Painted Like Mondrian.* Arbor House, 1983.
>
> *The Burglar Who Traded Ted Williams.* Dutton, 1994.
>
> *The Burglar Who Thought He Was Bogart.* Dutton, 1995.
>
> *The Burglar in the Library.* Dutton, 1997.
>
> *The Burglar in the Rye.* Dutton, 1999.

The Burglar on the Prowl. Morrow, 2005. 0060198303.

> Talked into committing another burglary by an old friend, Rhodenbarr finds himself back on the job. When he is forced to hide in a woman's apartment when she unexpectedly returns home, he overhears a date rape. Drawn into the case as an unofficial detective when he is caught on a security tape, Rhodenbarr sets off to find the bad man. Sidetracked by a shooting outside his bookstore and a number of other unrelated crimes, he eventually calls together all the suspects to prove he is still a master detective.
>
> *Burglary • Date rape*

Child, Lee ✍

Jack Reacher

Reacher is a drifter, set loose upon the world by a series of circumstances that make him a wanderer who does not fear action. He is a survivor, using the skills he accumulated as a military policeman. But despite his loner ways, he steps in when he feels situations need to be corrected. He is not unwilling to use violence to adjust the balance of society. See the author's Web site at http://www.leechild.com. **HB**

> *Killing Floor.* Putnam, 1997.
>
> *Die Trying.* Putnam, 1998.
>
> *Tripwire.* Putnam, 1999.
>
> *Running Blind* (UK: *The Visitor*). Putnam, 2000.
>
> *Echo Burning.* Putnam, 2001.
>
> *Without Fail.* Putnam, 2002.

Persuader. Delacorte, 2003. 0385336667.

> Reacher is set up by the Feds to hunt for one of their missing agents in Maine. Forced to look into the dealings of tycoon Zachary Beck, he is surprised to find himself in opposition to an old nemesis, Francis Quinn.
>
> *Maine • Wealthy*

 The Enemy. Delacorte, 2004. 0385336675.

> As the year 1989 comes to a close, Reacher is at Fort Bird when a general is found dead in a motel. Missing from the general's effects is a very important briefcase containing military secrets that have to be recovered. The young MP and his African American female partner Summer begin an investigation that shows Reacher might be one of the suspects. Meanwhile, he has to deal with the cancer that has struck his mother.
>
> **BA**
>
> *African American • Cancer • Historical (1900–1999) • Military • Mothers and sons • North Carolina, Fort Bird • Soldiers*

One Shot. Delacorte, 2005. 9780385336680.

> When Gulf War sniper James Barr is accused of taking down five people, he has only one request: Reacher. Reacher knows Barr,because he brought him down for a similar incident while they were both in the military. Against his better judgment, Reacher finds himself working for the defense.
>
> *Indiana • Snipers*

The Hard Way. Delacorte, 2006. 9780385336697.

> Reacher is convinced to help ex-army officer Edward Lane and six Special Forces veterans find Lane's kidnapped wife and daughter. Lane has already lost one wife to a kidnapping and botched rescue, so he will not abide failure on this mission. The problem is that the ransom has been picked up, the clock is ticking, and Lane may not have told Reacher everything he needs to know.
>
> *Kidnapping • New York, New York*

Bad Luck and Trouble. Delacorte, 2007. 9780385340557.

> When members of his old unit are being murdered, Reacher gets a signal from former Sergeant Frances Neagley to help. Now of the original eight, there are only four left. When the remaining gang gets together, Reacher falls in line to help find out who is murdering the investigators one at a time.
>
> *California, Los Angeles • Military police • Nevada, Las Vegas • Revenge*

Nothing to Lose. Delacorte, 2008. 9780385340564.

> While drifting, Reacher settles in Despair, only to be run out of town as a vagrant. The town appears to be under the thumb of a scrap metal king whose religion believes the end of the world is coming. Moving just down the road to Hope, Reacher meets a female police officer, and with her help

he heads back to Despair to discover what is going on behind the well-guarded walls of the man's compound.

> *Colorado, Despair* • *Colorado, Hope* • *Religion*

Gone Tomorrow. Delacorte, 2009. 9780385340571.

While riding the subway one night, Reacher realizes he is looking at a woman who matches all the behavioral characteristics of a suicide bomber. When he finds out the woman has links to the Pentagon, Reacher begins to see a reason for her behavior. The problem is that he is assaulted by forces from the police, the FBI, and the military while trying to deal with a terrorist threat tied to the Afghan war.

> *Afghanistan War* • *Al-Qaeda* • *New York, New York* • *Terrorism*

61 Hours. Delacorte, 2010. 9780385340588.

When a tour bus spins out of control on an icy road, Reacher acts to save his fellow passengers and finds himself in Boulton, South Dakota. When the local cops seems outmatched by a Mexican drug lord's methamphetamine factory ensconced in an old military facility, it is up to Reacher to bring them down.

> *Drugs* • *Meth labs* • *Methamphetamine* • *Organized crime* • *South Dakota, Boulton*

Worth Dying For. Delacorte, 2010.

While recovering from injuries incurred during his last adventure, Reacher finds himself in Nebraska in a small town dominated by the Duncans. They have a criminal hold over the town, and their organization is sending something out of this county that is not corn. In order to bring down this crop of bad guys, Reacher is going to have to figure out what happened to an eight-year-old child decades ago. When the locals send for reinforcements, Reacher finds himself badly outnumbered but mad enough to stick around.

> *Children in jeopardy* • *Nebraska* • *Organized crime*

Gash, Jonathan (pseud. of John Grant) ✍

Lovejoy

The world of antiques brings out the rogue in everyone, and no one is better able to manipulate things to his advantage than Lovejoy. His special talent as a divvie gives him a sixth sense about antiques and murder. He is also a rogue with women, but his charm seems to override his arrogance around the opposite sex. His appearances on television have increased his popularity. Readers may also enjoy Lawrence Block (Bernie Rhodenbarr) and Simon Brett (Melita Pargeter). See a fan Web site at http://www.frii.com/~saunders/gash.htm. **TR** Series subjects: **Antiquities** • **England**

> *The Judas Pair.* UK: Collins, 1977. (US: Harper & Row, 1977).

> *Gold from Gemini.* UK: Collins, 1978. (US: *Gold by Gemini.* Harper & Row, 1978).

> *The Grail Tree.* UK: Collins, 1979. (US: Harper & Row, 1980).

Spend Game. UK: Collins, 1980. (US: Ticknor, 1981).

The Vatican Rip. UK: Collins, 1981. (US: Ticknor, 1982).

Firefly Gadroon. UK: Collins, 1982. (US: St. Martin's, 1984).

The Sleepers of Erin. UK: Collins, 1983. (US: Dutton, 1983).

The Gondola Scam. UK: Collins, 1984. (US: St. Martin's, 1984).

Pearlhanger. UK: Collins, 1985. (US: St. Martin's, 1985).

Moonspender. UK: Collins, 1986. (US: St. Martin's, 1987).

The Tartan Ringers. UK: Collins, 1986. (US: *The Tartan Sell.* St. Martin's, 1986).

Jade Woman. UK: Collins, 1988. (US: St. Martin's, 1989).

The Very Last Gambado. UK: Collins, 1989. (US: St. Martin's, 1990).

The Great California Game. UK: Century, 1991. (US: St. Martin's, 1991).

The Lies of Fair Ladies. UK: Century, 1992. (US: St. Martin's, 1992).

Paid and Loving Eyes. UK: Century, 1993. (US: St. Martin's, 1993).

The Sin Within Her Smile. UK: Century, 1993. (US: Viking, 1993).

The Grace in Older Women. UK: Century, 1995. (US: Viking, 1995).

The Possessions of a Lady. UK: Century, 1996 (US: Viking, 1996).

The Rich and the Profane. UK: Macmillan, 1998. (US: Viking, 1999).

A Rag, a Bone, and a Hank of Hair. UK: Macmillan, 1999. (US: Viking, 2000).

Every Last Cent. UK: Macmillan, 2001. 978-0333905296.

Rumor has it that Mortimer, the local honest antiques divvy, is none other than Lovejoy's son. The boy's honesty is disturbing to the other antiques dealers, and when their concern turns to murder, Lovejoy must scramble to save his occupation, and maybe his relations.

The Ten Word Game. St. Martin's Minotaur, 2003. 0312323476. (UK: Allison & Busby, 2003).

Life is tough when Lovejoy has to steal back a forgery that he sold, clerk in a store, and hide from a bounty hunter. Lured by kidnappers and taken aboard a cruise ship, he finds himself forced to divvy up the collection of the St. Petersburg Hermitage.

Cruises

Faces in the Pool. Minotaur, 2009. 9780312384111. (UK: Allison & Busby, 2008).

Languishing in jail is not to the taste of divvy and bon vivant adventurer Lovejoy. When a divorced millionaire named Ellen Jaynor offers him a get-out-of-jail free card to work for her, he jumps at the chance. Who would not want to be a shill in a speed dating service? Who would not want to marry a rich woman? Perhaps hunting down her ex-husband as a result is not so grand, but there is the possibility that the some of the people he seeks are the Forgotten Tribes. They own a lot of antiques—enough said?

Divorce • Relationships

Wilson, Robert ✍

Bruce Medway

West Africa is home to expatriated "fixer" Bruce Medway. As he tries to balance his own self-interest against the potential for financial gain, he always finds himself up against the challenges and corruptions of this part of the world. Readers who enjoy Robert Wilson may also enjoy Lee Child's Reacher and Graham Greene. See Robert Wilson's Web site at http://www.robert-wilson.eu. **HB** Series subjects: **Africa, West**

Instruments of Darkness. Harvest, 2003. 0156011131. (UK: Collins, 1995).

Bruce Medway has just completed a transportation deal for Jack Obuasi when he finds it has put him in opposition to the powerful Madame Severnou. He now must stay one step ahead of the hoods she has sent to punish him. In the meantime, he launches a search for a missing expatriated Brit named Steven Kershaw, who has many mysteries in his background. He finds himself needing the help of a legitimate detective, Inspector Bogado.

Missing persons

The Big Killing. Harvest, 2003. 0156011190. (UK: Collins, 1996).

Medway is cooling his heels in the Ivory Coast when he finds himself pulled in three directions. Fat Paul, a porn merchant, wants a tape delivered. He needs to act as a bodyguard for Ron Collins, a young diamond trader. Someone wants him to find a missing plantation manager. When these cases start to leave people dead and the civil war in Liberia heats up, staying out of trouble becomes the number one concern for the "fixer."

Ivory Coast • Jewels • Pornography

Blood Is Dirt. Harvest, 2004. 0156011255. (UK: Collins, 1997).

Napier Briggs hires Medway to recover the $2 million he has lost in a confidence scheme, but before Medway can make a move his client is murdered. This brings to Cotonou his daughter, commodities broker Selina Aguia. When Medway finds himself caught between the vengeance-seeking Selina and some angry mobsters, he needs to scramble to save his own skin; what he seeks is a deadly substance that can endanger everyone.

Benin, Cotonou • Organized crime • Toxic waste

A Darkening Stain. Harvest, 2004. 015601131X. (UK: Collins, 1998).

When a mobster named Roberto Franconelli wants Medway to find a missing man named Mariner in forty-eight hours, he tries to stay on topic. But with the entire region aware that young schoolgirls have gone missing, he finds himself pulled into that case.

Children in jeopardy • Organized crime

1

2

3

Appendix

Bibliographies

Adey, Robert. *Locked Room Murders and Other Impossible Crimes: A Comprehensive Bibliography.* Revised and expanded ed. Crossover Press, 1991. 0962887005.

An outstanding example of a dedicated fan publishing his own notes for the edification of other fans.

Albert, Walter. *Detective and Mystery Fiction: An International Bibliography of Secondary Sources.* Brownstone Books, 1985. 094102802X.

The printed version of this bibliography attempts to guide the researcher to widely distributed information about the mystery.

Albert, Walter. *Detective and Mystery Fiction: An International Bibliography of Secondary Sources.* Locus Press, n.d.

This CD-ROM version is an updated version that can be used on any PC or Apple with a CD-ROM drive and a standard Web browser. It is a second edition, revised and expanded, from the original print work.

Barzun, Jacques, and Wendell Hertig Taylor. *A Catalogue of Crime: Being a Reader's Guide to the Literature of Mystery, Detection, and Related Genres.* Harper & Row, 1989. 0060157968.

Get an arrogant and delightfully opinionated look at the mystery by reading the reviews of these experts.

Bleiler, Richard. *Reference Guide to Mystery and Detective Fiction.* Libraries Unlimited, 1999. 1563083809.

This work does a fine job of reviewing available reference sources for research in the genre.

Bourgeau, Art. *The Mystery Lover's Companion.* Crown, 1986. 0517556022.

Philadelphia bookstore owner Bourgeau lists his favorites.

Breen, Jon. L. *What About Murder? A Guide to Books About Mystery and Detective Fiction.* Scarecrow, 1981. 0-8108-1413-7.

Breen, Jon. L. *What About Murder? (1981–1991): A Guide to Books About Mystery and Detective Fiction.* Scarecrow, 1993. 0-8180-26090-7.

If you want evaluations of books that discuss mysteries, Breen's annotated bibliography is the best place to go.

Burgess, Michael, and Jill H. Vassilakos. *Murder in Retrospect: A Selective Guide to Historical Mystery Fiction.* Libraries Unlimited, 2005. 1-59158-087-0.

Contento, William G. *Mystery Fiction Miscellany: An Index.* Locus Press, 2000.
   This CD-ROM combines Contento's *Index to Crime and Mystery Anthologies* with two works by Martin H. Greenberg, *Index to Ellery Queen Mystery Magazine* and *Mystery Short Fiction: 1990–2000.*

Contento, William G., and Martin H. Greenberg, ed. *Index to Crime and Mystery Anthologies.* G. K. Hall, 1991. 0816186294.
   This book is a great place to check for hard-to-find mystery short stories. Check out the expanded coverage in the CD-ROM version, listed below.

Cook, Michael L. *Monthly Murders: A Checklist and Chronological Listing of Fiction in the Digest-Size Mystery Magazines in the United States and England.* Greenwood Press, 1982. 0313231265.
   This massive work attempts to list all the short stories in the field.

Cook, Michael L. *Mystery Fanfare: A Composite Annotated Index to Mystery and Related Fanzines, 1963–1981.* Bowling Green State University Popular Press, 1983. 0879722290.
   Fans with a sense of dedication produce a lot of writings about the field, and dedicated bibliographer Cook indexed their work for this period.

Gannon, Michael B. *Blood, Bedlam, Bullets, and Badguys: A Reader's Guide to Adventure/ Suspense Fiction.* Libraries Unlimited, 2004. 1563087324.
   A readers' advisory guide to the world of suspense and thrillers.

Green, Joseph, and Jim Finch. *Sleuths, Sidekicks and Stooges.* Scolar, 1997. 9781859281925.
   This enormous work organizes the genre by the characters. Its strength is that besides the lead characters, it gives equal tribute to the sidekick assistants and the authorities that the detective defies.

Hagen, Ordean A. *Who Done It? A Guide to Detective, Mystery and Suspense Fiction.* R. R. Bowker, 1969.
   The first book-length bibliography published in the field. Errors occurred, but it was the first major effort to list titles in the field.

Hubin, Allen J., ed. *Crime Fiction II: A Comprehensive Bibliography, 1749–1990.* Garland, 1994. 0-8240-6891-2. 2 vols.
   The best list of published mysteries ever compiled. It is indispensable to serious mystery researchers.

Hubin, Allen J., ed. *Crime Fiction IV: A Comprehensive Bibliography, 1749–2000.* Locus Press, 2003.
   The CD-ROM version of this work is an updated version that can be used on any PC or Apple with a CD-ROM drive and a standard Web browser.

Machler, Tasha. *Murder by Category: A Subject Guide to Mystery Fiction.* Scarecrow, 1991. 0810824639.

> Machler, a bookstore owner, organized some mysteries into about 100 subject categories.

Melvin, David Skene, and Ann Skene Melvin. *Crime, Detective, Espionage, Mystery, and Thriller Fiction and Film: A Comprehensive Bibliography of Critical Writing Through 1979.* Greenwood, 1980. 031322062X.

> Gathering secondary source references into one index, the compilers of this work included English- and non-English-language sources.

Menendez, Albert J. *The Subject Is Murder.* Garland, 1986. 0824086554.

Menendez, Albert J. *The Subject Is Murder: Volume 2.* Garland, 1990. 0824025806.

> Volume 1 covers twenty-five subject areas, while the second volume adds some old and some new categories while trying to organize the genre by subject.

Mundell, E. H., and G. Jay Rausch. *The Detective Short Story: A Bibliography and Index.* Kansas State University Library, 1974.

> In this expansion of the Queen title listed below, Mundell and Rausch updated the old work and included items overlooked by Queen.

Niebuhr, Gary Warren. *Caught Up in Crime: A Reader's Guide to Crime Fiction and Nonfiction.* Libraries Unlimited, 2009. 9781591584285.

> A readers' advisory guide to the crime fiction genre.

Niebuhr, Gary Warren. *Make Mine A Mystery: A Reader's Guide to Mystery and Detective Fiction.* Libraries Unlimited, 2004. 1563087847.

> A readers' advisory guide to mystery books in series.

Pronzini, Bill, and Marcia Muller. *1001 Midnights: The Aficionado's Guide to Mystery and Detective Fiction.* Arbor House, 1986. 0877956227.

> P.I. authors and married couple Pronzini and Muller put together this comprehensive list of best books in the field.

Queen, Ellery. *Queen's Quorum.* Little, Brown, 1951.

> This history of the short story in the genre approaches the topic by listing the most important books published in the field.

Queen, Ellery, ed. *The Detective Short Story: A Bibliography.* Little, Brown, 1942.

> The master mystery authors and publishers of *Ellery Queen Mystery Magazine* provided an early overview of the state of the art in the short story.

Shephard, Richard, and Nick Jennison. *100 Must Read Crime Novels.* A & C Black, 2006. 073675845.

> Two freelance writers take their shot at listing their 100 favorites in the field.

Stiwell, Steven A., and Charles Montney, eds. *What Mystery Do I Read Next?: A Reader's Guide to Recent Mystery Fiction.* Gale Research, 1996. 0787615927.

> This separate volume from the authors' multi-genre title *What Do I Read Next?* tries to lead mystery readers to potential novels with similar appeals.

Book Review Sources

Booklist
>Each spring this magazine does a mystery issue that provides a great list of titles for selection purposes. It regularly reviews mysteries in a special review column.

Publishers Weekly.
>Each fall this magazine does a Mystery Category Closeup that provides an overview of the mystery genre from the industry point of view. It regularly reviews mysteries in a special review column.

>Additional book review sources are listed in the "Journals" section below.

Conventions

Bouchercon, the World Mystery Convention, is held once a year in the fall. The convention is named for Anthony Boucher, a respected mystery reviewer and author. This fan's convention has grown in its thirty-plus years to include the concerns of authors, agents, publishers, and booksellers as well. Each Bouchercon maintains its own Web site (http://www.bouchercon.info).

Left Coast Crime Conference is held each spring in the Western half of the United States. The convention is similar to a Bouchercon, but its emphasis is to celebrate the authors of that region. Each Left Coast Conference maintains its own Web site (http://www.leftcoastcrime.org).

Malice Domestic was created to extend the work being done to elevate the status of women in the genre. Its goal is to celebrate the soft-boiled mystery, but traditional mystery readers will find that most of their authors are eligible for discussion at this convention. The convention is held each spring near the nation's capital. The convention's Web site is http://www.malicedomestic.org.

Magna Cum Murder originated as an alumni activity for Ball State University. It has grown into a regional mystery convention that works very hard to bring attention to two or three major international mystery stars each year. The convention's Web site is http://www.magnacummurder.com.

Encyclopedias

Ashley, Mike. *The Mammoth Encyclopedia of Modern Crime Fiction.* Carroll & Graf, 2002. 0786710063.
>An overview of the genre from Agatha Christie through the 1900s.

Barnett, Colleen A. *Mystery Women: An Encyclopedia of Leading Women Characters in Mystery Fiction. Volume 1: 1860–1979.* Ravenstone, 1997. *Volume 2: 1980–1989.* Poisoned Pen, 2002. 1890208698. *Volume III (1990–1999) Part 1: A–L.* Poisoned Pen Press, 2004. 1590580494.
> This work assembles the greats from the beginning of the genre to 1999.

Brunsdale, Mitzi. *Gumshoes: A Dictionary of Fictional Detectives.* Greenwood, 2006. 0313333319.
> After an introductory overview of the genre, this work covers 150 post-1970s authors in the field.

DeAndrea, William L. *Encyclopedia Mysteriosa.* Prentice Hall, 1994. 0-671-85025-3.
> The late mystery critic put this tome together to update or replace the *Encyclopedia of Mystery and Detection,* but it may be limited by some factual errors and limited coverage. Both volumes should be kept. It did win the 1994 Edgar award for best reference book.

Green, Joseph, and Jim Finch. *Sleuths, Sidekicks and Stooges.* Scolar, 1997. 1859281923.
> This enormous work organizes the genre by the characters. Its strength is that besides the lead characters, it gives equal tribute to the sidekick assistants and the authorities that the detective defies. Its weakness, according to reviews, is that some errors occur in the listings.

Herbert, Rosemary, ed. *The Oxford Companion to Crime & Mystery Writing.* Oxford University Press, 1999. 0195072391.
> This work provides a comprehensive overview of the entire genre.

Murphy, Bruce F. *The Encyclopedia of Murder and Mystery.* St. Martin's Minotaur, 1999. 0312215541.
> A personalized look at the genre.

Penzler, Otto, Chris Steinbrunner, and Marvin Lachman. *Detectionary: A Biographical Dictionary of Leading Characters in Mystery Fiction.* Overlook, 1977. 0879510412.
> This dictionary-format work is divided into four sections: detectives, rogues and helpers, cases, and movies.

Rollyson, Carl, ed. *Critical Survey of Mystery and Detective Fiction.* Salem Press, 2008. 978-1587653971.
> This five-volume set provides a detailed analysis of the lives and writings of major contributors to mystery and detective fiction.

St. James Guide to Crime and Mystery Writers. St. James Press, 1996. 0786710488.
> The best single-volume reference work for fans and researchers.

Steinbrunner, Chris, Otto Penzler, Marv Lachman, and Charles Shibuk. *Encyclopedia of Mystery & Detection.* McGraw-Hill, 1976. 0070611211.
> The first, and still the best, mainstream attempt to outline the genre for the average reader.

Winks, Robin, and Maureen Corrigan. *Mystery and Suspense Writers.* Charles Scribner's Sons, 1998. 0684805219.

> This two-volume work is a compilation of scholarly articles on the entire genre.

Filmography

Cameron, Ian. *A Pictorial History of Crime Films.* Hamlyn, 1975. 0600370224.

> There is some text here, but the majority of this review is stills from all the great films.

Christopher, Nicholas. *Somewhere in the Night: Film Noir and the American City.* Free, 1997. 0684828030.

> This study attempts to identify the chief characteristics shared by all the films in this subgenre.

Crowther, Bruce. *Film Noir: Reflections in a Dark Mirror.* Continuum, 1989. 0826405045.

> This work is a topical approach to the subgenre and is heavily illustrated.

Everson, William K. *The Detective in Film.* Citadel, 1972. 0806502983.

> This well-illustrated guide to the films features the greatest detectives filmed from 1903 to 1972.

Hardy, Phil, ed. *The BFI Companion to Crime.* University of California Press, 1997. 0520215389.

> This British filmography offers a complete and detailed guide to crime on film.

Hirsch, Foster. *The Dark Side of the Screen: Film Noir.* Barnes, 1981. 049802234X.

> A study of the participants and practitioners in this subgenre.

Irwin, John T. *Unless the Threat of Death Is Behind Them : Hard-boiled Fiction and Film Noir.* Johns Hopkins University Press, 2006. 9780801884351.

> A study of the source material for the greatest film noir.

Martin, Richard. *Mean Streets and Raging Bulls: The Legacy of Film Noir in Contemporary American Cinema.* Scarecrow, 1997. 0810833379.

> This study attempts to show how the subgenre of film noir has influenced crime and mystery films since its heyday in the late 1940s and early 1950s.

Silver, Alain, and Elizabeth Ward. *Film Noir: An Encyclopedic Reference to the American Style.* 3rd ed. Overlook, 1992. 0879514795.

> For each individual film, its production details are listed, with a brief summary of the plot.

Stephens, Michael L. *Film Noir: A Comprehensive Illustrated Reference to Movies, Terms and Persons.* McFarland, 1995. 0899508022.

> This subgenre receives a comprehensive treatment in an encyclopedia format that covers the directors, actors, films, plot devices, and themes.

Tuska, Jon. *The Detective in Hollywood.* Doubleday, 1978. 0385120931.
>   This is an overview with lots of pictures, by renowned film critic Tuska.

Guides

Benvenuti, Stefano, and Gianni Rizzoni. *The Whodunit: An Informal History of Detective Fiction.* Macmillan, 1979. 002509260X.
>   This historical guide was compiled by two Italian critics in the field.

Breen, Jon L. *Novel Verdicts: A Guide to Courtroom Fiction.* 2nd ed. Scarecrow Press, 1999. 0-8108-3674-2. 0810817411.
>   Lifelong reader and review Breen has put together a comprehensive guide to this subgenre.

Charles, John, with Joanna Morrison and Candace Clark. *The Mystery Readers' Advisory: The Librarian's Clues to Murder and Mayhem.* ALA, 2001. 083890811X.
>   This work introduces librarians to everything in this genre, from collection development to programming and marketing tips.

Gorman, Ed, with Martin H. Greenberg, Larry Segriff, and Jon L. Breen. *The Fine Art of Murder: The Mystery Reader's Indispensable Companion.* Carroll & Graf, 1993. 0-88184-972-3.
>   This Anthony Award–winning title is a cornucopia of mystery trivia for any fan, similar in style to the groundbreaking *Murder Ink.*

Grape, Jan, with Dean James and Ellen Nehr. *Deadly Women: The Woman Mystery Reader's Indispensable Companion.* Carroll & Graf, 1998. 0-7867-0468-3.
>   A compilation of articles by and about women in the mystery field. An absolutely delightful bedside book full of trivia.

Heising, Willetta L. *Detecting Men and Detecting Men Pocket Guide.* Purple Moon Press, 1998. 0-9644593-3-7 & 0-9644593-4-5.

Heising, Willetta L. *Detecting Women 3 and Detecting Women 3 Pocket Guide.* Purple Moon Press, 1999. 9780964459359.
>   These readers' guides and checklists feature more than 600 series by women and men. The pocket guides can be carried into a bookstore or library as a shopping guide.

Jakubowski, Maxim, ed. *100 Great Detectives: Famous Mystery Writers Examine Their Favorite Fictional Investigators.* Carroll & Graf, 1991. 0881847291.
>   Famous mystery writers examine their favorite mystery characters in this guide edited by London bookstore owner Jakubowski.

King, Nina, and Robin Winks. *Crime of the Scene: A Mystery Novel Guide for the International Traveler.* St. Martin's Press, 1997. 0312151748.
>   There can be no better outline for travelers as they try to find books to match locations.

Nichols, Victoria, and Susan Thompson. *Silk Stalkings: More Women Write of Murder.* Scarecrow Press, 1998. 0-810-83393-X.

   A delightful spin through the accomplishments of women within the mystery genre, this book is the second edition of this guide.

Niebuhr, Gary Warren. *Read 'Em Their Writes: A Handbook for Mystery and Crime Fiction Book Discussions.* Libraries Unlimited, 2006. 1591583039.

   A guide for book discussion leaders.

Oleksiw, Susan. <u>A Reader's Guide to the Classic British Mystery</u>. G. K. Hall, 1988. 0-8161-8787-3.

   Each of the volumes in this series offers annotated titles in its area, with special indexes to guide a reader through the genre.

   Lachman, Marvin. *A Reader's Guide to the American Novel of Detection.* G. K. Hall, 1993. 0-8161-1803-5.

   Niebuhr, Gary Warren. *A Reader's Guide to the Private Eye Novel.* G. K. Hall, 1993. 0-8161-1802-7.

   Vicarel, JoAnn. *A Reader's Guide to the Police Procedure.* G. K. Hall, 1995. 0-8161-1801-9.

   Johnson Jarvis, Mary. *A Reader's Guide to the Suspense Novel.* G. K. Hall, 1997. 0-8161-1804-3.

   Stone, Nancy-Stephanie. *A Reader's Guide to the Spy and Thriller Novel.* G. K. Hall, 1997. 0-8161-1800-0.

Ousby, Ian. *Guilty Parties: A Mystery Lover's Companion.* Thames & Hudson, 1997. 0500279780.

   As much fun as *Murder Ink*, this fan-oriented review of mystery fiction is full of surprises and is wonderfully illustrated.

Penzler, Otto. *The Private Lives of Private Eyes: Spies, Crime Fighters, and Other Good Guys.* Grosset and Dunlap, 1977. 0448143259.

   Using the characters as the approach, famed bookstore owner and collector Penzler outlines the lives of these fictional people.

Penzler, Otto, ed. *The Great Detectives: A Host of the World's Most Celebrated Sleuths Are Unmasked by Their Authors.* Little, Brown, 1978. 0316698830.

   This work includes the words of the creators dissecting their own creations.

Siegel, Jeff. *The American Detective: An Illustrated History.* Taylor, 1993. 0878338292.

   This colorful approach to the detective includes reproductions of book covers, as well as media stills and posters.

Sobin, Roger. *The Essential Mystery Lists.* Poisoned Pen Press, 2007. 9781590584576.

   A list of all the award winning contributions to the crime and mystery field.

Stine, Kate, ed. *The Armchair Detective Book of Lists*. Mysterious Press, 1995. 0-89296-423-5.

> A small book of lists full of the kind of trivia that mystery fans will just love to read.

Swanson, Jean, and Dean James. *By a Woman's Hand: A Guide to Mystery Fiction by Women*. 2nd ed. Berkley, 1996. 0425154726.

> An informal encyclopedic look at female authors who have made an impact on the genre.

Swanson, Jean, with Dean James and Anne Perry. *Killer Books: A Reader's Guide to Exploring the Popular World of Mystery and Suspense*. Berkley, 1998. 0425162184.

> For the fan reader, this book is a marvelous overview of the field, including books, movies, and TV shows.

Trott, Barry. *Read On . . . Crime Fiction: Reading Lists for Every Taste*. Libraries Unlimited, 2008. 9781591583738.

> More than just a bibliography of titles and annotations, this work by a nationally renowned librarian and readers' advisor contains elements of the appeal of works in this field.

Winn, Dilys. *Murder Ink: The Mystery Reader's Companion*. Workman, 1977. 2nd ed. issued in 1984 by Workman. 0894807684.

> This classic volume was one of the first fan-oriented publications in the field. It is full of trivia about the field. It was revised in 1984 in a second edition that was equal in fun and facts.

History and Criticism

Bailey, Frankie Y. *Out of the Woodpile: Black Characters in Crime and Detective Fiction*. Greenwood Press, 1991. 0313266719.

> From slaves to assimilation, Bailey tries to trace the path of African American characters in mysteries.

Ball, John. *The Mystery Story*. University of California–San Diego, 1976. 0891630198.

> Examining every facet of the mystery story, including origins, history, subgenres, authors, and characters, this work was produced as a companion to a reprint series the university was issuing in the 1970s.

Binyon, T. J. *Murder Will Out: The Detective in Fiction*. Oxford, 1989. 019219223X.

> Tracing the history of mystery from Poe to the present, this work provides an overview of the development of the genre.

Bloom, Harold, ed. *Classic Crime and Suspense Writers*. Chelsea House, 1995. 0791022315.

> This work contains excerpts from essays on Ambler, Buchan, Cain, Chandler, du Maurier, Fleming, Greene, Hammett, Hornung, John D. MacDonald, Ross Macdonald, Thompson, and Woolrich.

Bloom, Harold, ed. *Classic Mystery Writers*. Chelsea House, 1995. 0791022358.
This work contains excerpts from essays by Berkeley/Iles, Chesterton, Christie, Collins, Crofts, Doyle, Freeman, Poe, Post, Rinehart, Sayers, Van Dine, and Wallace.

Bloom, Harold, ed. *Modern Crime and Suspense Writers*. Chelsea House, 1995. 0791022471.
This work studies Bloch, Condon, Dahl, Deighton, Ellroy, Harris, Highsmith, le Carre, Leonard, Ludlum, Parker, Spillane, and Vachss.

Bloom, Harold, ed. *Modern Mystery Writers*. Chelsea House, 1995. 0791023761.
This works studies Allingham, Blake, Brown, Carr, Crispin, Gardner, Himes, Innes, Marsh, Millar, Queen, Stout, and Tey.

Cassuto, Leonard. *Hard-Boiled Sentimentality: The Secret History of American Crime Fiction*. Columbia University, 2008. 9780231126915.
An academic study of the hard-boiled fiction genre.

Collins, Max Allan. *The History of Mystery*. Collectors Press, 2001. 1-888054-53-0.
An overview of the history of the genre supplemented with beautiful photographs.

Craig, Patricia, and Mary Cadogan. *The Lady Investigates: Women Detectives and Spies in Fiction*. Oxford, 1981. 0312464266.
The majority of this work is an analysis of women characters in the formative years of the mystery.

Davis, David Brion. *Homicide in American Fiction, 1798–1860*. Cornell, 1957.
This critical study looks at the formative fiction that led to the creation of the modern mystery.

Dove, George N. *The Reader and the Detective Story*. Bowling Green State University Popular Press, 1997. 0879727314.
This critical work takes the unique approach of tying the mystery to the process of reading and enjoying fiction.

Eames, Hugh. *Sleuths, Inc.: Studies of Problem Solvers*. Lippincott, 1978. 0397012942.
This work studies the contributions of Doyle, Simenon, Hammett, Ambler, and Chandler.

Geherin, David. *Scene of the Crime: The Importance of Place in Crime and Mystery Fiction*. McFarland & Co., 2008. 9780786432981.
Using the works of fifteen authors, Geherin provides an analysis of setting.

Haycraft, Howard. *The Art of the Mystery Story: A Collection of Critical Essays*. Carroll & Graf, 1946.
A collection of major essays created by practitioners in the field.

Haycraft, Howard. *Murder for Pleasure: The Life and Times of the Detective Story*. D. Appleton-Century, 1941.
This classic work of criticism and history was considered the standard by which all other criticism was measured for many years.

Horsley, Lee. *Twentieth-Century Crime Fiction*. Oxford University, 2005. 0199253269.
Horsley is a senior lecturer in English literature at Lancaster University in England, and this is his academic-oriented look at the field.

James, P. D. *Talking About Detective Fiction*. Knopf, 2009. 9780307592828.
Master fiction writer James provides a delightful overview of the important works and trends in the genre.

Klein, Kathleen Gregory. *Great Women Mystery Writers: Classic to Contemporary*. Greenwood, 1994. 0313287708.
Essays and bibliographies on major female contributors to the genre are provided by an impressive list of mystery fans and scholars.

Klein, Kathleen Gregory. *The Woman Detective: Gender and Genre*. University of Illinois, 1988. 0252015223.
A study of women's role in the history of the genre.

Lachman, Marvin. *The American Regional Mystery*. Crossover, 2000. 096288703X.
A guide to the locations of mysteries set in the United States, with critical commentary.

Landrum, Larry. *American Mystery Novels and Detective Novels: A Reference Guide*. Greenwood Press, 1999. 0313213879.
This book does a very thorough job of explaining the forces that created the mystery as a modern genre from its roots to the literary influences that shape it today.

Lehman, David. *The Perfect Murder: A Study in Detection*. University of Michigan, 1999. 0472085859.
The book examines the reason readers enjoy reading about murder. It is an enlarged and expanded update to the original 1989 edition.

Lindsay, Elizabeth Blakesley. *Great Women Mystery Writers*. 2nd ed. Greenwood, 2007. 9780313334283.
Essays and bibliographies on major female contributors to the genre are provided by an impressive list of mystery fans and scholars.

Moore, Lewis D. *Cracking the Hard-Boiled Detective: A Critical History from the 1920s to the Present*. McFarland, 2006. 0-7864-25681-4.
A critical review that traces the hard-boiled form from its birth in the 1920s to the present.

Murch, A. E. *The Development of the Detective Novel*. Philosophical Library, 1958.
From its earliest ancestors through the Golden Age, this work attempts to trace the origins of the contemporary mystery.

Overmier, Judith, and Rhonda Harris Taylor. *Managing the Mystery Collection: From Creation to Consumption*. Haworth Information, 2004. 9780789031532.
A guide to the genre for librarians.

Panek, Leroy Lad. *The American Police Novel: A History*. McFarland & Company, 2003. 978-0786416882.

    A study of the police procedural.

Panek, Leroy Lad. *An Introduction to the Detective Story*. Bowling Green University Popular Press, 1987. 0879723777.

    This overview of the history of the mystery looks at early contributors and then covers the various subgenres.

Panek, LeRoy Lad. *The Origins of the American Detective Story*. McFarland, 2006. 0-7864-2776-0.

    From turn-of-the-century publications, theories are drawn about the evolution of the mystery novel as we know it.

Panek, Leroy Lad. *Probable Cause: Crime Fiction in America*. Bowling Green University Popular Press, 1990. 0879724854.

    Panek provides an overview of the first 100 years of crime fiction in America by putting together basic facts and observations that explain how the literature developed.

Schwartz, Saul. *The Detective Story: An Introduction to the Whodunit*. National Textbook, 1978. 0844256099.

    A textbook for teaching the mystery.

Symons, Julian. *Bloody Murder: From the Detective Story to the Crime Novel*. 3rd ed. Mysterious Press, 1992. 0-89296-496-0.

    The most respected contemporary analytical look at the detective story by the late British critic and writer of mystery fiction.

Symons, Julian. *Great Detectives: Seven Original Investigations*. Abrams, 1981. 0810909782.

    Symons has spent a lifetime studying the mystery novel, and here he concentrates on seven of the best.

Thomson, H. Douglas. *Masters of Mystery: A Study of the Detective Story*. Collins, 1931.

    This work may be the first attempt to create an overview of the field.

Walton, Priscilla L., and Manina Jones. *Detective Agency: Women Rewriting the Hard-Boiled Tradition*. University of California, 1999. 0520215079.

    A look at the effect of women in an area of the genre that traditionally was reserved for men.

Willett, Ralph. *The Naked City: Urban Crime Fiction in the USA*. Manchester University, 1996. 0719043018.

    City by city, this guide provides an overview of crime-related fiction as it developed in urban America.

Winks, Robin W. *Detective Fiction: A Collection of Critical Essays*. Prentice Hall, 1980. 0132026899.

    This collection contains most of the major essays on the field through the publication of this work, including the famous Edmund Wilson essay, "Who Cares Who Killed Roger Ackroyd?"

Winks, Robin W. *Modus Operandi: An Excursion into Detective Fiction.* Godine, 1982. 0879234067.

A collection of contemporary criticism of the field by a historian and reviewer.

Mystery Journals

Alfred Hitchcock Mystery Magazine
PO Box 54011
Boulder, CO 80322-4011
Fiction, some reviews

Crimespree Magazine
536 South 5th Street, Suite 1A
Milwaukee, WI 53204
http://www.crimespreemag.com.
Fiction, reviews, and commentary

Deadly Pleasures
PO Box 839
Farmington, UT 84025-0839
http://www.deadlypleasures.com/
Interviews, reviews

Ellery Queen Mystery Magazine
PO Box 54625
Boulder, CO 80322-4625
http://www.themysteryplace.com
Fiction, some reviews

Mystery Readers Journal
Published by Mystery Readers International (see under "Organizations")

Mystery Scene
331 West 57th Street, Suite 148
New York, NY 10019-3101
http://www.mysteryscenemag.com/
Commentary

Online Resources

General Guides to the Genre

Stop, You're Killing Me: http://www.stopyourekillingme.com

Reviews

Mystery Reader: http://www.themysteryreader.com

Mystery Listservs

Dorothy-l: http://www.dorothyl.com—a mailing list for mystery readers

Fiction-l: http://www.webrary.org/rs/flmenu.html—a mailing list for general readers' advisory questions, including mystery fiction

Organizations

Mystery Readers International
http://www.mysteryreaders.org
PO Box 8116
Berkeley, CA 94707

Mystery Writers of America
http://www.mysterywriters.org
17 East 47th Street, 6th floor
New York, NY 10017

Private Eye Writers of America
http://pwanewsandviews.blogspot.com
4342H Forest DeVille Drive
St. Louis, MO 63129-1833

Sisters in Crime
http://www.sistersincrime.org
PO Box 442124
Lawrence, KS 66044

Author Index

Title Index

Subject Index

Character Index

Location Index

About the Author

GARY WARREN NIEBUHR is the Library Director for the Village of Greendale, Wisconsin. He is the author of *A Reader's Guide to the Private Eye Novel, Read 'Em Their Writes, Caught Up in Crime,* and the original *Make Mine a Mystery,* which received the Anthony, Macavity, and Kenneth Kingery Awards.